CANADIAN SOCIAL POLICY

An Introduction

Second Edition

John R. Graham
University of Calgary

Karen J. Swift
York University

Roger Delaney
Lakehead University

Prentice Hall

Toronto

National Library of Canada Cataloguing in Publication Data

Graham, John R. (John Russell), 1964-
    Canadian social policy : an introduction

2nd ed.
Includes bibliographical references and index.
ISBN 0-13-067106-1

1. Canada—Social policy. I. Swift, Karen. II. Delaney, Roger. III. Title.

HV108.G735 2003   361.6'1'0971   C2002-901119-1

Statistics Canada information is used with permission of the Minister of Industry, as Minister responsible for Statistics Canada. Information on the availability of the wide range of data from Statistics Canada can be obtained from Statistics Canada's Regional Offices, its World Wide Web site at www.statcan.ca, and its toll-free access number 1-800-263-1136.

ISBN 0-13-067106-1

Vice-President, Editorial Director: Michael Young
Acquisitions Editor: Jessica Mosher
Marketing Manager: Judith Allen
Associate Editor: Patti Altridge
Production Editor: Tara Tovell
Copy Editor: Mary Teresa Bitti
Proofreader: Nadia Halim
Production Manager: Wendy Moran
Page Layout: Heidi Palfrey
Cover Design: Michelle Bellemare
Cover Image: KPT Power Photos

2 3 4 5   06 05 04 03

Printed and bound in Canada.

This book is lovingly dedicated to Russell and Jean Graham;
Peter, Julian and Evan Holland; and to the late
Dr. John Gandy, academic mentor and friend.

Contents

Preface

There are numerous books on social policy in the United Kingdom and United States. *Canadian Social Policy: An Introduction* is a response to the need for a Canadian perspective. It is a single volume introduction to a highly diversified field that provides a framework for analyzing social policies. The book stresses concepts, as well as consideration of the actual policies themselves, as parallel and equal means to a framework. Our thinking owes much to recent forces in social policy practice and scholarship, particularly as they relate to feminist, postmodern, and social diversity writings, widely construed, and to the concerns of social justice raised by this scholarship.

Social policy is a fundamental component of social work practice and should never be seen as an ethereal or aloof add-on to the curriculum. It is important in other ways, perhaps more so than at any other time either in our country's history or in the history of the social work profession. The now prolonged assault on universal programs, the ever more limited scope of policies, the ascendancy of neo-conservative ideology, globalization, the imperative of diversity—these, among other phenomena, will greatly influence social work practice and social policy analysis in future years. It is essential, therefore, that students introduced to Canadian social policy understand these dynamics and have at their disposal an analytical frame of reference that will make them sensitive to the nuances of policy work and to the diverse needs of society's most marginalized.

Canadian Social Policy: An Introduction examines major social policy considerations in Canada. It is intended for an audience of graduate, senior undergraduate, and senior community college students in social work, and for professionals who want to update their knowledge of current policy contexts. It is also intended to offer insights to students and practitioners of other disciplines, such as anthropology, business administration, Canadian studies, clinical psychology, development studies, divinity, economics, education, geography, history, nursing, occupational therapy, political science, public administration, rehabilitation studies, and sociology.

We greatly appreciate the supportive and most useful advice from reviewers and from readers, which significantly influenced this second edition. The second edition builds upon and updates data from the first edition, including two additional stand-alone chapters on welfare state institutions and social policy analysis/implementation, respectively. Some chapters lend greater attention to the demographics of poverty and to policy-making processes, among other areas. The introductory chapter outlines some conceptual ideas that are a foundation for social policy analysis and application. Chapter 2 considers historic influences on Canadian social policies; Chapter 3, some of the country's major social welfare programs; and Chapter 4, significant policy-related ideological, social, and economic facets. Chapter 5 covers globalization, the environment, social inclusion, and social movements. Chapter 6 introduces the key notion of diversity to social policy formation, and Chapter 7 presents how social policies are applied to social work practice and to social service delivery in general. The final two chapters examine the policy-making process in Canada, from stages and structures through to analysis, implementation, and assessment.

This textbook has been a number of years in the making. It started out as a proposal submitted by Roger Delaney. Once a publishing contract was received and the work begun, Roger invited John Graham and Karen Swift to be co-authors. The textbook's initial focus then expanded in order to place greater emphasis on the historical origins of Canadian social policies and on the impact of social diversity on all aspects of policy formation and analysis. The writing process has been truly collaborative, with each author contributing to the others' sentences, paragraphs, references, and ideas, and acting as a sounding-board over all matters related to authorship. Roger took the lead in Chapters 1, 8, and 9; John in Chapters 2, 3, 4, and the first part of Chapter 5; and Karen in the latter part of Chapter 5 and in Chapters 6 and 7; but the entire final product has each scholar's imprint.

Acknowledgments

Many people, too numerous to mention, were extremely influential in the completion of this text. Special thanks are extended to Helen Boukos, Cathryn Bradshaw, Xiaobei Chen, Stefanie Kaiser, Patricia Bianchini, Susan Morgan, and Louise Querido in particular, for extremely helpful and timely research assistanceship. John Graham's father, Russell Graham, read the entire first-edition manuscript and provided, as always, exceptionally valuable editorial advice. Staff at Pearson Education Canada were unendingly cooperative and encouraging. In the early 1970s, the late Albert Rose of the Faculty of Social Work, University of Toronto, conceived a social policy chart for teaching purposes. In light of substantial policy changes since then, part of the conceptualization in Chapter 3 is loosely based on Dr. Rose's original chart and is dedicated to his memory. Keith Brownlee, Paul DeBakker, David Este, Gayle Gilchrist-James, Jacqueline Ismael, Jane McMichael, and Margaret Sellick were among colleagues who provided much-appreciated support and advice. Funding from the University of Calgary Starter Grant for newly recruited faculty provided money for research assistanceship; particular thanks are extended to the University of Calgary and the Alberta government for this critical support. Grateful acknowledgment is extended for grant support from SSHRC to the Caring Labour Network. A Senate Research Grant from Lakehead University was likewise instrumental in moving the manuscript toward completion. Finally, thanks are extended to the Caledon Institute of Social Policy, the Canadian Council on Social Development, the National Council of Welfare, Statistics Canada, and those publishing companies that allowed us to cite various research.

The editors and authors would like to thank the following reviewers for their helpful commentary on the previous edition: Robert Marino of King's College, University of Western Ontario; Francis Turner of Wilfrid Laurier University; and Brian Wharf of the University of Victoria. The editors and authors would also like to thank the following reviewers for their helpful commentary on this manuscript: Michael J. Holosko of the University of Windsor; Lynda E. Turner of Kwantlen University College; and Thérèse Jennissen of Carleton University.

Chapter (1)

Introduction to Canadian Social Policy

Social policy is premised in the past, implemented in the present, and directed toward the future. It is profoundly influenced by societal values and ideologies, and should be sensitive to the diversities that constitute Canadian society. A thorough understanding of social policy is essential to effective social work practice. This text, therefore, presents Canadian social policy from a framework that takes into account the imperatives of history, diversity, and relevance to direct practice in Canada. Likewise, the book consciously affirms the empowerment of all Canadians—particularly those who have been historically marginal within local, regional, national, and international power structures

For a beginning student, one of the most immediate means of understanding social policy is through terminology. This chapter, therefore, introduces several key concepts, and concludes with a look at the relationship of policy to direct practice, a theme that is elaborated in Chapter 5. The student is also encouraged to refer to the glossary at the end of the book, which contains core definitions used in the present chapter and throughout the text.

Human beings believe in a wide range of religions and philosophies, organize around a wide range of political and social principles, and value different human attributes and characteristics. So numerous are these differences that even core issues for human beings are responded to by as many questions as answers. What is the purpose of our existence on earth? What is the purpose of suffering? Are human beings born intrinsically good, evil, both, or neither? Are all people equal? The contemplation of these questions, and others like them, produce different interpretations or world views (Delaney, 1995, McPherson and Rabb, 1994).

World views are constructed from values drawn from religious, political, social, and physical information about humans and the societies they create. Once accepted by a group of people, these world views become *agreement realities* (Babbie, 1986, 1977). Agreement realities become the *truth* for all those with a similar world view and this truth is passed down from generation to generation.

The study of social policy helps us to understand how world views influence the way in which members of social arrangements (i.e., societies, communities, families, or clubs) feel about such things as:

➤ social power, including personal powers and freedoms;

➤ social justice, including social equality, social status, roles, and prerogatives;

➤ human, civil, and social rights;

➤ human and social diversity;

➤ the nature of society;

➤ the relationship between people and society; and

➤ the nature of human relationships.

Conversely, an understanding of such issues can translate into effective social policy, which in turn may reshape a world view.

If you were born and raised only in Canada after 1970, then the many elements that currently make up Canadian society probably make sense to you. If you live in an organized community (such as a city or town) that elects officials (such as mayors, reeves, and aldermen) to govern the community, this process of governance seems normal to you. Other things that would be normal to you would include electing provincial and federal members to provincial, territorial, and federal parliaments to represent you (representative democracy); having your basic health care costs paid for by government (medicare); having free public education to grade 12; being free to travel throughout Canada without a passport; working for a salary or profits in a competitive marketplace; and having police forces that are accountable to elected officials.

You would become acquainted with the rules that govern people's conduct in Canada, such as criminal laws that make such activities as murder, theft, kidnapping, and physical and sexual assault illegal. You would become aware of rules that govern conduct in the workplace, such as those dealing with harassment, exploitation, and injury. You would become aware that there are rules that also protect the vulnerable, such as children and the elderly, from being exploited or injured. Finally, you would also discover a number of rules that govern our activities, such as traffic laws, snowmobile and boating laws, and hunting and fishing laws.

You would also be aware that Canada is made up of many different people who speak different languages, believe in different religions, live different lifestyles, and value different things, all of which are protected from discrimination by Canada's Charter of Rights and Freedoms.

More importantly, in addition to these shared world views, how you experience all of the above elements of Canadian society is influenced by such factors as whether you are rich or poor; white or a person of colour; male or female; heterosexual or gay or lesbian; married or single; renting or owning; working, unemployed, or retired; young or old; citizen or immigrant; professional or minimum-wage worker; full-time employed or part-time employed; or healthy, injured, or ill. Most of us will experience life in Canada from perspectives shaped by many combinations of the above attributes over the course of our lives.

Because people experience Canada differently, they can also differ about what they believe is in Canada's best interest. If people are rich, powerful, and respected, they may very well want Canada to remain as it is or to change in a way that benefits them. Philosopher Karl Mannheim (1936) calls this *ideological thinking*. On the other hand, if people are poor, unemployed, and living in slum conditions, they may very well want Canada to change drastically and in a way that benefits them. Mannheim (1936) called this *utopian thinking*.

Social policy is about making decisions that are, in the perception of those making them, in the best interests of Canada and Canadians. Because these perceptions are so subjective, it is essential to ask certain questions in order to understand what impact social policies will have on society. Specifically, who has the power to make social policy decisions? Whose views of life in Canada are driving the policy-making process? Who is benefiting from these policies? Who is not benefiting from these policies? How consistent are these policies with societal norms?

One of the most important aspects of social policy for beginning students is the multitude of approaches available to study it. Among the many approaches that will be explored throughout the book are the contrasting perceptions of social policy as comprehensive versus incremental, global versus local, and value-driven versus scientifically derived. These variances in approach reflect the social work profession's and society's confusion about just what social policy is.

What Are Social Policies?

The late British scholar Richard Titmuss (1974) examines social policy by first exploring the meaning of the terms *social* and *policy*. To him, *social* refers to all of the non-economic factors that affect people in society and relate to people as social beings. *Policy*, Titmuss insists, is about enduring the dilemmas of choice created when one objective must be selected over others.

Exploring various definitions and perceptions about social policy can be a frustrating journey into subtle abstract differences or esoteric debates. Moreover, many social workers and human service workers often confuse just what social policy is. For example, it is not uncommon to hear social workers talk about their agency's social policy.

The following is intended to provide you with a framework to ground your study of social policy. Throughout the book, you will be able to use this to analyze social policy debates.

Social policy describes societal visions, that is, values and beliefs that people hold about what a society should look like based upon some notion about human beings, about the nature of society and how society and humans interact. For example, different political parties talk about different programs or policies that they believe will benefit society. Different interest and advocacy groups also have a vision about what a society should look like. So we can identify a social policy position related to different competing groups in a society. We can also assume that most like-minded people will support a common vision and will disagree with a different vision being espoused by another group of like-minded people with their common vision. If we all agreed on a societal vision, then we would have only one social policy position.

However, those elected to form a government are in a unique position. They can translate their social policy vision into law, thus creating new public policies that reflect their vision, revising existing public policies to adjust to their vision, or simply repealing existing public policies. Public policies guide public programs and laws are binding to all citizens. Therefore, if you gain power, you can implement your social policies and require all citizens to live under the societal vision reflected in your social policies. People who disagree with Canadian laws are left with limited options, including supporting a party with your policy vision to win the next election, using social and/or economic power to prevent or discourage an elected government from implementing public policies with which you disagree, or revolting against the existing government and taking power.

Public policies inform social programs and define both the nature of the programs and the citizens for whom the programs serve. Agencies or government departments or ministries (the formal social organizations) are empowered and financed to provide these social programs within the framework provided by the enabling act and subsequent regulations. In turn, agencies and government services have organizational cultures that influence how services are delivered even within their guiding legislation.

In summary, social policy positions influence legislation, which in turn influences programs, which in turn influence services. Whoever has the power to implement his or her social policy position or to prevent others from implementing their position determines the quality, range, and availability of social programs. The next section deals with varying definitions of social policy as espoused by a wide range of theorists.

Defining Social Policies

Titmuss

Richard Titmuss (1974) argues that social policy is basically about "choices between conflicting political objectives and goals and how they are formulated" (49). These choices are influenced by views of what constitutes a good society based on that which "culturally distinguishes between the needs and aspirations of social man [sic] in contradiction to the needs and aspirations of economic man [sic]" (49). Titmuss argues that social policy can best be understood by looking at it in terms of one of the following three models or functions:

➤ *The Residual Welfare Model of Social Policy* argues that the private market and the family are responsible for meeting an individual's needs. Only when these break down should social welfare institutions come into play. As will be discussed in Chapter 3, proponents of neo-conservative and liberal ideologies favour this model.

➤ *The Industrial Achievement-Performance Model of Social Policy* argues that social needs should be met on the basis of merit, work performance, and productivity. Known as the "Handmaiden Model," it is favoured by positivists (Federico, 1983) and other economic and psychological theorists who advocate incentives, effort, and reward.

➤ *The Institutional Redistributive Model of Social Policy* argues that social welfare should be a major integrated institution in society, providing universal services outside the market, based on the principle of need.

Since policy can emerge from various alternative approaches, choices must exist. Without choices, we do not have a policy; rather we have a law, either natural or legislated. For example, since we cannot control the weather, we have no policy concerning weather control. However, should science ever learn how to control weather, then choices about how to control the weather would have to be made. Continuing with this example, a tension might arise between people who want warm sunshine and farmers who want rain (*preferential choices*). Further, the means of controlling the weather might cause some form of ecological distress, such as sterilizing some insects or wildlife (*anticipated consequences*). And finally, controlling the weather might even have detrimental effects that are not even known (*unanticipated consequences*). In this example, the choice to control weather would result in an anticipated consequence for insects and wildlife, some potential unanticipated consequences, and a decision about whether the farmer gets rain or the public gets sunshine.

Rein—Value-driven Policy

This example shows that values and beliefs are important aspects of making the choices necessary for social policy. Indeed, the American scholar Martin Rein (1974) suggests that "social policy is, above all, concerned with choice among competing values" (298). From Rein's perspective, society consists of people holding diverse values (world views) who are in competition with each other and, therefore, each other's values, in an effort to achieve maximum power. So ingrained are values in every aspect of social, economic, and public policies that many social policy theorists, such as Rein, Gil (1998), Wharf, and MacKenzie (1998) warn that a major role of policy-makers is to learn how to control their own values and prejudices. This warning is further discussed in Chapter 8.

Rein suggests that values influence social policy in five major ways:

1. Values influence how the purpose of the policy is defined, especially for policies that deal with "moral" decisions. An example would be policy addressing the abortion debate.

2. From among many possible choices of action, values influence priorities by assigning greater "value" to some courses of action over others. An economic example would be reducing the rate of inflation by increasing interest rates (assigning the protection of the status quo and business interests a higher value than maintaining employment levels).

3. Once a position is articulated and the means to bring it about are put in place, people will assign it importance (which is value-derived) simply because it exists (has form) and therefore society can be asked to change in order to allow that form to exist. For example, the North American Free Trade Agreement has caused significant changes to the Canadian economy,

leading to the closure of some industries, the increase in some markets, the decrease in others, and so on.

4. Policy-makers can become preoccupied with the value of usefulness and become overly concerned with political feasibility rather than societal need. A current example is the federal government's Axworthy social policy reform document of 1994, which is seen by many to have done little to change many social policies, since few proposals were implemented.

5. Values influence the way in which outcomes are interpreted and evaluated. One example is the claim that certain poverty lines do not really describe poverty. As Chapter 3 elaborates, there are many different poverty lines in Canada, each with its own threshold below which a person's annual income is declared "in poverty"; ultimately the threshold level is determined by some value of what is seen to be fair (adapted from Rein, 1974, 298).

Since social policy is often articulated as public policy, the values that gain dominance greatly affect the choices made in our public policy statements. Public policies are legislated acts, regulations, and by-laws (including all associated policies in the ministerial, agency, and public arenas) at the federal, provincial, and municipal levels of government (Doern and Aucoin, 1971). As such, public policies are *social statements* reflecting the values and ideology of the political party/parties sponsoring them. Because the bases of public policies are legislated acts and their regulations, they have three distinct attributes:

1. Public policies are *legitimate*. Although an issue may be heavily debated—as gun control is, for example—once it is legislated, it is the law and is right or legitimate. Those who opposed the issue must now accept it even if they are working to change it.

2. Public policies apply to everyone.

3. Because government *controls* (much, but not all) *coercion* in society, public policies can be enforced. Governments control enforcement agencies, such as the police, government investigators (e.g., income tax and welfare fraud investigators), and, in the case of the federal government, the army. These enforcement agencies ensure that the government can and will enforce the law.

Public policies in effect provide boundaries and controls to regulate a citizen's behaviour, either directly (game and fishing policy, housing policy, taxation policy) or indirectly (foreign policy). As such, public policies play an instrumental part in all aspects of societal life.

Gil—Social Justice

David Gil (1970), who, along with Rein and Wharf and MacKenzie, is discussed in greater length in Chapter 8, suggests that social policies are not only concerned with the life-sustaining activities that ensure minimum basic needs, but also with life-enhancing activities that stimulate our human potential. But the range of possibilities for these activities is as great as the range of world views that influence them. From a polycentric perspective, this variation in views allows a more complete world view to emerge. A polycentric perspective, first articulated by McPherson and Rabb (1994), argues that

radically different world views not only reveal something about culture and language, but about reality itself and the ways different people have come to know it. Therefore, each world view reveals something about the total picture, which can never be fully known. An accurate picture of reality is only possible by attempting to accommodate and reconcile as many world views as possible (Delaney, 1995, 13).

Moreover, Gil (1998) sees the necessity of a social transformation where systemic inequalities based on world views supporting "inequality, individualism, selfishness, domination, competition, and disregard for community (from local to global)"(35) are replaced by world views "affirming equality, individuality, liberty, cooperation, community and global solidarity" (35). Fundamental to this perspective is the view that human beings have physical, emotional, and spiritual dimensions and that human social functioning is impeded if resources that meet these physical, emotional, and spiritual dimensions are not available. The result would be humans whose potential is limited or at least constrained. Should one group of people attempt to ensure that their physical, emotional, and spiritual dimensions are satisfied at the expense of another group, then this would be an act of oppression.

Other approaches to social policy tend to reflect the comprehensive–incremental continuum.

Mishra—Society and Social Policy

Mishra (1981) defines social policy in comprehensive terms as referring "to the aims and objectives of social action concerning needs as well as to the structural patterns or arrangements through which needs are met" (x). Social policy is seen to be concerned with deliberately and rationally matching ends and means through social institutions designed for that purpose.

Braybrooke and Lindbloom—Incrementalism

Braybrooke and Lindblom (1963), in turn, emphasize *incrementalism*. These authors suggest that the world is just too complex and organic to allow comprehensive policy and planning. For one thing, comprehensive policy-makers themselves have to fill in variables about society and people about which they do not have valid and reliable information, thus allowing their own values to influence the design of social policies. Instead, they suggest that, historically, people simply corrected problems as they came up, and, over time, made substantive changes. Known as incrementalism, this approach to social policy analysis is limited to considerations of alternative policies that are only incrementally different from the status quo. Because there is no major framework, the overall policy approach tends to be disjointed. Because different people are preparing policies for different problems independently, the term *disjointed incrementalism* is often applied to examples of this approach, which displays the following characteristics:

1. Analysis is limited to a few familiar alternatives.
2. Analysis of policy goals is intertwined with empirical aspects of the problem.
3. Analysis is concerned with remedying ills rather than with seeking positive goals.
4. A sequence of trials, errors, and revised trials is undergone.
5. Analysis of only some of the important consequences of those alternatives is considered.
6. Analytical work is fragmented among many partisan participants in policy-making (Hogwood and Gunn, 1984).

Some observers argue that incrementalism closely approximates functionalism. This latter theory, functionalism, suggests that every social system must meet four functional prerequisites in order to persist. These four prerequisites apply to all social systems. They are:

1. *adaptation* to the external environment;
2. *goal attainment* to coordinate collective activities to reach certain goals;
3. *integration* of members to maintain solidarity and harmony; and
4. *pattern maintenance* (or *latency*) to ensure the activities required by members are performed with optimum compliance.

Functionalists view social welfare activities as helping to create harmony among social institutions and individuals, and hence maintaining communal solidarity. The essential framework is to value stability and continuity above social change. In other words, society, as it currently exists, is considered to be good, and therefore only when something goes wrong should it be changed.

Critics of functionalism, such as Mishra (1981), suggest that the increase in poverty, privilege, and exploitation in the United States and the universal problems of racism and sexism have served to undermine the validity of the functionalist model. Mishra and other scholars might argue that the dominant metaphor for social organization is conflict between groups in society, rather than social stability, as functionalists imply. Nevertheless, incrementalist approaches still provide a basis for social policy-making in Canada and are especially effective when combined with comprehensive policy-making. But regardless of which approach is adopted, a more important issue is how power is being shared and who determines the priorities, the structure, and the method of implementation of social welfare programs.

Turner; Yelaja

Canadian scholar Francis Turner views social policy as

statements of the social goals and objectives to which various groups—professional, governmental or private—are committed. They are the mission statements of various groups, and....vary widely in a country such as ours....[A]s responsible citizens in a democratic country, we have a responsibility to understand this important component of our lives. This responsibility exists whether our goal is to become a social worker, a member of other related professions, a better-informed recipient of services, an advocate for social change, or a fully participating member of society (1995, 10).

Turner's view, while reflecting the competition among values held by various groups for domination, also identifies social policy as being culturally relevant, that is, social policies in Canada are not the same as social policies found in other countries.

Another rather comprehensive definition of social policy comes from Canadian scholar Shankar Yelaja (1987) whose definition of social welfare reflects a social administration approach. For Yelaja, social policy is concerned with

the public administration of welfare services, that is, the formulation, development and management of specific services of government at all levels, such as health, education, income maintenance, and welfare services. Social policy is formulated not only by government, but also by institutions such as voluntary organizations, business, labour, industry, professional groups, public interest groups and churches. Furthermore, social policy is to be understood within the framework of societal ends and means, which are interdependent (2).

According to this perspective, social policy reflects social reality within a cultural context.

Gilbert and Specht; Marshall

American scholars Gilbert and Specht (1974) focus on social welfare policy in an effort to provide social workers with an understanding of how these policies affect the populations with which social workers have historically worked. They define the institution of social welfare as "that patterning of relationships which develops in society to carry out mutual support functions" (5). Another social policy theorist with social administration orientations, this time from the United Kingdom, is T. H. Marshall (1965), who notes that social policy is not a technical term with an exact meaning, but refers to

the policy of governments with regard to action having a direct impact on the welfare of the citizens by providing them with service or income. The central core consists, therefore, of social insurance, public (or national) assistance, the health and welfare services, housing policy (7).

Marshall argues that the best way of assuring the welfare of citizens is to cultivate among all citizens a sense of the right to have (also called a sense of entitlement to) the following three things:

➤ civil rights, which guarantee individual liberty and equality before the law;

➤ political rights, which ensure the right to vote and seek political office; and

➤ social rights, which ensure equal access and opportunities to all social institutions.

In assuring people these rights, social policy advocates would rely on the legal system to monitor and correct any abuses of these rights. However, Drover (2000) warns that globalization requires a redefinition of Marshall's notion of social citizenship because of the restricted ability of nations to respond to the rights of their citizens. Rice and Prince (2000) envision a co-operative union between the forces driving economic policies and social policies where social policy is seen as a viable partner with economic policy rather than a drain of national and international economies.

In a similar argument, Lafitte (1962) claimed that social policy is "an attempt to steer the life of society along lines it would not follow if left to itself" (9). Freeman and Sherwood (1970) view social policy as consisting of "conclusions reached by persons concerned with the betterment of community conditions and social life, and with the amelioration of deviance and social disorganization" (13).

Quality-of-Life

Another perspective that allows comparisons of the impact of social policies is the *quality-of-life approach*. This approach is used by the United Nations, which, on the basis of data collected on quality-of-life indicators, makes statements about the social health of nations. Examples of these quality-of-life indicators are:

➤ physical and mental health;

➤ education and occupational achievements;

➤ development in the arts and science;

➤ production and consumption;

➤ wealth and income (including child poverty);

➤ conditions of the natural environment;

➤ patterns of recreation;

➤ patterns of social participation;

➤ patterns of social morality; and

➤ social deviance and alienation.

The quality-of-life indicators allow social workers to compare how their country's social welfare programs fare when compared internationally. In recent years, Canada has slipped considerably in the amount of money spent on social programs and, conversely, has increased in the number of poor children and families.

The various social policy theories we have introduced all seek to explore the following questions: Is society organized around the needs of human beings? Are human beings organized around the needs of society? Are the needs of human beings and the needs of society interdependent? While these questions may sound rather simplistic, their resolution is not simplistic, as each question is supported by a set of ideologies and world views that seeks to make it the key question in all social policy statements. For example, the prevailing view in Canada today corresponds to the economic model of people, which advocates that human beings be organized around the economic needs of society. To challenge this view is to also challenge the power establishment not just in Canada, but internationally. As globalization results in more and more treaties among nations giving substantial power to economic interests, countries are having less say about the quality of life and social program issues that affect their people.

Social Policy in a Time of Mistrust and Cynicism

One of the unfortunate consequences of the replacement in the 1990s of the Canada Assistance Plan (CAP) with Canada Health and Social Transfer (CHST) was the unleashing of the ideology of mistrust. CAP, which was hailed by many countries as positive and progressive social welfare legislation, provided a standard of social assistance across Canada for people in need or likely to be in need. Originally designed to share welfare costs with the provinces on a fifty-fifty basis, CAP had slowly begun to decrease cost sharing with the provinces during the late 1980s and early 1990s. With the passing of CHST, responsibility for the funding of social services devolved from the federal government to the provinces and to local communities in some of these provinces. Moreover, the removal of CAP hailed a widespread increase in the privatization of social services across Canada. This will be discussed further in Chapter 7.

The ideology of mistrust suggests that people are "guided by an 'acquisitive instinct,' that is, they are out to get all they can by any means" (Macarov, 1995, 147). Mistrust has existed for centuries. The Law of Less Eligibility (also referred to as *wage stop*) is one example. Passed in 1834, this law required all people receiving charity to be given less money or goods than the lowest paid worker in the parish. This law was designed to starve those who were "lazy" or "immoral" back to work. The workhouses, which encouraged brutal and cruel treatment of unemployed workers, are another example of social policy being driven by the ideology of mistrust. Furthermore, the "ideology of the elite" argues that while most people are deserving and trustworthy, those people receiving charity or social assistance are not trustworthy or deserving because they lack moral character and cannot plan and think for themselves. This view also supports "the politics of conduct," which argues that a person's conduct should determine both the quality and quantity of services provided.

The resulting mistrust of people can lead to public announcements that welfare cheats are being hunted down and will be punished. Certainly the news media is more attracted to welfare cheaters being caught than to the many stories of those who are trying to both subsist and exist as people, while being provided with social assistance. You only need to think about how often you have heard people who are not poor speak knowingly about the youth who are abusing Employment Insurance, the women who are having babies in order to live off the public purse, the immigrants who are sending their welfare money to support terrorists, the youth who are committing horrible crimes and getting away with it, the homeless who are all mentally ill or lazy people, the unions who are trying to destroy business, the gays who want equal human rights, or the children of the poor who are so much like their parents—just no good.

As the ideology of mistrust becomes more pervasive in our society, so too is our society becoming more cynical. It quickly becomes evident that people who are rich demand and have opportunities that those who are not rich do not have. For example, while medicare attends to the health needs of the general population, those with sufficient money can go to the United States and receive medical attention and procedures quickly.

Political and Social Consequences

Lerner (1997) believes that the current ethos of selfishness and cynicism has led to an economy-first attitude in which people are becoming more and more insecure if they are not among those who are "winning" in today's economic marketplace. He envisions that the shrinking middle class will have to create an alliance with the poor to combat the ethos of selfishness, materialism, and corporatism (Saul, 1995) that is being espoused not just by the rich, but by multinational conglomerates. For Lerner, the politics of meaning is a political process aimed at achieving the following goals:

1. to create a society that "encourages and supports love and intimacy, friendship and community, ethnic sensitivity and spiritual awareness" (55);
2. to redefine production and profit in terms of practices that foster spiritual harmony, loving relationships, mutual recognition, and work that promotes the common good;
3. to construct social conditions that promote the material, emotional, and spiritual uniqueness, sanctity, and infinite preciousness of every human being;
4. to design a society that recognizes the need and provides for the opportunity to develop our inner lives; and
5. to create a society that instills awe and joy in how we relate to the world and each other.

For social workers whose value and ethical base is grounded in principles of social justice, social equality, and respect for the inner being of all humans, these goals, while seemingly idealistic, speak to the very heart of our profession. Many other twentieth-century writers, such as Fromm (1967, 1955), Theilhard (1998), de Chardin (1955), Freire (1994, 1985, 1968), Frankl (1969), Gil (1998, 1992, 1970), and Titmuss (1970) have all supported some aspect of Lerner's five goals.

One interesting look at the effects of encouraging altruism is a study done by Titmuss (1970) , who noted that the donation of blood in countries such as Britain and Canada is done voluntarily and without financial payment, while in other countries, such as the United States, donors are paid for their blood. This provided Titmuss with the opportunity to study whether the altruistic act of donating blood created different results than did the market mechanism of purchasing blood. Titmuss concludes that the selling of blood

represses....altruism, erodes the sense of community, lowers scientific standards, sanctions...the profits in hospitals and clinical laboratories, legalizes hostility between doctor and patient, subjects....medicine to the laws of the marketplace, places immense social costs on those least able to bear them...[and] increases the danger of unethical behaviour (245–246).

In effect, blood systems that purchase blood may create a situation in which blood and blood products are transferred from the poor to the rich. Moreover, where blood is given voluntarily, supplies and the quality of these supplies of blood are expected to be superior to those within systems where blood is purchased.

As elaborated in Chapters 5 and 9, there are profound implications to the current ethos of cynicism, as it relates to the environmental movement, global economic and political structures, and the decrease of social service programs.

Social Policy and Social Welfare Policy

For many beginning students of social policy, there is often some confusion between the terms *social policy* and *social welfare policy*. What is apparent from the various approaches to social policy that we have discussed is the lack of consensus about how social policy ought to be defined. The generally prevailing view of social policy is that it is concerned with the "big picture" of society and with the big issues in society, such as social justice, social equality, human rights and freedoms, empowerment and human authenticity, progressive distribution of wealth, full employment, medicare, criminal justice, and mutual aid (Mullaly, 1993).

Because social policy deals with major social issues, it is concerned with the espoused visions and social remedies articulated by such groups as political communities, business communities, professional communities, labour communities, multicultural communities, interest groups, and special-needs communities representing people who are poor, people who are physically challenged, and people who are homeless.

Issues of social power and social control are also important concerns for social policy. In a very real way, social workers who work in the area of social policy become monitors of social conditions and public policies. In this capacity, they play an important role in educating the social work profession and society-at-large regarding anticipated or unanticipated consequences that might result from new or revised public policies or from changes in government and business practices in Canada.

Social policy is also concerned with "politics," with trade agreements, with environmental issues, with hiring practices, with taxation, with racism, with gender and sexual preference discrimination, with the economy, and with other related subjects. Advocates for social justice often use the social policy forum to promote political solutions for social problems (Gil, 1998; Carniol, 1995; Mullaly, 1993) and view the role of the social worker as one of promoting social justice and social equality not only in the service community, but in the population at large. Social change based on humanistic values drives this agenda for change and promotes a collaborative partnership in Canadian policy-making.

Social welfare policy, on the other hand, is concerned with social welfare programs and the relationship between public and business policies and social welfare programs. As such, it is less abstract and global than social policy and deals with very concrete issues, such as the quality and effectiveness of social service programs, citizen participation in policy and service issues, the role of community, and the actual impact of public policies on people. By studying social welfare policy, social workers directly observe the impact of public policies on the lives of people. As a result, a major role for social welfare policy advocates is the deconstruction of the social myths that drive many of Canada's social programs today and the direct involvement of people in finding solutions to their life problems.

Social welfare policy advocates are very concerned with the role of the community in the lives of its members (Delaney, Brownlee and Sellick, 1999; Wharf and McKenzie, 1998; Cassidy, 1991). Wharf and McKenzie (1998) describe community governance using the metaphor of a three-rung ladder. The first rung includes programs, such as water and sewage, garbage, parking, and recreation programs and facilities that are essentially under community control. The second rung refers to those programs for which the power to operate lies in the provincial, territorial, or federal government levels, but the operating responsibilities belong to the community. This level, they suggest, includes such programs as child welfare and health services. The third rung, which is concerned with principles of equity, requires a collaborative partnership between senior levels of government and the community. Included on this rung are programs such as Social Assistance and Employment Insurance. Wharf and McKenzie conclude by affirming that community governance models provide "an opportunity to reform the policy process and policy outcomes by involving people who are significantly affected by these outcomes" (125).

It is in the area of citizen participation that social welfare policy excels. While social policy tends to deal comprehensively in the political and societal arenas, social welfare policy lends itself to involving people in a process toward policy development and renewal. The issues that social welfare policy addresses are issues that people know about and that affect everyday living. People can more readily see the cause-effect relationship between how programs operate and how these programs affect them. It is much easier to involve people in actions that are clear, local, and achievable. On the other hand, advocacy in social policy is generally national, provincial, or territorial, ideological, value-based, and complex. This makes it much harder to involve people. For example, in a university or college setting, it is always much easier to get students to participate in a march against raising tuition fees than it is to get students involved with a political party to influence its educational policies in favour of lowering or stabilizing tuition fees.

A final consideration is the distinction between policy-making and policy advocacy. Jansson (1999) suggests that policy advocates must have analytical skills (for policy evaluation and development), political skills (for development and implementation of political strategies), interactional skills (for development of collaborative partnerships), and values-clarification or ethical-reasoning skills. Both policy advocates and policy-makers must be able to perform six policy tasks (setting agendas, analyzing problems, making proposals, enacting policy, implementing policy, and assessing policy). As Jansson notes:

When presenting problems to agency, community, and legislative decision makers, the [policy practitioners and policy advocates] engage in agenda-setting tasks. When they use social science research....practitioners use problem-analyzing tasks. They also analyze social problems, such as homelessness, in classifying homeless persons, gauging the problem's prevalence in various communities, and seeking its causes (13).

All schools of social work have at least one course that deals with social policy. One reason is that social policy and social welfare policy govern not only the environment in which most social workers will work, but also the quality of services that will be available to the people we serve and the attitudes that will prevail among those who rely on these services for their well-being. As the following section discusses, there are other reasons why social policy must be addressed.

Social Work and Social Policy

As subsequent chapters will reiterate, every social work intervention—be it with an individual, a family, a group, an organization, or a community—is somehow referenced to a social policy. Assisting a family to seek adequate housing invariably relates to social housing policies; assisting an individual to re-enter the community after a prolonged period of incarceration may relate to vocational policies. These considerations therefore influence the nature of Canadian social work education.

From a curriculum perspective, the Educational Policy Statements of *The Manual of Standards and Procedures for the Accreditation of Canadian Programs of Social Work Education* (1996), approved by the Canadian Association of Schools of Social Work, state that the social work curriculum at the first university level shall ensure that social work students will learn "critical analysis of social work and social welfare history and social policy as socially constructed institutions and their implications for social work practice" (CASSW, 1996, 3). Accreditation Standard Article 5.8 (d) states that social work students in the first university level shall have "transferable analysis of the multiple and intersecting bases of oppression and related practice skills" (CASSW, 1996, 6).

Although this explains why schools of social work teach social policy, it does not explain why you should study social policy. Perhaps the following narrative will help.

While driving home from work one day, I heard on the radio that the city was going to increase swimming pool rates from 10 cents per child to 25 cents per child. I thought to myself that inflation is striking everywhere and while annoyed, gave this no further thought. After all, a 15-cent raise is not the end of the world.

Three days later, I was listening to the same station's call-in show, and I heard a mother relate the following. She was a single mother with five children, living on Social Assistance. Each summer, she saved money to allow her children to go swimming three times a week at a cost of $1.50. However, with the new rates, this would now cost her $1.25 per day or $3.75 for the three days. She could not afford this and would have to cut back the time her children could go swimming.

She was greatly distressed, as swimming was one of the few activities to which she could afford to send her children. Now her children would become even more isolated from other children and she was helpless to do anything about it. When asked why she could not just save more money, the mother replied that she was giving up meals for herself in order for the children to go swimming under the old rates.

I was embarrassed as I listened to this mother, and angry that she even had to tell such a story. As a social worker, I should have been more sensitive to the price hike. Worse, since I could afford to pay the extra 15 cents, I did not even consider that there were those who could not. This is one policy I vowed to fight and one new awareness that allows me to assess policies better. I just hope I did learn.

The study of social policy can increase our sensitivity to the people we serve. Because we know the circumstances under which many of our clients live, we can become proponents for policies that will enhance their well-being and advocates against policies that negatively impact them.

The study of social policy also allows you to gain greater understanding of how social inequalities, disempowerment, marginalization, and oppression can seep into political agendas and how these can affect those least able to fight against them. Bishop (1994) sees these elements as part of a "power-over" agenda. This agenda seeks to create a world of systems designed to keep people in unjust and unequal positions, using four types of power over people. The first type, political power, results in power being in the hands of fewer and fewer people because those making decisions favour their own group, giving themselves increasing power. The second type, economic power, occurs where one group has access to more economic resources than others. The third type, physical force, backs up economic and political power. The fourth type, ideological power, allows an individual or group to influence others' concepts of reality, and their ideas of what is possible and what is valuable (36–37).

Understanding how those forces that are opposed to social welfare and the welfare state attempt to gain social, economic, and political power through social policy is important for social workers. Wharf (1990) suggests that social work practice that is insufficiently oriented to social change fails to address the four following problems. First, it makes the assumption that once a problem is identified, change will occur and the problem will be solved. This is rarely the case in real practice. Second, it ignores power and its distribution in Canada. Third, social workers are not assigned responsibility by society for bringing about change and, in reality, some agencies may be the problem and not the solution. Fourth, the issue of auspices is not addressed. In other words, because social workers are employed in agencies that receive their mandates from those holding political power, the social worker's efforts to change the system are limited by each agency's political and social agendas (Wharf, 1990, 23–25).

By understanding the policy-making process, social workers can learn how to advocate for social changes that benefit those in society least able to fend for themselves. Many of our current beliefs about leadership, privilege, hierarchy, power, and wealth have been forged in history and have created patterned inequalities in the allocation of status and the distribution of rights among people (Gil, 1992, 1970). By exposing these inequalities and confronting the metaphors that support social inequality, social workers can participate in the policy debate. In fact, both the American and Canadian Social Work Codes of Ethics make the study of social justice a practice requirement.

It is important for social workers to understand and be sensitive to the different life experiences of Canadians. Understanding how social policies impact on issues of human diversity is critical for social workers who live in a pluralist society. Social workers are asked to play a variety of practice roles—teacher, enabler, facilitator, mediator, organizer, advocate, case manager, and administrator, among others. Social policy gives an added contextual dimension to these roles because it places the client situation within the social arena—an arena that too often has little or no regard for the client or the client's situation.

The following story outlines one of the authors' experiences with social policy and its direct impact on people.

One day, I reported to my deputy minister who informed me that a prominent author was coming to the province to assist us with reforms to our institutions for children. A major presentation involving the Premier, several provincial and federal Ministers, and the prominent author was being planned and I was asked to be the spokesperson for the province. Flattered but anxious, I read every article and book written by this prominent author until I had prepared a speech that I believed would reflect both the province's and the author's position on reform.

On the day of the presentation, which was being held in the province's largest children's institution, I arrived in a very nervous state. As I walked down the rather dingy corridor leading to the elevator, I could not help but notice the children wandering in the corridor. As I looked at each child, I told myself that I was giving this speech for this child. I kept repeating this thought child by child and I began to feel energized and confident. After all, I had a cause.

Just as I approached the elevator, I saw a young girl stretched out in a wheelchair. The child had no recognizable face. Her skin was pale and wrinkled and her nose was two holes on her face. Mucous was running from her nose into a gaping mouth.

As I was giving my speech, I noticed the smiles from the officials on the stage, including the author. I was pleased. After the speeches were finished, the moderator asked if there were any questions. Among the several hundred people in the audience was a woman who, after a few polite and complimentary questions had been asked by others, said, "This is all well and good, but these children need someone to love them, to hold them, to comfort them. How are your changes going to achieve this if you don't give us more staff?" Politely brushed off, she repeated the same question in many ways until those sitting near her began to physically indicate by their body positions that they were not with her.

I was really angry with this woman because I sensed she had taken the edge off the presentations and, after all, I had been one of the presenters. However, the Deputy Minister came over to me, shook my hand, congratulated me on an excellent speech, and invited me to join the dignitaries for lunch. Flattered, I said I would be along shortly but I wanted to help package our equipment first. Actually, I just needed to work off energy.

Eventually I went into the elevator and upon leaving had this overwhelming urge to turn around. When I did, I saw the woman who had irritated me holding the little girl who had been in the wheelchair in her arms while she was feeding her. I saw the love on this woman's face as she gazed into the girl's eyes and I sensed the love this little girl returned. I stood transfixed, totally shattered, shamed, and humbled.

This is one of those events in my life that was a gift, albeit a very painful one. Before my eyes was a reminder to me that I chose to be a social worker and I had unconsciously drifted from my own values and belief in human beings. I told myself over and over that social and public policies are about people, and policy and people cannot be compartmentalized. As a policy analyst, I use this moment to understand the human face in policy and the beauty that this rugged woman taught me. I wish every policy analyst and social planner had a moment like mine when the intellect is awakened to human potential and the power of love.

I did not go to lunch. I did not give another speech for five years. But I did learn a beautiful but painful lesson about the human spirit and about the purpose of social policy.

This story is a reminder that policy is about people, not just facts, statistics, laws, rules, manuals, power, and politics. Social workers whose values put people first and promote the human imperative to become more fully human (Freire, 1968) are positioned to play a vital role in the development of Canada's social policy and social welfare policy.

Finally, social policy provides a wealth of information on such issues as how our current social structures came to be; who is benefiting from these structures; who has the real power to make social changes; what the most effective approaches to citizen participation are; who is being oppressed, isolated, or ignored in society; and what array of ideological powers exist to maintain the current social agenda regarding the distribution of wealth, powers, and privilege.

Conclusion

Social policy helps social workers to better understand people. It does this by describing both the social context in which people live and the forces that created this context. It allows us to appreciate that the world in which we live did not just happen. Rather, it was created on the basis of decisions people made about what this society would look like and what values and beliefs would drive the development of this society. The inequalities that exist in Canada are not accidental. Moreover, as this chapter points out, there are different ways of conceptualizing social policy, differences between social policies and social welfare policies, considerable interface between all levels and fields of social work practice and social policies, and the profound significance of such social values as cynicism and ideology in how social policies are created and carried out. The next chapter discusses how an understanding of the historic origins of social policies is critical to an appreciation of how social policies evolved, what the major factors in this evolution were, and what might be a reasonable basis for thinking about their present and future development.

Discussion

To help you explore the issue of equality and its importance to social policy, the following is intended to provide a source of discussion.

Are You a Number One?

Issues of equality are of enormous concern to advocates of progressive social welfare in Canada. However, for beginning (and sometimes advanced) students of social policy, this concept can be deceptive, simply because a "living" society is enormously difficult to understand. The following examples use the number 1.0 to illustrate just how complex this concept is.

But first, equality does not view human beings as the "same," which is what the political right attempts to say. In fact, it is just the opposite. Equality recognizes that every human being is unique and capable of human development. In essence, equality promotes the notion that every person is entitled to the same chance to develop and evolve her/his human potential.

Now, let's get back to the number 1.0 and start with an easy example. Assume that a society assigns every human being in that society the value of 1.0. In a democracy, every eligible citizen has one vote and therefore a 1.0 value. But the term "eligible citizen" suggests that there must be people who are not eligible to vote and who politically are assigned a value of less than 1.0, or in this case, 0. Canada, at the turn of the twentieth century, did not allow the mentally ill, criminals, women, children, immigrants, refugees, and others the right to vote. Advocacy groups fought to gain the value of 1.0 for some of these people but not for all. At the turn of the twenty-first century, some of those listed here are still assigned the value of 0. In other words, they have no voice in the Canadian political election system.

Now, let's use another example that examines power and privilege assigned to people in political office—the very people who can highly influence policy decisions. People who hold political office are given a value greater than 1.0. The Office of the Prime Minister gives this citizen greater powers and prerogatives than an ordinary citizen and he or she may therefore be viewed as a 2.5. A major, cabinet minister, or other elected official, may have a rating somewhere between 1.1 and 2.4. However, when these people leave office, they (we assume) return to 1.0. In a dictatorial society, the leaders assign themselves values even higher than 2.5 and most others in that society a value of 0. In a feudal system, the king may be a 5.0 or 10.0, the nobility somewhere between 1.1 and the king's value; and freepersons may have a value of 1.0, but serfs are 0s.

When considering how policy is made in Canada, who else influences the policy-making process and what value do they have? For example, the National Business Council currently exerts greater influence than the National Anti-Poverty Association. Northern communities have complained that the views of southern communities dominate policy decisions and disempower and disrespect northern realities and people. Even within social movements that espouse equality, inequality can exist among those who have influence and those whose voices are not heard. Inequalities and injustices can occur within and between different social, political, and economic arrangements in society.

Another perspective from which to consider the issue of equality involves everyday life situations. For example, consider something as simple as applying for a job. If my mother owns the company and I apply for a job, my value may be a 10.0. Other applicants may be 1.0s because they are well qualified and some, equally qualified, may even be less than 1.0 if colour, religion, gender, or other variables are being used to select candidates. In a like manner, some people try to assign their status, job, wealth, family name, religion, race, or other attribute a value greater than 1.0 in order to achieve superiority and advantage over others. Can you think who these people would be and provide some examples that illustrate this?

Let us examine yet another dimension. As a college or university student, what value is being assigned to you, to your professors, or the school's administrators? Are different academic units viewed as having greater value than 1.0? For example, is medicine viewed as equal to social work? Is law viewed as equal to psychology? Is psychology equal to social work?

Now, let's examine one more level of complexity. An individual may have a number of different values for different social situations. For example, an unemployed white male who lives in a home with a family of three and who is the star hockey player may be viewed (in a right-wing society) as a 0.4 because he is unemployed, a 1.0 because he is a white male, a 1.5 because he dominates his family, and a 2.0 by the community for his hockey skills.

However, perception of social worth is also an issue. For example, the son of a rich family with a social status of 3.0 may view himself as being only a 0.5. On the other hand, the daughter of a peasant family with a social value of 0.1 may view herself as a 1.0. It is obviously a difficult chore for the rich son to understand that others will see him as a 3.0 regardless of how he sees himself and he may very well believe that he is underprivileged. The same is true for the peasant's daughter. Perception can blind one's view of justice and equality. A millionaire who is the poorest in her neighbourhood may believe she is only a 0.8.

You can apply the number 1.0 to assess how any situation values participants. The above examples deal with individual value, social value, organizational value, and human value at political, civil, and social levels of societal interactions. Obviously, this can become very complex, very quickly. Experiment by using the number 1.0 to analyze family situations, relationships, social groups, and others. You may wish to read Gil (1998), Saul (1995), Swift (1995), and/or Bishop (1994) to get more information on equality.

Chapter 2

Historical Influences

Social policies are in a constant state of change, but their roots may be traced to the earliest stages of human evolution. Familiarity with history therefore provides the reader with some of the necessary tools to think about how social policies could be constructed for today and tomorrow. Rather than being constrained by the present-day circumstances of time or place, the human imagination is set free. Prevailing assumptions thus may be more readily challenged, rather than benignly accepted. Creative approaches may be considered, rather than overlooked or assumed to have been untenable.

This chapter examines several areas of English Canadian social welfare history; further elaboration of the experiences of Aboriginal peoples and of French-speaking Canada appear in Chapter 6. Although this chapter also presents data in chronological order, the following 12 themes are evident throughout:

1. Policies are in a constant state of evolution—they have taken on different forms during different periods of history.

2. Social policies are "cultural constructs"—they are profoundly influenced by myriad cultures, values, and ideologies in a society.

3. Social policies sometimes represent the highest aspects of being human. At their very best, they reflect a basic concern for other people, a recognition of our interdependence, and an impulse to act upon this recognition.

4. There is a contradictory nature to social policies. Among recipients, some aspects have been beneficial, while others, as will be seen, have not. Motivations among proponents of social policies, whether conscious or not, have been just as variable. Social policies, as a result, may reflect motivations and/or have consequences that are troubling: the drive to contain social unrest, to maintain social control, or to reproduce social inequalities with respect to gender, ethnicity, race, range of mental or physical ability, or other areas of diversity.

5. Social policies have different impacts on different groups in society. Recipients of a particular policy, for instance, may have an experience disparate from that of the person who is paid to carry out the policy.

6. Various concepts in the history of policy development remain with us to the present day, such as the distinction between deserving and undeserving poor, or the local responsibility for social welfare.

7. In contemporary times, social policies have mirrored the growing social and economic complexity of modern life: the increasing mobility of people, the spread of urbanization, the deep impact of industrial capitalist development, and the gradual appreciation of human diversity. Corresponding also with industrial capitalist development has been the increasingly atomized, stratified nature of society, and the rise of bureaucratic structures, of which social work has been an important part.

8. The arrangements of capitalism in the past several decades have eroded the range of social policies and their comprehensiveness. Across the globe, more flexible forms of capital accumulation, labour market organization, and consumption patterns have prevailed. These, in turn, are seen by many observers to have compromised the range of social policy choices available to political leaders. International industrial capitalism and its multinational corporations have been increasingly freed from earlier notions of national responsibility. Environmental policy, workplace conditions, job security, wages, and social policies may well be determined less by national policy and more by the market-driven, lowest-bidder ethos of an increasingly international and competitive industrializing world.

9. The state has increasingly relinquished social service delivery to the private realm, often called the privatization of social services. This development reflects current national and international trends that emphasize the private marketplace over the direct role of government.

10. More and more, the economy requires a flexible workforce made up of part-time jobs, underemployment, and limited employment in the form of contract jobs of short duration. Social workers, like their clients, will be expected to respond to this new workplace environment, where, among other things, lifelong learning and vocational flexibility prevail.

11. Reflecting the inherently political nature of social policies, the Constitution of Canada is significant in determining which level of government has a particular administrative or financing authority. At the beginning of the twentieth century, local or municipal governments funded and administered most social services. But over the course of the century social welfare responsibilities gradually emerged among provincial and, in particular, federal jurisdictions.

12. The conceptualization of social welfare has transformed from a "residual" to an "institutional" (Wilensky and Lebeaux, 1958) and finally to a "post-institutional" perspective.

It is this final theme that provides a framework for exploring the preceding ones, as these terms—residual, institutional, and post-institutional—describe approaches that represent the three major periods in which Canadian social welfare history occurs.

The Residual Approach

In Canada, a residual concept of social welfare predominated until the twentieth century. During instances of sickness, unemployment, or other causes of interrupted or insufficient income, the family and the economic marketplace were considered the "normal" channels of help. For example, if sickness made it impossible for a family member to go to work, alternative sources of income—credit, a loan, or a different family member taking on additional employment—were sought. Alternatively, the family could turn to relatives for temporary assistance. Only after these sources were exhausted would other parties intervene, including members of the immediate community, religious institutions, or, later, charities. This residual model of social welfare is contrasted by the institutional approach. The institutional model emphasizes the role of government in responding to social needs, and is elaborated later in this chapter.

Classical Civilizations

The impulse to come to another's assistance is a fundamental part of what it is to be human. Indeed, anthropologists have observed that sharing is an essential characteristic of some of the earliest forms of human organization. Among early hunting-gathering societies, when food became scarce and hunger acute, generosity and sharing prevailed over hoarding. This is more than a simple matter of etiquette, for the maintenance of social bonds is essential to determining a group's fertility and rate of survival (Dolgoff and Feldstein, 1984, 16, 26). Given the threat of raids from other tribes or species, and the hazards of eking out an existence amidst a harsh physical climate, an individual literally could not survive without belonging to the collective. In a very real life and death context, this awareness underscores the symbiotic benefits of doing good unto one's neighbour.

The present discussion of hunting-gathering societies indicates how the responses we make to those in our identified group differ from those we make to people who are considered outsiders. Traditional societies often differentiate their treatment of members inside their own group from those outside it. In the same manner, contemporary social policies provide benefits for members of Canadian society, yet not to members of other societies. Social welfare assistance is an example of a program that only applies to Canadians living in Canada. Canadian social policies have other subtle ways of distinguishing between insiders and outsiders. As will be seen, particularly in Chapter 6, various areas of diversity, such as race, ethnicity, gender, range of ability, sexual orientation, and others, influence social policies.

Many ancient cultures throughout the world expressed social responsibilities in religious terms. As early as 2000 BC, Sumerian society placed a divine value on the protection of widows, orphans, and the poor. In fourth-century-BC China, Confucian ideals of humane and righteous leadership compelled rulers to target public funds toward the care of the aged, poor, orphans, or those affected by natural disasters, as well as toward the creation of public lands for the gathering of wood and herbs (Dolgoff and Feldstein, 1984, 28–30). Aboriginal societies in present-day North America continue to use such symbols as the Medicine Wheel to express the sacred bond between humanity and the physical and spiritual planes of existence (Feehan and Hannis, eds., 1993; Bopp et al., 1985). In the Judeo-Christian tradition, several Old Testament injunctions compel part of an annual harvest to be donated to the poor (Leviticus 19: 9–10) and to the widowed and strangers (Deuteronomy 24:19–22). The New Testament instructs Christians to care for the disadvantaged (Matthew 25: 31–46) and to forsake the love of material possessions (Luke 6: 20–38). Muslims also have a strong tradition of concern for the poor. In fact, one of the Five Pillars of Islam, alms-giving, is described not as a tax or a charity, but as a religious duty (Sura 9: 60).

Such widespread religious ideals were manifest in tangible forms. Ancient Grecian temples served as medical centres and care stations for the poor. In Roman society, a system of public charity was so advanced that during the second century AD, as much as half of Rome's population relied on some form of public assistance. In the Byzantine east, a complex system of maternity hospitals, medical facilities, and food rationing was provided from the revenues of the Orthodox Christian patriarchs (Dolgoff and Feldstein, 1984, 31–40). In our own time, social legislation is the bedrock of the welfare state, and, it should be stressed, is far from a historical aberration, or a peculiarity of our own time. Indeed, one of the earliest explicit social policies occurred in medieval England, the 1349 Statute of Labourers, which, in the aftermath of the Black Plague, froze workers' wages to their pre-plague levels, and limited the mobility of labour outside of one's home parish (de Schweinitz, 1943, 1–2).

The Medieval and Elizabethan European Heritage

Indeed, many of the direct roots of Canadian social policy are derived from a European heritage. Three non-governmental forms of institutionalized charity gradually developed and were particularly significant. The first of these were the medieval guilds, representing various merchant classes and artisans. Acting as mutual aid societies and charitable organizations for their members, the guilds built and maintained hospitals, distributed food to the needy, provided lodgings for the travelling poor, and gave other forms of incidental help. The second form of charity, the private foundations, were established by affluent benefactors and devoted to the construction and maintenance of hospitals, almshouses, and other such institutions. By the early sixteenth century there were some 460 such foundations in England alone. The third source of charity was the Church, providing assistance through various monastic orders among the thousands of local parishes across the continent. In Western Europe, among other parts of

Christiandom, tithing to the Church was compulsory, and a third of all collections went to the poor (Dolgoff and Feldstein, 1984, 39–44). The tithe may be seen as an early precursor to the contemporary income tax system, which helps to finance the modern welfare state.

This elaborate system of medieval charity was turned upside down by the sixteenth-century Protestant Reformation. In England, as in other parts of Europe, Protestant sects emerged, and Roman Catholic monasteries were dissolved. A new system of English social welfare was established and enshrined in the Elizabethan Poor Laws of 1601. Earlier, voluntary modes of charity fell to the local (parish) governments on a national scale, with accompanying punishments for non-compliance. Each parish was required to appoint an overseer of the poor, who, in consultation with church wardens, dispensed relief to the poor. The significance to the present day is twofold. Firstly, the overseer was an obvious precursor to the modern-day social worker. There is also an evident social control function to the role of the overseers. Indeed, overseers provide an excellent reminder that not all of social work's roots are strictly altruistic. Secondly, for the first time in history, social welfare responsibility had become, in practice and in legislation, a formalized, local arrangement. Voluntary forms of charity, including orphanages, hospitals, and almshouses for the old, remained alongside other local arrangements (Leiby, 1978, 38–41). Establishing a more comprehensive role for the state, a concept that emerged in its complete form in the twentieth century, saw its beginnings, therefore, in the sixteenth century. Up to the present time, this strong presence of local jurisdictions in social service delivery has persisted.

Other aspects of the Elizabethan Poor Laws are with us today. Later in the century, the principle of local residency was legislated, requiring that an individual receiving alms (or in contemporary usage, welfare) within a particular parish had to be a resident of that parish. In our own time, local governments as well as provinces have legislated that recipients must live within a particular province or municipality for a certain length of time before being entitled to receive Social Assistance.

A final feature of Elizabethan welfare, established in the late 1590s, was the differentiation made between deserving and undeserving poor, an aspect that had been part of previous forms of charity, but which was now outlined in legislation. While present-day terminology and practices may be different, one continuity has been this compulsion to distinguish between those who are worthy and those who are not. In Elizabethan times, the classification was threefold: the impotent poor, that is, those who could not work (pregnant women, extremely sick men or women, those over the age of 60) were allowed to live in what became known as poorhouses; any able-bodied people who could not seek employment or were temporarily unemployed were consigned to workhouses; and "unregenerate idlers" were placed in houses of correction (Bruce, 1961, 26; Dolgoff and Feldstein, 1984, 46). In contemporary times, various income security programs differentiate between classes of eligibility. Able-bodied individuals who temporarily cannot work due to work-related illness or injury may apply for Workers' Compensation. Able-bodied individuals capable of work but between jobs may be eligible to receive Employment Insurance (EI), or if EI entitlements run out, provincially/locally administered Social Assistance programs under various names, including General Welfare Assistance. Those who cannot work due to physical or psychiatric incapacity may receive Workers' Compensation long-term disability, Canada Pension Plan long-term disability, or provincially administered income security programs. Those who cannot work due to the responsibilities of single parenthood may receive benefits from provincially administered income security programs (Graham and Al-Krenawi, 2000). The Elizabethan Poor Laws also distinguished between men and women; there are numerous references, for instance, to women within the impotent poor classification. In our own time, as will be seen, social policies have continued to be constructed differentially for men and women.

In the 1600s, as in previous centuries, the plight of the poor was deplorable. Hospitals, poorhouses, workhouses, and other such institutions were invariably overcrowded, lacked minimum public health standards familiar to the contemporary reader, and were the loci of such deadly diseases as cholera, tuberculosis, and typhoid (Desert, 1976; Gonthier, 1978). Marginalized members of society—vagrants, those who were sick or disabled, among others—were forced into poorhouses that were as wretched as, and were sometimes one and the same as, local jails. Levels of alms were deliberately minimal. To seek assistance beyond the residual bounds of one's immediate family or the economic marketplace could be the source of frequent and intense public derision. Idle men refusing work were whipped, sent to prison, or both. Others were permanently maimed in an effort to rid them of their idleness. For these and other reasons, people were known to turn to prostitution, theft, or other crimes to avoid the disgrace and hardships of receiving alms (de Schweinitz, 1943, 20–22; Dolgoff and Feldstein, 1984, 49).

Before leaving the Elizabethan period in England, one final point should be emphasized: the Reformation Protestant theology of Calvin, Luther, and other thinkers influenced virtually all aspects of society, social welfare included. This thinking, moreover, continues to resonate in those twenty-first-century countries, such as Canada, where the historic influence of a Protestant theology remains vital to many people. Work, in Calvinist terms, became a divine vocation and therefore a religious activity. Idleness and worldly temptations were seen to interfere with the glory of God. Personal responsibility, discipline, and intense individualism were all revered (Weber, 1930, trans. 1958). As for social welfare, a legacy of punitive and repressive approaches found new rationalization. Pauperism, in this Protestant world view, was thought to result from the character defects of an individual or the flaws of a family. For moral and religious reasons, indiscriminate alms giving was condemned, and the poor were visited by poor law overseers, or by other community representatives, such as clergy, to root out the drunk, idle, or other undesirables (Dolgoff and Feldstein, 1984, 46–7).

The Nineteenth-century European Heritage

For several centuries, the principles established during the Elizabethan era predominated. But in the early nineteenth century, changes came about due to two issues of public concern: the rising costs of British poor relief and the rising numbers of relief recipients. A three-year royal commission was struck, resulting in the

Poor Law Reforms of 1834. Several principles were then established. The first was named "less eligibility," and stated that the basic provisions that one received while on relief were to be *less* than the lowest-paying available job. The rationale was to dissuade people from receiving relief, and to encourage self-reliance via the economic marketplace. This less-eligibility principle continues to dominate social welfare thinking in our own time. Economists and other analysts, for example, refer to policies that encourage the swift return to work, rather than reliance on an income security program (Burns, Batavia, and DeJong, 1994; Lewin and Hasenfeld, 1995; Shah and Smith, 1995; Schansberg, 1996; Smith, 1993). To this end, some politicians and policy analysts call for further reductions in social welfare entitlements.

The second 1834 principle was a delineation between outdoor and indoor relief, the forerunner of the current Canadian system of provincially/municipally administered Social Assistance. Outdoor relief provided material assistance to a select category of recipients who were allowed to live at home: the sick, the aged, the orphaned, or widowed. Indoor relief, in contrast, was limited to able-bodied men who were deemed employable. It could not be received at home. Recipients were obligated to live in workhouses and to undertake hard, manual labour—for example, breaking piles of large stones—in compensation for work. The intention was to punish and to limit the appeal of relief so as to encourage the able-bodied to fend for themselves.

This distinction in legislation between outdoor and indoor relief spelled out different categories of the poor, and was reminiscent of comparable Elizabethan notions. Also present were various assumptions anchored to the Protestant Reformation: that those poor who had been responsible for their own poverty were morally at fault, but, at the same time, were capable of "uplift," to use a term from the Victorian era, through discipline, thrift, hard work, and righteous living.

Three prominent thinkers of the nineteenth century also reinforced Poor Law thinking. The first was the Reverend Thomas Malthus who, in the late eighteenth century, wrote that the human population was increasing at a greater rate than such means of subsistence as the food supply. This, to many, was a clarion call to limit the appeal of relief: if the dependent classes were "coddled," or so the thinking went, they would multiply too quickly and start to exert undue pressure on society's limited material wealth. The second was economist Adam Smith, who saw a natural harmony between the self-seeking of an individual and the well-being of society. His view was typical of the strongly individualist outlook of the eighteenth and nineteenth centuries, which encouraged minimal standards of relief. The third thinker was philosopher Jeremy Bentham, who introduced the utilitarian notion that society should promote the greatest possible good for the greatest possible numbers (Bruce, 1961, 46–7, 78): a form of collectivism, but one that tended to promote the views of the majority, and to minimize the benefits for those who were poor or in other ways disempowered.

A final historical experience bears emphasis. The Speenhamland experiment of 1795 was a remarkable example of a social policy that challenged prevailing assumptions. Due to a short harvest and a severe winter, local justices of the peace of the Speenhamland area of England decided to pay subsidies to low-income employed individuals who had families to support—setting a minimum based on the price of bread and scaled according to family size. The Speenhamland experiment, as it later became known, spread to other parts of England. Following its implementation, familiar criticisms led to its abolition. Some argued that individual initiative would cease, the numbers of dependent people would grow, productivity would drop, and costs of relief would rise inordinately. Others argued, in hindsight, that its major problems were the maintenance of artificially low market wages, and the creation of artificial barriers to labour mobility (Bruce, 1961, 41, 76–7; de Schweinitz, 1943, 72–3; Dolgoff and Feldstein, 1984, 55). While historically brief, the Speenhamland experiment highlights the issue of wage supplementation for low-income citizens, which contemporary governments continue to debate. Some Canadian provinces have provisions in their welfare programs to defray additional expenses that recipients face when they start working, such as day care, transportation, work clothing, and tools. Others have considered programs that ease the transition from welfare to work via a "top-up" income supplementation program during the initial re-entry into the workforce (National Council of Welfare, 1993, 38–39). The Speenhamland experiment demonstrates that wage supplementation is part of our history.

Canada up to 1945

These aspects of a European heritage blended with a North American context and created a distinctly Canadian approach to social welfare. One of the most significant, and tragic, aspects of North American history is the colonization of Aboriginal peoples. Sporadic attempts at tenth-century Viking habitation along the northeast coast were followed by the permanent settlement of French habitants in the sixteenth century. This occurred largely along the St. Lawrence River, in a land they named New France. The French, and after the 1759 conquest of New France, the British, forever changed North America. The continent's Aboriginal peoples, decimated by disease and war, were forced onto reserves of land in the late nineteenth and early twentieth centuries, where they were further marginalized—economically, politically, and socially. As elaborated in Chapter 6, the resolutely Eurocentric orientation of Canadian social policies contributed much to the tragedy of colonization of Aboriginal peoples.

New France, and later, British North America, possessed an isolating geography, tormenting physical elements, and numerous forms of social misfortune: poverty, vagrancy, alcoholism, illegitimate births, and debtor classes, among others. Long-standing models of European social organization, however, could only be adapted haphazardly to the patterns of sparse inhabitation of frontier settlement. In Nova Scotia and New Brunswick there were poor laws administered by locally financed overseers of the poor. Present-day Quebec, like Newfoundland, relied upon the Roman Catholic Church to administer and dispense a complex system of social welfare, in addition to public education and health services. In Ontario, in the absence of either poor law legislation or a strong Roman Catholic influence, spontaneous forms of community concern had to prevail (Boychuk, 1998; Graham, 1995; Splane, 1965).

These machineries of social welfare carried on into the seventeenth, eighteenth, and early nineteenth centuries. But they were later transformed, mirroring the ferment of economic, social, and political changes of the day. Throughout this period, a series of primary economic staples dominated the economy. The cod fisheries of present-day Newfoundland became important in the sixteenth century, and were supplemented in the sixteenth to nineteenth centuries by the fur trade, corresponding with the slow but persistent westward pattern of human settlement. The latter gave way to a timber trade in the nineteenth century, and then to a wheat staple, first in present-day central Canada, and then after the 1880s, in Western Canada. Over the last quarter of the nineteenth century and into the twentieth, Canada experienced an industrial revolution, making Montreal and Toronto the leading urban centres of a growing network of national cities (Easterbrook and Aitken, 1956).

During this time there were several waves of immigration, highlighted by Loyalist settlement from south of the border following the American Revolution, significant British immigration during the middle of the nineteenth century, followed by a more diverse European settlement, much of it westward bound, during and after the 1880s (Lower, 1958, 187). From a scattered population of 70 000 in 1759, there appeared significant demographic growth. In 1851, present-day Ontario, Quebec, and the Maritime provinces had combined populations of 2.5 million people. In 1901, Canada's population had risen to 5.37 million, and in 1921, to 9 million (Easterbrook and Aitken, 1956, 395, 400; Prentice, Bourne, Cuthbert Brandt, Light, Mitchinson, and Black, 1988, 108). Meanwhile, the percentage of Canadians living in urban centres steadily climbed from 13 percent in 1851, to 35 percent in 1901, 47 percent in 1921, and to 52.5 percent by 1931 (Artibese and Stelter, 1985, 1887).

In 1867 the former colonies of British North America united to form Canada. Equally significant, the effects of the Industrial Revolution, urbanization, and demographic growth transformed it from a small, resource-based mercantilist economy into an industrializing nation. As society became increasingly complex, social welfare had to adapt accordingly. Houses of Industry—in effect, workhouses for the poor—emerged in Canada in the 1830s, through the influence of the British Poor Law Reforms of that decade. These tended to be administered on a local basis, and, alongside local and provincial hospitals, signalled governments' growing responsibility for social welfare. The voluntary sector, at the same time, remained vital, and a profusion of publicly and privately founded specialized charities were established over the next 80 years, among them, Houses of Providence, Boys' and Girls' Homes, city missions, Protestant and Roman Catholic orphanages, Jewish philanthropic organizations, hospitals for the sick, and refuges for the old. A distinct form of charity also came into being in the late nineteenth century—the settlement house, wherein the well-to-do, often university students, lived among and sought to help a city's poor. These could be significant loci of community social change (Irving, Parsons, and Bellamy, 1995).

Social welfare institutions and social movements were inextricably linked. Religious organizations, as an example, provided tangible services, a moral rationale for expanded activities, and proved to be a political force compelling greater state intervention into the country's social milieu. The Social Gospel Movement, a loose coalition of Protestant denominations influenced by British and American counterparts, emerged in the 1890s to apply Christian principles to prevailing social and economic issues. Similar forces were evident in twentieth-century Quebec, where, through the *Semaines sociales*, Roman Catholic clergy and laity discussed social issues. The Social Service Council of Canada, so named in 1913, was a public education and advocacy organization, originally created in 1907 and including representatives from the Anglican, Methodist, Presbyterian, and Baptist churches as well as the Trades and Labour Congress of Canada (Guest, 1997, 34). Protestant clergymen had been particularly important in the creation, leadership, and perpetuation of the Cooperative Commonwealth Federation (renamed the New Democratic Party in 1961), a social democratic political party elected to national and provincial legislatures and advocating a more comprehensive welfare state (Allen, 1970).

In the late 1880s, what has become known as an urban reform movement emerged—a loose coalition of journalists, clergy, charity workers, government officials, and other interested parties. It sought a broad array of public causes: public control of utilities, including public transit; better public health provisions, including the expansion of public health nursing services, improved sanitation, improved housing standards, and improved standards of meat processing and water quality; the establishment of more green spaces in urban areas—parks and playgrounds; and improved standards of relief, child welfare, and other social programs (Stelter and Artibese, eds., 1977). A leading proponent was Toronto *Globe* journalist J.J. Kelso, founder of the Toronto Humane Society in 1887, later renamed the Children's Aid Society (Fingard, 1989, 171; Jones and Rutman, 1981). Another was Herbert B. Ames, a well-to-do Montreal manufacturer who published an 1897 study, *City on the Hill*, documenting the deplorable living conditions endured by the city's working class (Copp, 1974).

The working class itself did much to assist the working poor: nineteenth-century workers organized fraternal societies, each member contributing a small, regular amount to a fund from which they could draw if sickness or an accident interfered with work. Canadian trade unions helped to raise standards of living, protect workers' wages, and improve workplace conditions (Kealey, 1980; Palmer, 1979). Women were responsible for fundraising and service provision within many local charities. By the end of the nineteenth century these activities had expanded to include a number of reform organizations, many now national in scope. The National Council of Women (established 1893), the Woman's Christian Temperance Union (1874), and the Young Women's Christian Association (established nationally in 1895), to name three, sought numerous social improvements, including women's right to vote (obtained federally in 1918 and provincially shortly before and afterwards), and social policies that would assist women and children (Kealey, 1979; Strong-Boag, 1976).

One of the most important social effects of industrialization was the segregation of people according to gender. In earlier economies, a family's income would often focus on agricultural production and take place at home, relying on the work of men, women, and children within families. But in an industrial economy, a family's livelihood depended more and more on men's employment outside the home; some literature refers to this as the phenomenon of the "breadwinner male." Women in an industrial economy remained at home, and focused their attention increasingly on domestic work such as raising children, cooking, laundering, sewing, and less so on producing goods for trade or barter; certain literature refers to this phenomenon as "women's domesticity," or "the domestication of women." In an industrial society there emerged a gendered split between the public realm outside the home, dominated by men, and the domestic realm. Women's social advocacy and charitable activities, it should be stressed, did take women outside the home. And they were important precedents to the growing presence of women employed outside the home during the post-1960s period.

The Canadian social work profession has strong roots in national organizations that represented women, churches, and trade unions. It was also influenced by the Charity Organization movement, which was preceded by American and British counterparts and which sought to rationalize charity, to make it more efficient, more humane, and more proficient in its techniques. The world's oldest schools of social work opened in Great Britain in 1890 and the United States in 1903, and Canada's first school appeared soon afterwards, at the University of Toronto in 1914. It was followed by similar schools at McGill University (1918), the University of British Columbia (1928), the Université de Montreal (1939), and at an independent institution that ultimately became affiliated with Dalhousie University in Halifax, Nova Scotia (1941). The Canadian Council on Child Welfare was founded in 1920 (renamed the Canadian Welfare Council in 1935 and the Canadian Council on Social Development in 1969). The Canadian Association of Social Workers followed in 1926. These were among the myriad organizations that sought more comprehensive social policies at the provincial and national levels (Graham, 1996b).

Social Policies

Among the most significant pieces of social policy legislation before World War II was the Workman's Compensation Act of 1914, first established in Ontario but soon emulated by other provinces. It provided injured workers with regular cash income as a right, rather than as something that followed often lengthy litigation against an employer. As early as 1919, the federal government had furtively pledged national systems of health insurance and unemployment insurance (UI, now named Employment Insurance or EI). A national system of health insurance did not come into being until 1966. Unemployment Insurance finally came into force in 1940, several decades after the establishment of comparable programs in Britain and other advanced industrialized nations. Its introduction had been delayed for decades because of the federal government's reluctance to amend the Canadian Constitution, allowing the federal government jurisdiction in this area. Meanwhile, in 1916 Manitoba was the first province to introduce Mother's Pensions, a selective program providing a small, means-tested income to widows and divorced or deserted wives and their children (Guest, 1997). The next major piece of legislation—also selective—was the 1927 Old Age Pensions Act, the cost of which was shared on a fifty-fifty basis by the federal and provincial governments.

Under section 92 of the Canadian Constitution (the British North America Act, 1867, renamed in 1982 the Constitution Act, 1867), the areas of education, health, and welfare were (and remain to this day) provincial prerogatives. But by strength of precedent, local governments continued to take on funding and administrative responsibilities for many social programs. As creatures of the provinces and having no constitutionally prescribed autonomy of their own, municipalities could be created and disbanded by provincial writ, and tended to have a limited tax base. But because of the unprecedented extent and duration of unemployment during the 1930s, local governments could not withstand the financial and administrative commitments of unemployment relief, among other social programs for which they had always been held responsible. Over the course of that decade, higher levels of government consequently took on greater financial responsibility (Graham, 1995). In the process, social welfare was massively transformed.

The Institutional Approach

Canada, 1945–1973

Canada changed dramatically after World War II. Immigration levels increased significantly. New immigration selection practices came into effect in 1962, intending to introduce principles that were universal and non-discriminatory; in 1967 further selection practice changes led to the introduction of what was intended to be a more objective points system. This is not to suggest, however, that Canadian immigration practices became entirely objective. Indeed, as several scholars point out, there remain discriminatory standards, sometimes less obvious and sometimes different from earlier practices. An excellent current example is the preference given to potential immigrants with proficiency in English or French, with particular educational/vocational backgrounds, or with certain amounts of disposable investment capital (Henry, Tator, Mattis, and Rees, 1995; Section 7(1) of Canada's Immigration Act, **cicnet.ci.gc.ca/english/pub/anrep99e.html# legislative**).

The country's growing racial and ethnic diversity, which is discussed in Chapter 6, was further reinforced by the federal government's introduction of an official policy of multiculturalism (1971), the Charter of Rights and Freedoms (1982), and the Canadian Multiculturalism Act (1987). In addition to being significantly more diverse, the country's population was also more numerous. In 1971, Canada consisted of 21.6 million people, nearly a twofold increase from 1941. In the same year, 1971, the percentage of Canadians living in urban centres had increased to 76.1 percent.

Social work grew proportionately. In 1941, the census reported 1767 social workers in Canada. By 1981, there were more than 27 590 (Drover, 1988, 2034). An earlier reliance on a two-year, post-BA diploma (and before this a one-year,

FIGURE 2.1 Total Social Spending in Canada 1945–1992/93

Billions (constant $1994)

Source: Caledon Institute of Social Policy (1995). The Comprehensive Reform of Social Programs: Brief to the Standing Committee on Human Resources Development. Ottawa, ON: Renouf Publishing.

FIGURE 2.2 Total Social Spending in Canada Per Capita, 1945/46–1992/93

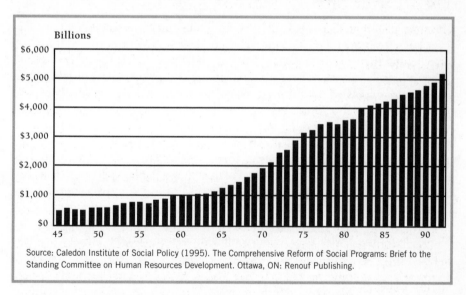

Billions

Source: Caledon Institute of Social Policy (1995). The Comprehensive Reform of Social Programs: Brief to the Standing Committee on Human Resources Development. Ottawa, ON: Renouf Publishing.

post-BA certificate) gave way, in the post-war era, to the dominance of the Bachelor of Social Work/Master of Social Work sequence.

The country's first Doctor of Social Work program was inaugurated at the University of Toronto in 1952. Moreover, by 1949 there were eight Canadian social work schools—nearly a threefold increase over a 10-year period—and by 1970 there were 12 (Graham, 1996a, 129). Numerous social workers forever changed the face of Canadian society. Harry Cassidy (1900–51) an economist at the

FIGURE 2.3   Total Social Spending in Canada as Percentage of GDP, 1945/46–1992/93

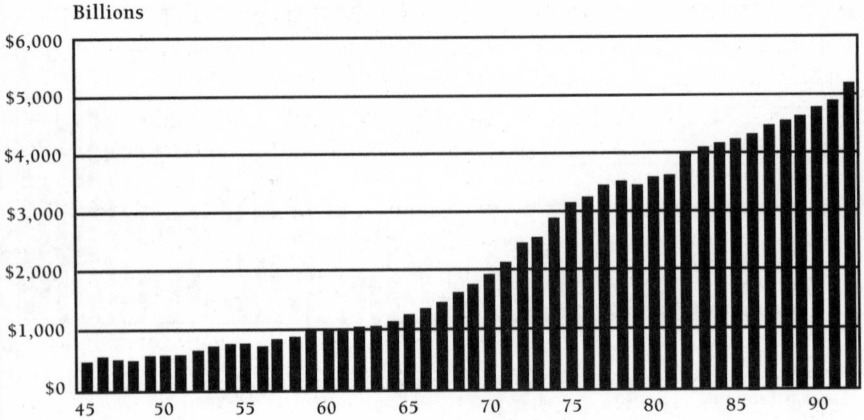

Billions

Source: Caledon Institute of Social Policy (1995). The Comprehensive Reform of Social Programs: Brief to the Standing Committee on Human Resources Development. Ottawa, ON: Renouf Publishing.

University of Toronto School of Social Work, wrote numerous studies on Canadian social security programs. Charlotte Whitton (1896–1975), director and driving force behind the Canadian Welfare Council (later named the Canadian Council on Social Development), reflected several aspects of the profession's history. While she crusaded endlessly for improved standards of child welfare and for changes in social policies, she also advocated harsh welfare assistance eligibility requirements for single mothers, among other practices that might be considered less than progressive by today's standards (Rooke and Schnell, 1987). Bessie Touzel (1904–1997) trained in the 1920s at the University of Toronto, held a succession of appointments of increasing responsibility such as Chief of the Ottawa Public Welfare Department, Executive Secretary of the Toronto Welfare Council, and Executive Director of the Ontario Welfare Council. A staunch advocate of improved casework practices, she wrote numerous policy studies, was an adviser to the Marsh Commission (see below), and served with the United Nations in Tanzania (Obituaries, *The Globe and Mail*, April 26, 1997).

Social Policies

Everything changed after the 1943 *Report on Social Security for Canada* (the Marsh Report), written by economist Leonard Marsh, who taught social work at McGill University. The Marsh Report echoed the famous 1942 Beveridge Report in Great Britain. Both were blueprints for a comprehensive and largely universal welfare state in their respective countries. And both provided a rationale for what scholars describe as an institutional model of social policy. The institutional approach, in contrast to the residual approach, saw the welfare services as normal, "first line" functions of modern industrial society, a proper, legitimate function of modern industrial society in helping individuals achieve self-fulfilment (Wilensky and Lebeaux, 1958, 138). The tendency to construct stigmatizing programs was much reduced, and means tests, under a universal program, no longer prevailed as the primary requirement for eligibility. Under universal programs, a sense of entitlement, or right of citizenship, prevailed (Graham and Al-Krenawi, 2000).

As noted in Figures 2.1 through 2.3, spending for social programs increased markedly over the following several decades (Caledon Institute, 1995, 3, 4). Following the introduction of UI, the next major Marsh Report proposal, a universal Family Allowances (FA) program, came into being in 1944: regardless of family income, *all* Canadian mothers of children under the age of 16 would receive a monthly allowance. The next major development after that was the conversion, in 1951, of the Old Age Security Program from selective to universal. As of that year, all seniors over the age of 70 would receive a pension, regardless of their level of income.

A universal system of health insurance first appeared in Saskatchewan, under the political leadership of the first social democratic government elected in North America: the Cooperative Commonwealth Federation. In 1945, Premier Tommy Douglas set up a social assistance medical care plan covering old age pensioners, recipients of mothers' allowances, blind pensioners, and wards of the state. This selective program was supplemented in 1947 by the introduction of universal, state-administered hospital insurance, and in 1959 by universal, province-wide medical insurance. Meanwhile, in 1956, the federal government initiated the Hospital Insurance and Diagnostic Services Act, a negotiated cost-sharing agreement between Ottawa and the provinces covering a basic range of in-patient hospital services. Again, following the lead of Saskatchewan, the federal government installed a universal health care system in 1966, and by 1972 every province and territory was administering its own health services. The story of social policy has been one of intense competition between groups in society, and health care was no exception. Companies that had provided private health insurance resisted what some perceived to be the intrusion of the state. So, too, did many physicians acting individually and through professional associations, claiming that physicians' autonomy would be compromised and access to comprehensive health care services would be reduced (Naylor, 1986).

Health insurance, along with education and welfare, was cost-shared equally, on a fifty-fifty basis, by the federal government and each province under the Canada Assistance Plan (CAP) program, inaugurated in 1966. Under the CAP, provinces also set up and administered such social services as child welfare protection, rehabilitation, home support for the elderly and people who are disabled, employment programs, child care, and Social Assistance. The federal government, with massive revenue sources from the income tax system, corporate taxes, and tariffs, was expected to provide otherwise vulnerable programs with a solid basis of funding.

As early as 1966, the federal government had introduced the Canada Pension Plan (CPP), providing social insurance protection for retirement and disability, as well as survivors' benefits. A national program (with the exception of Quebec, which legislated the equivalent in the Quebec Pension Plan), this compulsory plan was tied to workplace earnings and was portable if the individual moved or took on a different job within Canada. The CPP and OAS were supplemented in 1966 by an income-tested pension plan for low-income earners, the Guaranteed Income Supplement.

The Post-institutional Approach

By the late 1960s and early 1970s, it seemed as though many of the basic programs had been established, and continued policy initiatives would simply fill in the gaps that had been overlooked or had developed. The Unemployment Insurance program was considerably expanded in 1971 by increasing benefit rates, widening the program's compulsory coverage to include nearly all employees, and easing qualifying conditions. During the same decade, the Canada Pension Plan benefit rates were also elevated, and OAS benefits were extended to recipients' widows (Guest, 1997, 173, 188). A growing awareness of female poverty led to the 1975 introduction of the Spouse's Allowance, a means-tested supplement paid to old age pensioners' spouses. Several studies in the late '60s and '70s , including a Senate Committee report, *Poverty in Canada* (1971), revealed as many as one in five Canadians living in poverty (Guest, 1997, 156). The report called for a Guaranteed Annual Income (GAI), which would have provided, had it been adopted, a minimum threshold of income below which no individual would fall. There also emerged a gradual recognition of poverty and inequality as a reflection of such social diversities as gender,

FIGURE 2.4   Total Government (Federal, Provincial, and Municipal) Income Security Expenditures, 1980–81 to 1998–99

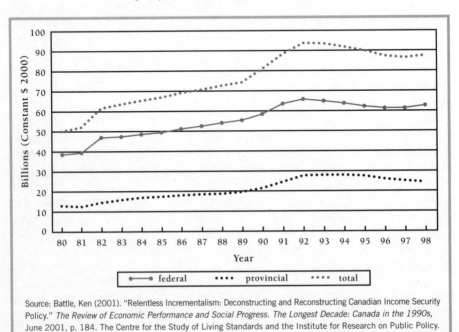

Source: Battle, Ken (2001). "Relentless Incrementalism: Deconstructing and Reconstructing Canadian Income Security Policy." *The Review of Economic Performance and Social Progress. The Longest Decade: Canada in the 1990s,* June 2001, p. 184. The Centre for the Study of Living Standards and the Institute for Research on Public Policy.

FIGURE 2.5 **Total Government (Federal, Provincial, and Municipal) Income Security Expenditures Per Capita, 1980–81 to 1998–99**

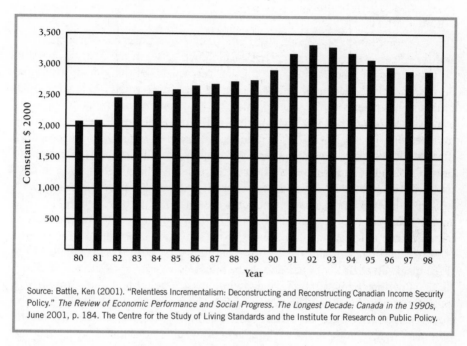

Source: Battle, Ken (2001). "Relentless Incrementalism: Deconstructing and Reconstructing Canadian Income Security Policy." *The Review of Economic Performance and Social Progress. The Longest Decade: Canada in the 1990s,* June 2001, p. 184. The Centre for the Study of Living Standards and the Institute for Research on Public Policy.

FIGURE 2.6 **Total Government (Federal, Provincial, and Municipal) Income Security Expenditures as % of GDP and Total Spending, 1980–81 to 1998–99**

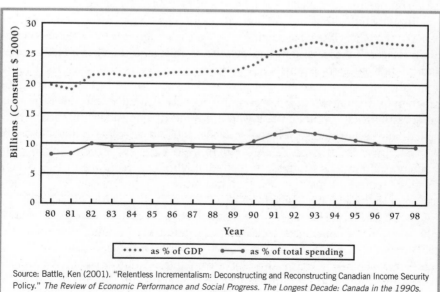

Source: Battle, Ken (2001). "Relentless Incrementalism: Deconstructing and Reconstructing Canadian Income Security Policy." *The Review of Economic Performance and Social Progress. The Longest Decade: Canada in the 1990s.* June 2001, p. 185. The Centre for the Study of Living Standards and the Institute for Research on Public Policy.

ethnicity, race, Aboriginal status, range of ability, and geography. These, given their critical significance, are examined in greater depth in Chapter 6.

Social Policies

Other factors, however, conspired to gradually erode Canadian social policies, and this erosion marks the underlying difference between the institutional and post-institutional models of social policy. Seven aspects of this post-institutional model are of particular significance. The first is that government funding for social programs has fallen steadily. The decline of federal government transfer payments to provinces, under the CAP, began in the 1970s and gathered further acceleration, to the extent that by 1992–93, the federal share of CAP transfers to the country's three wealthiest provinces was down to 28 percent in Ontario and 36 percent in British Columbia and Alberta (National Council of Welfare, 1995, 7). The CAP itself was replaced in 1996 by a Canada Health and Social Transfer (CHST), which further reduced federal government contributions to education, health care, and social welfare by 15 percent during the first two years of its implementation (Graham and Al-Krenawi, 2000). The CHST also reduced the federal government's ability to enforce standards as to how the money is spent and to which of the three major block areas money should be allocated (National Council of Welfare, 1995). Provincial governments, meanwhile, have tended to reduce transfers to local governments for the delivery of programs administered and partially financed by municipalities. These vary from province to province, but, depending on the province, may include child welfare, general welfare assistance, home-making, rehabilitation services, and others. The cumulative effect of these reductions among the different tiers of government leveled off social spending during the late 1970s and afterwards, as noted in Figures 2.4 and 2.5, which analyze income security payments. At the same time, the contributions of individuals and their employers to various programs such as UI (see below) and CPP have increased steadily.

Funding reductions of CAP, and of social programs not associated with CAP (e.g., UI, FA, CPP, OAS), have helped to create a second feature of the post-institutional model: the persistent and definite shrinkage in the comprehensiveness and extent of social programs. For example, after 50 years of funding the UI program, the federal government removed its financial support in 1990, making the program fully funded by employer and worker contributions. In the same year, more restrictive eligibility criteria were introduced, alongside shortened benefit periods, higher premiums, and more severe penalties to claimants quitting their jobs without "just cause" (Chappell, 1997, 49). In 1996, UI was changed to Employment Insurance, and various reforms, intended to produce further savings of $1.9 billion, sought to reduce the maximum stay on insurance, penalize repeat users, and take back a proportion of payments from wealthier recipients (Battle, 2001).

While health care has undergone significant erosion in its funding base, the federal government, nonetheless, released an important 1984 policy document, the Canada Health Act (CHA), widely viewed as an instrument to maintain federal standards. The document reaffirms five principles of our universal health care system: its universality, comprehensiveness, accessibility (minimal barriers to services), portability (transferability of services from province to province), and public administration. Despite, or perhaps because of health care cutbacks and recent attempts by physicians' groups to extra-bill patients above and beyond medicare premiums, a recent survey indicated that more than 80 percent of Canadians support these CHA principles (*The Globe and Mail*, October 26, 1995, A21). At the same time, in light of CHST block funding arrangements, the federal government's ability to enforce these standards may be impaired. Recent policy documents, such as the Alberta government's 2002 report *A Framework for Reform: Report of the Premier's Advisory Council on Health*, intend to lead to policy decisions "on what health services are publicly insured in addition to those required under the Canada Health Act." Also in the report is a mandate to examine how to "diversify the revenue stream" for health care delivery. "Instead of rationing health services, we need to find better ways of paying for the health services Albertans want and need" (**http://www2.gov.ab.ca/home/health_first**).

A third, related aspect of the post-institutional model is the elimination of universal programs and their replacement with those that are selective. An excellent example is the 1992 substitution of the universal Family Allowances (FA) with a Child Tax Benefit, combining the former FA and child tax credits with one refundable, income-tested child tax credit. The 1989 introduction of a clawback on OAS payments to upper-income Canadians essentially abolished the universal basis of this program. As one policy document observes, the de-indexing against inflation of the threshold beyond which the OAS is taxed back, will mean that an increasing number of Canadians will receive partial or no benefits (Battle and Torjman, 1993a, 4). These are but two examples of the growing trend away from universal programs and toward those that are selective.

A fourth aspect underlying many of the above changes is the growth of government debt. The debt is a cumulative, multiyear calculation based on the total amount of money that is owed. It is differentiated from a deficit, which is a yearly calculation based on annual operating costs, and occurs where spending exceeds revenue. While all levels of government experience debts and deficits, the present analysis, for sake of illustration, considers only the federal scene. In 1995, the federal government's total debt was $550 billion, or $18 535 for every Canadian. This is a considerable increase from 1965, when the deficit was $17 billion, or roughly $860 per person. Between 1965 and 1975, the federal government deficits were still below 2 percent of Gross Domestic Product (GDP, the value of goods and services produced in the economy based on earnings inside the country), and the debt was a low 18 percent. A combination of circumstances—a recession, accelerated borrowing, and an inability to match revenues with expenses—increased the debt to 48 percent of GDP by 1982, and by 1994 it was 71 percent (*The Globe and Mail*, February 13, 1995, A11). Since then, through a combination of circumstances, including reduced interest rates on the debt and reduced program expenditures, the 2001 debt ratio is down to 53 percent, and is projected by federal government officials to fall to 47 percent by 2003 (*The Globe and Mail*, May 21, 2001, B7). It is not debt in itself that matters, however, but rather how policy analysts, politicians, and others interpret the causes and significance of debt.

A fifth theme is the gradual recognition, through federal and provincial human rights legislation, the 1982 Charter of Rights and Freedoms, and other policy initiatives, of the rights of historically disempowered peoples: Aboriginal peoples, members of ethnoracial and religious minority communities, women, gays and lesbians, and people with disabilities, among others. As Chapter 5 points out, new conceptions of community and individual rights are developing. Likewise, to turn to a sixth theme, and as elaborated in Chapter 4, there is the rise of a neo-liberal ideology. A seventh and final theme, also elaborated in Chapter 5, is the impact upon social policy of globalization, and new relationships between civil society and the state (Rice and Prince, 2000).

Conclusion

As this chapter demonstrates, the historical experience is profoundly important in shaping the current nature of social policies. To best understand the present, it is imperative to learn about the past, and to have some commensurate appreciation, therefore, of social policies' future prospects. The next chapter, which emphasizes ideological, political, social, and economic aspects of Canadian social policies, will enable the reader to better appreciate the contexts in which social policies are conceived, carried out, and changed.

Chapter 3

Contemporary Welfare State Institutions

This chapter examines major welfare state institutions in Canada. The welfare state is an important part of social service delivery in Canada and refers to those governments that commit themselves to the development of social policies for the collective well-being of all. Welfare state institutions include, but are not limited to, income security, health, and education. These cover a wide range of programs and services. Armitage (1996) outlines seven:

1. Cash programs such as Old Age Security, Canada Child Tax Benefit, Canada Pension Plan, and postsecondary student loans.
2. Fiscal measures including tuition-fee deductions, child-care expense deductions, and RRSP exemptions.
3. Goods and services measures, such as hospital insurance, legal aid, and education.
4. Measures related to employment, including minimum wage legislation and employment equity programs.
5. Occupational welfare measures (e.g., pension and insurance plans, sports and recreational facilities).
6. Family care and dependency programs, such as home-care provisions.
7. Voluntary/charitable programs typified by shelters, soup kitchens, and food banks.

This chapter and the next touch on many such components, with brief mention of health and education programs, and particular focus on income security. The chapter first introduces the political and fiscal arrangements in Canada that make contemporary welfare state institutions possible. It then pays particular attention to programs in the areas of income security, and concludes with comments on several related, emerging social policy issues in Canada.

Fiscal and Political Arrangements

The Context

Most of the world's countries are unitary; that is, political power is centralized in one central or national level of government. Canada is among the world's approximately 20 countries that are federal states; political power in Canada is divided between a central or national level of government and a number of provincial levels of government (Inwood, 1999, 125). In Canada, there are 10 provinces, as well as three territories: the Northwest Territories, Yukon Territory, and Nunavit. Territories do not have the constitutionally proscribed autonomy that provinces have; each of the territories is governed by the federal government and by territorial governments that have delegated authority. Since the 1970s, the federal government, through the minister of Indian and Northern Affairs Canada, has increasingly devolved responsibilities to territorial legislatures. Likewise, as elaborated in Chapter 6, Aboriginal peoples have assumed either delegated or inherent powers to raise revenues and deliver services to people living on reserves.

The Canadian Constitution (named in 1867 the British North America Act, renamed in 1982 the Constitution Act of 1867) defines the framework for working out social policy within the federal political system in which the national and provincial governments have sovereign yet interdependent jurisdictions. As a pre-welfare state document, the Constitution was not entirely clear as to whether the federal or provincial governments were responsible for social welfare. Sections 91 through 95 of the Constitution outline the main division of powers and responsibilities; powers not expressly given to the provinces were to remain the domain of the federal government (Irving, 1987). Under Section 91, the federal government had jurisdiction over quarantine and marine hospitals, penitentiaries, and Aboriginal peoples; Section 92 made provincial governments responsible for building and maintaining hospitals, asylums, charities, and public or reformatory prisons (Chappell, 1997, 80).

Major legal decisions tended to assert social welfare as a provincial jurisdiction (Irving, 1987; Thomlison and Bradshaw, 1999). Irving (1987) posits two factors that influenced this judicial interpretation. First, the Depression highlighted the imbalance between social welfare initiatives and the ability to pay for these, and second, a growing reliance on the property and civil rights mandate of the provinces to deal with social problems over the "peace, order, and good government" mandate of the federal government developed. Thus, the responsibility for social welfare, health care, and employment services was to be principally under provincial control.

Many social policies, such as Unemployment Relief, were historically delivered at the municipal or local level of government. In some jurisdictions, this level of government has continued to be responsible or co-responsible for the funding and delivery of Social Assistance, supported housing, home care, day care, and other services. Types of Canadian local governments include cities, towns, villages, and municipalities (which range from rural municipalities to regional and metropolitan governments that serve major urban areas). Under the Constitution, local governments are creatures of the provinces; they can be created or disbanded by a provincial government, as recent efforts at amalgamating several major urban centres such as Toronto, Ottawa, and Montreal illustrate. Municipal powers are set out by provincial legislation often known as the Municipal Act, the Local Government Act, the Cities and Towns Act, or some similar name. Local governments, like their higher counterparts, are democratically accountable; legislation determines cycles of municipal elections of mayors, councillors, or their equivalents. Local councils make and carry out policies and receive revenue, principally through municipal taxes on real property and grants from provincial governments.

Local governments receive specific-purpose transfers from the federal government, usually for infrastructure and transportation services, as well as transfers from provincial governments. In both cases, specific rates generally tend to be imposed by the higher level of government, rather than being negotiated by autonomous levels of government, as is the case with federal-provincial transfers. Just as the federal government has been criticized for offloading responsibilities for funding major social programs to provincial governments, so too have provincial and federal governments—particularly provincial governments—been criticized for offloading to local governments, without comparable increases in cash transfers (Graham, 1995). Municipal budgets have been constrained. Between 1996 and 2001, municipal revenues in Canada increased by only 7.7 percent, compared with federal and provincial increases of 33 and 26 percent respectively (*The Globe and Mail*, October 22, 2001, A10). The dynamics of downloading from higher to lower levels of government are occurring in many advanced industrial countries, not just Canada, with commensurate impact upon the social and economic well-being of cities worldwide (Kahn and Kamerman, 1998).

Higher levels of government got involved more extensively in the welfare state over the course of the early twentieth century, and with accelerated presence in the aftermath of the 1930s' Great Depression. As the need for health and welfare services increased across Canada during that calamitous decade, the financial burden became too heavy for the provinces and their municipal counterparts to carry (Graham, 1995). Most taxation powers resided with the federal government. A constitutional dilemma ensued: how to develop strategies for securing federal moneys without violating the provincial jurisdictions of social welfare delivery. After World War II in particular, with the rise of a comprehensive welfare state, the federal government developed cost-sharing programs as a means of providing financial assistance for the delivery of social programs by the provinces and territories. These arrangements facilitated the development of our current welfare state. Particularly important federal powers related to social policy, including the responsibility for public debt and property, and the ability to raise moneys by taxation. Through the spending power of the federal parliament, social welfare transfer moneys have been made available to the provinces and territories without changing much of the original constitutional jurisdiction.

A final comment bears emphasis. Not all social programs are cost shared and provincially delivered, as the following pages will show. Several, such as Employment Insurance, are federal in administration and employer-employee funded.

The Fiscal Context

Intergovernmental finance refers to the web of financial flows that link governments in a federal system. Since the federal government has especially comprehensive tax-raising capacities, a considerable portion of intergovernmental finance involves federal to provincial transfers; provincial to municipal, and federal to municipal transfers also occur.

The literature often refers to seven terms (also noted in the glossary at the end of this book). Some intergovernmental grants are *block grants* (or general-purpose grants), while others are *specific-purpose grants*. A block grant is a cash transfer provided by one level of government to another, the amount of the transfer being fixed independently of the purpose to which the funds are put. Its opposite is a specific-purpose grant, the amount of which is tied to its intended purpose; an example would be a matched or shared-cost program.

Thirdly, there are unconditional grants, or *equalization payments*, which require no particular commitment by the recipient government to tie the grant to an expected type of expenditure. Equalization payments are intended to address two types of imbalances. The first is a *horizontal imbalance* between provinces, denoting differences in fiscal capacity between "richer" and "poorer" provinces. The second is *a vertical imbalance*, denoting any difference in fiscal capacity between the federal government and a particular province. By *fiscal capacity*, we mean a particular level of government's ability to change the total or composition of its revenues (e.g., taxes) or expenditures (e.g., a social program). The final term requiring definition is a type of transfer that is a *conditional grant*, which is tied directly to an expected type of service delivery. An example of a conditional grant is the Canada Assistance Plan (1966–96), which provided federal transfers to provincial governments to cover the latter's delivery of health, education, and social services.

Horizontal imbalances between provinces can be addressed in two ways. The first is by the federal government taking over a particular responsibility; Unemployment Insurance, inaugurated in 1941 as a federal (rather than a provincial) social program, is an example. A second way of addressing a horizontal imbalance is by the direct transfer of federal moneys to a province, via either an unconditional grant (equalization payment) or a conditional grant. Vertical imbalances are ordinarily addressed by equalization payments from the federal government to "poorer" provinces.

As indicated in Figure 3.1, in the 2001–02 fiscal year, the federal government transferred roughly $47 billion to provincial and territorial governments, which included $34.6 billion for the CHST, $10.4 million for equalization payments, a further $1.7 billion for other expenditures, and $1.5 billion for territorial funding for various programs. These transfers account for about 23 percent of aggregate provincial and territorial estimated revenues. Precise values vary by province, and are more significant to poorer provinces and less so to those that are more prosperous. According to the federal government's Department of Finance, in 2001 federal payments represented 40 percent of revenue in Newfoundland, compared to just 15 in Alberta (**www.fin.gc.ca/FEDPROV/FTPTe.html**).

FIGURE 3.1   Total Federal Transfers, 2001–02: $47 billion to Provinces and Territories

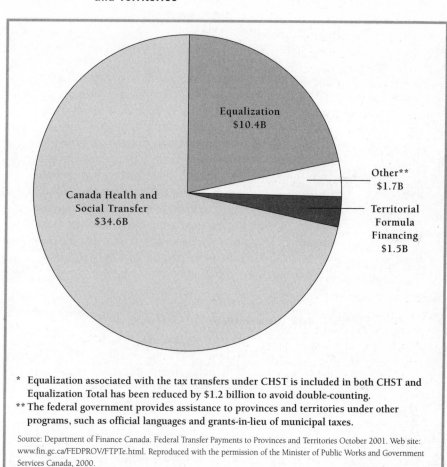

*   Equalization associated with the tax transfers under CHST is included in both CHST and Equalization Total has been reduced by $1.2 billion to avoid double-counting.
** The federal government provides assistance to provinces and territories under other programs, such as official languages and grants-in-lieu of municipal taxes.

Source: Department of Finance Canada. Federal Transfer Payments to Provinces and Territories October 2001. Web site: www.fin.gc.ca/FEDPROV/FTPTe.html. Reproduced with the permission of the Minister of Public Works and Government Services Canada, 2000.

Equalization Payments

Initial arrangements for Canada's system of intergovernmental finance were set out in the Canadian Constitution, and revised periodically as federal-provincial relations and governmental services became more complex. The first formal equalization program was introduced in 1957 in order to ensure that per capita revenues of all provinces from a variety of taxes—personal income taxes, corporate taxes, succession duties—matched those of the country's wealthiest provinces, which were then British Columbia and Ontario. In the first of the required five-year revisions to these arrangements, the level to which these transfers were equalized became the all-province average, rather than matching the wealthiest two provinces. Also in this first of many five-year revisions, recipient provinces were guaranteed revenues equal to 50 percent of the all-province per capita of resource revenues. The system evolved during the 1960s until the present time, with a number of different actuarial formulas for determining how to measure a fair transfer of revenue. Such changes were generally determined via conferences of federal and provincial first ministers. The most recent five-year arrangement took effect in April 1999 and will be revised in 2004 (Courchene, 2000).

At the time of writing this chapter, one of the more contentious issues of equalization is a perceived disincentive for equalization-receiving provinces to develop revenue capacities. For example, Ottawa would "claw back" in equalization payments the amount that a province such as Newfoundland or Nova Scotia collected in offshore oil or onshore mineral production projects (*The Globe and Mail*, July 18, 2001, B9). Others complain that wealthy provinces end up transferring considerable funds to Ottawa that are then distributed to poorer provinces. In 1998, Alberta's contribution to Ottawa amounted to more than $2,000 per capita, Ontario's was $1,700, and British Columbia's, $700 (*The Globe and Mail*, July 18, 2001, B9). Yet the Constitution is clear regarding Ottawa's responsibility to ensure delivery of reasonably comparable levels of public services at reasonably comparable levels of taxation to Canadians, regardless of where they live. This, to many, is the rationale for continuing equalization, in the face of some observers' calls for its modification.

The Canada Health and Social Transfer (CHST), 1996

Perhaps the apex of the creation of a universal welfare state in Canada occurred after the 1966 introduction of the Canada Assistance Plan (CAP, 1966–1996). The CAP was a funding agreement that enabled the federal government to cost-share with the provinces those constitutionally proscribed provincial responsibilities for the delivery of education, health, and social service commitments. The CAP was a landmark social policy, allowing the federal government to ensure minimum standards of service delivery, relatively equal standards of services across the provinces, and a reliable funding base to achieve these ends.

The CAP started to unravel in the mid-1970s, as reductions in cost-sharing arrangements eroded the amount of money transferred to provinces. By 1992–93, the federal share of CAP transfers to the country's three wealthiest provinces was down to 28 percent in Ontario and 36 percent in British Columbia and Alberta (National Council of Welfare, 1995, 7). The CAP had ceased to be a fifty-fifty cost-shared relationship. And many provinces, in turn, downloaded significant financial responsibility to local governments for the funding and delivery of social service programs such as Social Assistance, supported housing, home care, day care, and other services.

The CHST, which replaced the CAP in 1996, resulted in a 15-percent decrease in federal transfers to provinces intended for health, postsecondary education, and social services over the proceeding two years (Scott, 1998, xv). Provinces, for their part, have reduced benefit rates for Social Assistance and other programs. The CHST also erodes enforceable federal government standards, and so provinces are free to allocate received money in whatever way they wish—even if this means substantial reductions in program entitlements, and restrictions on eligibility and access. One of the country's foremost social policy think-tanks, the Caledon Institute of Social Policy (CISP), contends that this change in enforceability "constitutes one of the worst mistakes in the history of our social security system." It turns back "the social policy clock" to a period of minimal standards and far greater risks for society's most vulnerable (Torjman and Battle, 1995a, 5). "There will be no guarantee of a safety net in the country," a second CISP document points out (Torjman and Battle, 1995b, 2). This one piece of legislation—passed in the federal House of Commons in 1995 and creating the CHST—highlights the profound significance of social policy to direct social work practice, and to the lives of many social work clients.

Federal government cutbacks to provincial governments for the cost-shared funding of health, social service, and education, under the CHST, has had an impact upon provincial government delivery of services, as well as on the relative role of each level of government in social policy. One observer insists that the "relative power of the provinces over social policy" has increased as a result of these cutbacks, as well as its devolution of labour market social programs, such as employment training, to the provinces (Battle, 2001, 16). Ottawa, so the argument goes, "dominates income security policy," and yet the provinces deliver "most welfare, social service, and health care" policies, via cost-sharing arrangements with the federal government (Battle, 2001, 16). Federal-provincial fiscal and administrative relations are in "full evolutionary flight." Another expert points out: "There is no status quo" (Courchene, 1996, cited in Inwood, 1999, 128). The relative balance of participation of these levels of government, and the dynamics that lead to these ever-shifting arrangements, are examined in greater detail in the next section.

Federal-Provincial Relations

Canadian federalism has never been static. With the increased scope of the post-World War II Canadian welfare state, and as federal and provincial responsibilities for social welfare became more complex, federal-provincial relationships have become increasingly important to government and to the country's policy-making processes. Indeed, most of the important areas of contemporary social policy cut across loosely defined boundaries of federal and provincial jurisdiction. National policies can often only be carried out with some degree of provincial cooperation; and provincial responsibilities rely on some degree of federal cooperation—in social policy, this often means the transfer of federal moneys to provinces.

The Political Context

Federal-provincial relations take place in many arenas. They range from informal, sometimes daily, contact between federal and provincial civil servants, to formal contact that includes large-scale conferences of provincial and federal first ministers (i.e., the prime minister and provincial premiers). Contact itself covers the widest gamut of jurisdictions—from international trade, to fiscal arrangements, to economic development. Formal contacts usually number in the hundreds on a yearly basis, while less formal contacts are far more numerous. Joint federal-provincial agreements are essential to various types of social policies—particularly in relation to joint funding arrangements.

The tone and nature of federal-provincial relations vary significantly over time. Some scholars argue that from the end of World War II until the early 1960s an era of "cooperative federalism" occurred, where federal-provincial relations were relatively cordial. During the late 1960s and 1970s an era of "executive federalism," as one scholar describes it, emerged: federal-provincial relations were more acrimonious (Smiley, 1976, 54). Several factors may have precipitated this changing dynamic. Provincial responsibilities had grown in scope and magnitude. Likewise, a Quiet Revolution was occurring in the 1960s in Quebec, in which a renewed sense of nationality propelled the Quebec government to assert its right to withdraw from certain federal social welfare programs such as the CPP (and to create its Quebec counterpart, the QPP), and to modernize Quebec social and political affairs (Trofimenkoff, 1983). In Western Canada, provincial rights were likewise increasingly asserted in the 1970s and afterwards (Inwood, 1999, 129). Executive federalism has also coincided with increasingly visible federal-provincial constitutional struggles, and with more elaborate and formal federal-provincial "diplomacy": institutionalized first ministers' conferences, and entire bureaucracies composed of specialists to support these enterprises (Inwood, 1999, 129).

Several major attempts at re-establishing a Canadian constitutional framework over the past 30 years have had a significant, incremental impact upon federal-provincial relations. In 1976, the Parti Québécois was elected in Quebec, and in 1980 it held a provincial referendum on sovereignty association with Canada. Sovereignty association was to include political sovereignty with economic and other types of ties with Canada, including a common currency, a free trade zone, a common tariff, and a court of justice composed of equal numbers of Canadians and Québécois to oversee this associative arrangement. The referendum was defeated by a 60 percent No to 40 percent Yes return. During that referendum, in which Prime Minister Trudeau campaigned for the No side, Trudeau promised to repatriate Canada's Constitution—then called the British North America Act and held in London. In 1982, the federal government repatriated the Canadian Constitution and introduced, in the process, a Charter of Rights and Freedoms. The government of Quebec never agreed to the repatriation process and its premier, Réné Lévésque (whose government had lost the 1980 referendum), publicly expressed a feeling of betrayal by the other premiers and Prime Minister Pierre Trudeau.

In 1987, a new federal government under Brian Mulroney sought to establish a Meech Lake Accord set of constitutional reforms designed to induce the government of Quebec to officially accept repatriation of the Constitution. The Accord's five basic points, proposed by Quebec Premier Robert Bourassa, included a guarantee of Quebec's special status as a "distinct society" and a commitment to Canada's linguistic duality. Other provisions would increase provincial powers with respect to immigration, provide for provincial input in appointing Supreme Court judges, restrict federal spending power, and restore the provincial right to constitutional veto. Prime Minister Brian Mulroney and all the provincial premiers agreed to the Accord on April 30, 1987, although strong doubts were expressed by the premiers of Ontario and Manitoba and by several women's and Native rights groups. The Accord died on June 22, 1990, when the legislatures of Newfoundland and Manitoba failed to approve it. This led to a national referendum in 1992 over a proposed constitutional renewal (the Charlottetown Accord), which had a number of provisions, including Quebec's special status within the Canadian federation. The Charlottetown national referendum of 1992 was defeated nationally by 54 percent of votes cast. It did, however, receive approval in New Brunswick, Newfoundland, Prince Edward Island, the Northwest Territories, and, by the narrowest of margins, Ontario. Three years later, in 1995, the sovereigntist government in Quebec held a referendum on whether or not Quebec should become sovereign after having made a formal offer to Canada for a new economic and political partnership, and narrowly lost by a vote of 50.6 percent against and 49.4 percent for.

Since then, federal-provincial relations have been relatively cordial, but Quebec has remained on the periphery of some federal-provincial agreements. One example is the 1999 social union agreement struck between the federal government and all provinces except Quebec. It intends to improve each layer of government's level of transparency, accountability, and mutual collaboration in social policy, and is an important benchmark for current federal-provincial relations in this area (Inwood, 1999, 128).

An excellent example of this spirit of intergovernmental cooperation is the Canada Child Tax Benefit (CCTB) program, consisting of the Canada Child Tax Benefit, providing federal income support to all low- and middle-income families with children, and the National Child Benefit (NCB) supplement for low-income families (National Council of Welfare, 2001, 43). The CCTB is the culmination of a much simplified federal approach to child poverty, with the previous folding together of older programs (Family Allowances, children's tax exemption, and the refundable child tax credit) into one federal Child Tax Benefit. Moreover, it also introduced new provincial income-tested child benefits that were administered on behalf of the provinces by the federal government through the income tax system (Battle, 2001, 40); administrative data sharing also occurred through federal and provincial governments.

At the best of times, some analysts assert that Canada's federal system creates a form of "institutional fragmentation" that limits the state's capacity to create social policies (Banting, 1985, 49). This is precisely what the CCTB is attempting to overcome. But there is a long historical legacy of fragmentation, as the following section on income security illustrates. The federal government is responsible for such programs as Employment Insurance, Old Age Security, and the Canada Pension Plan. Provinces have jurisdiction over Social Assistance and Workers' Compensation. These different federal and provincial roles, as pointed out in Chapter 2, evolved for historically specific reasons.

Income Security Programs

Canadian social policies cover a wide range of health, education, and income security measures. The present chapter, for purposes of brevity, concentrates on income security programs—that is, those social programs that provide cash payments to recipients. As Chapter 2 emphasizes, prior to the development in the 1940s and 1950s of a comprehensive welfare state, Canadians living in poverty had few places to which they could turn. They were expected to be self-reliant. If, however, they had no options but to seek help from others, they would ordinarily go first to family, then to friends, and then to community sources such as the church or a charity (Graham, 1992; Splane, 1965). When these were exhausted, "unemployment relief"—the precursor to contemporary Social Assistance—was accessed (Graham, 1996; Struthers, 1983).

In today's world, a far more elaborate system of income security exists, encompassing all three levels of government (and hence different offices with which a social worker might be in contact), and applying to a wide spectrum of categories. Different income security programs have been designed for:

➤ single-parent families (the CCTB and Social Assistance, the exact name varies by province);

➤ single individuals who have been unemployed for a long term (Social Assistance, the exact name varies by province);

➤ individuals who recently lost their job (Employment Insurance);

➤ youth who do not live with a parent or guardian (Social Assistance, the exact name varies by province);

➤ individuals who experience a workplace injury (Workers' Compensation);

➤ people with a disability (Social Assistance, the exact name varies by province; or Canada Pension Plan; or Workers' Compensation);

➤ the elderly (Canada Pension Plan, Old Age Security, Guaranteed Income Supplement; some provinces have top-up programs for the elderly poor);

➤ government-assisted refugees new to Canada (Resettlement Assistance Program);

➤ veterans of wars (War Veterans' Allowance);

among other categories.

Social workers need to have comprehensive familiarity with this system in order to help clients identify the particular programs for which they are eligible, and ensure prompt and full access to these programs. The success with which social workers undertake this task may be of crucial significance to the client. It may make the difference, for example, between a client going hungry or having food, being homeless or being able to secure accommodations, being in despair or feeling hopeful, being trapped in poverty or having the means to better their standard of living.

Some Key Terms and Concepts

Selective Programs

There are two major forms of income security programs: selective and universal. Each has its own assumptions. Selective programs have a long history, extending to Elizabethan poor relief in England, and brought to Canada with European colonization. "Unemployment Relief" was a selective program, as is its contemporary successor, general welfare assistance, also called "Social Assistance" or "a social allowance." The usual form of a selective payment involves a transfer of money from a level of government to an individual. Eligibility for selective programs is based on a means test. Means tests are carried out to evaluate, firstly, a person's financial resources—such as income, assets, debts, and other obligations—and secondly, other criteria, such as number of dependants or health status of the applicant.

Selective programs are subject to several criticisms. One such criticism is that they may personalize problems of poverty, rather than focusing attention on broader societal structures beyond an individual's control that may create the conditions for poverty. The economy is one example of a societal structure. Say, for instance, that a weak economy leads to the closure of a pulp and paper mill in a one-industry town. This in turn would lead to the loss of a job for the applicant of a selective program.

What is more, selective programs, critics contend, may stigmatize people who, through factors outside their immediate control, experience temporary or permanent loss of income. These programs devote considerable administrative resources to monitoring the lives of individual clients, rather than focusing on broader community and societal changes that might improve the opportunities of a client. Proponents, on the other hand, believe that selective programs are the most efficient means of targeting money to those in need. As well, some believe means tests may motivate recipients to return to the workforce.

Universal Programs

Universal programs provide cash benefits to *all* individuals in a society who fall into a certain category. They differ from selective programs in that eligibility is a right of citizenship, rather than having to be proven through a means test. The implications are several-fold. A recipient's level of specific needs, or economic status, is not taken into account when determining eligibility. Where selective programs focus attention on an individual claimant's worthiness to receive benefits, universal programs operate under manifestly different assumptions. The state expresses responsibility to provide income security for all citizens, and society implicitly recognizes the presence of conditions beyond an individual's control that may impede economic well-being. Stigma has little place in a universal program, since all people, regardless of level of need, may have access to benefits as long as they fulfill eligibility conditions (such as being the required age in the case of Old Age Security).

While universal programs may target money to a greater number of people, including the well-to-do, many argue that it is the income tax system's role to counterbalance payments to the rich—and not the social program itself. In a progressive income tax system, the proportion of paid taxes increases with earnings; those with a greater ability to do so, pay more. In a regressive tax system, in contrast, taxes are not collected on an ability-to-pay basis. Regressive and progressive are relative terms, and the most extreme instance of a regressive tax—such as a sales tax—is one that is levied equally. How so? Whether a person paying a sales tax is below the poverty line or the president of a major bank, the sales tax charged remains the same. Canada's tax system is somewhat—although far from completely—progressive. Thus, higher income earners pay a greater proportion of their money on income tax than do those in lower income categories. The argument may be made that universal programs do *not* wrongfully direct moneys to the better-off, given the existence (or potential existence) of a progressive income tax system (Muszynski, 1987). What is more, with everyone receiving benefits from a universal program, some argue that the middle and upper classes are politically co-opted into supporting the program, and benefits are less likely—than in a selective program geared only toward the less politically powerful poor—to be reduced in scope or eligibility (Titmuss, 1958, 1987).

Universal programs came to the fore during the World War II period. But their presence has been systematically eroded over the past 25 years, as selective programs have found new favour. The reasons for this development are elaborated in Chapter 2.

Demogrant, Social Assistance, Social Insurance

Several other terms will be used to describe income security programs. Their knowledge and effective use are essential to social work practice. A demogrant is a cash payment to an individual or family based on a demographic characteristic (usually age), as opposed to need; an example, as will be seen, is Old Age Security. Social Assistance refers to selective income security programs that use a means or needs test to determine eligibility; these are often administered at the provincial or local governmental level, depending on province. Social Insurance refers to income security programs in which eligibility for benefits is determined by a previous record of contribution and on the occurrence of a particular contingency, such as unemployment, retirement, injury, or widowhood; examples include the Canada Pension Plan and Employment Insurance (Armitage, 1996, 190–195).

Major Income Security Programs in Canada

Several levels of government deliver income security programs. They constitute part of, but not the entirety of, transfers to persons and transfers to governments. The following programmatic descriptions are deliberately succinct and simplified, covering major aspects of eligibility and benefits but omitting minor details that are too numerous to discuss. Many programs are not discussed, due to the need for brevity. Greater elaboration is found in Graham and Al-Krenawi, 2000, Guest, 1997, or McGilly, 1998.

Federal Government Programs

Employment Insurance (EI, 1996–)

Previously known as Unemployment Insurance (1940–1996), there are three ways to obtain EI: loss of job due to termination, temporary disruption of work due to illness, and application for maternity/parental benefits. EI is based now on hours worked, rather than weeks worked—which is a fairer practice for part-time and multiple job-holding workers. The entrance requirements have become more stringent over the past 15 years but continue to vary depending on job type and rate of unemployment in the region where the claimant lives. For example, in areas with high unemployment (above 13 percent), a minimum of 420 hours will be needed, whereas in places of low unemployment (below 6 percent), 700 hours will be needed (**http://www14.hrdc-drhc.gc.ca/ei-ae/ratesc.htm**). A 1998 report indicates that only 43 percent of jobless individuals received benefits during the previous year due to increasingly severe restrictions on eligibility (*The Globe and Mail*, February 13, 1998, A3). Most recipients receive up to 55 percent of their average weekly insured earnings (up to a particular ceiling), the result of incremental drops in entitlement from as high as 64 percent of working wages in the 1970s. As of October 1, 2001, the maximum benefits payment is $413 per week. The program used to be funded by the federal government and employer-employee contributions; it is now funded only by employer and employee contributions.

Canada Pension Plan/Quebec Pension Plan (CPP/QPP, 1966–)

Canada and Quebec Pension Plans are insurance plans to which people must contribute during their working years. Both were created the same year and are similar in design; the QPP is administered by the Quebec provincial government and is solely for those working in that province, and the CPP is administered by the federal government and is for those in all provinces other than Quebec. CPP and QPP are also comprised of survivor's pensions for the spouses of deceased pensioners, disability pensions, and children's and death benefits. Eligibility is based on past contributions to the plan. In instances of retirement (as distinct from disability or spousal death), it is paid to contributing claimants over the age of 60, and is intended to replace about 25 percent of the income the claimant paid into the plan. As of July 1, 2001, the maximum benefits are $775 per month for retirement payments; $935.12 for disability payments; $465 for spousal survivors' payments (age 65 or over). The program is funded by employer and employee contributions. These contribution rates were low and level from 1966 to 1986, but rose gradually since then, and between 1997 and 2004 were anticipated to nearly double (Battle, 1997a). The program is considered Social Insurance.

Old Age Security (OAS, 1952–)

The Old Age Security pension is a monthly benefit for people 65 years of age or over. It originated in 1927 as a selective, means-tested program but was transformed into a universal program in 1951. As a universal program, employment history does not play a part in eligibility, and a claimant need not be retired. Those on an OAS pension pay both federal and provincial income tax. Those with higher incomes repay part or all of their benefit through the tax system (Government of Canada, 1999a). As such, some argue that OAS ceases to be a universal program due to the so-called "claw back" of benefits of higher-income-earning Canadians through the income tax system, precluding many people from full entitlement and a substantial number from ever receiving any compensation. Moreover, clawback amounts have systematically increased since the late 1980s. As of July 1, 2001, the maximum benefits are $436.55 per month. The program is financed from federal government general tax revenues, and is considered a demogrant.

Guaranteed Income Supplement (GIS, 1966–)

The GIS was established to supplement the earnings of low-income OAS recipients and is administered under the OAS program. Eligibility is determined by need and may increase or decrease according to a claimant's overall yearly income. As of October 1, 2001, the maximum benefits are $526.08 per month for a single applicant, and $342.67 for married applicants. The program is funded from federal government general tax revenues and is considered to be Social Insurance.

Spouse's Allowance (SPA, 1976–)

The SPA was established to provide income to the spouse of an OAS pensioner, or to a widow or widower. Like the GIS, eligibility is based on need, and is only provided to those within certain income limits. The SPA stops when the recipient turns 65 and becomes eligible for the OAS, or if the recipient leaves the country or dies. As of October 1, 2001, the maximum benefits are $785.33 per month for a beneficiary married to an OAS pensioner, and $867.02 for those widowed to a former OAS pensioner. The program is funded from federal government general tax revenues and is considered to be Social Insurance.

Veterans' Pensions (VP, 1919–)

Those members of the armed forces who incur a disability during wartime (Active Force), peacetime (Special Duty Area), or other military service are eligible for the VP. The amount of pension is determined by degree of disability and varies accordingly; maximum rates as of October 1, 2001 are $1,821.17 for single and $2,276.46 for married recipients. The program is funded from federal government general tax revenues and is considered a demogrant.

War Veterans Allowances (WVA, 1930–)

This income-related program ensures a minimum annual income for wartime/peacetime service veterans. Eligibility is based on need and a minimum qualifying age of 60 for a man and 55 for a woman. Survivors' allowances are also available. As of October 1, 2001, the maximum benefits are $1,058.15 per month for single claimants and $1,605.58 for those living with a spouse. This program is funded from federal government general tax revenues and is considered to be a form of Social Assistance.

Resettlement Assistance Program (RAP, 1998–)

Administered by the Ministry of Citizenship and Immigration (MCI), the Resettlement Assistance Program (RAP) provides financial assistance for up to one year after arrival to government-assisted refugees arriving to Canada. In many instances funding may also be provided via cost-sharing sponsorship agreements between MCI and sponsorship agreement holders at the local, regional, and national levels.

Almost all newcomers to Canada are independent-class immigrants or are sponsored by others, such as a Canadian family member. A small proportion are refugees, defined as having "a well-founded fear of persecution in his or her country of origin because of race, religion, nationality, membership in a social group or political opinion" (Canada, 1999b). RAP is only for refugee-class immigrants. "The funds help pay for basic household items, income support and a range of immediate essential services including port of entry reception services, temporary accommodation, assistance with locating permanent accommodation, financial orientation, links to mandatory federal/provincial programs, basic orientation and assessment and referral to broader-based services, to ensure where possible a continuum of service. Income support can last for up to 12 months or until the refugee becomes self-sufficient, whichever occurs first" (**www.cic.gc.ca/english/refugee/ref4-e.html**). It is parallel to the Immigrant Loans Program, also intended to assist the resettlement process. Local, regional, and national immigration-service organizations provide hands-on transition assistance in a refugee's securement of housing, education, employment, and other services; the RAP is delivered in collaboration with these organizations. The program is funded from federal government general tax revenues and is considered to be a form of Social Assistance.

Canada Child Tax Benefit (CCTB, 1993–)

The CCTB (formerly the Child Tax Benefit, 1993–98) replaced the following three things: the Family Allowance (1944–1992), a universal demogrant form of income security provided to all mothers of children under the age of 18, and refundable and non-refundable tax credits. Under the CCTB, the federal government provides payments to parents or guardians on behalf of children under the age of 18 through the CCTB. It is usually paid to the mother of the child if the child lives with her. The amount is different according to family income, number of children and their ages. This program also coincides with comparable programs at the provincial and territorial levels; eligibility for those programs is determined by information provided by the CCTB application. The two main components of the CCTB are the base benefit and the National Child Benefit (NCB) supplement. The base benefit is available to families with incomes up to a certain ceiling; in 2001 it was $67,000. The NCB supplement, an important component of the National Child Benefit system, is a federal, provincial, and territorial initiative designed to tackle child poverty, and is available to low-income families (**www.fin.gc.ca/budget99/pamphe/chilpae.html**). The CCTB is an excellent example of a formerly universal program (the Family Allowance) that has been replaced by a selective/income tested program (the CCTB). Some commentators criticize the program for providing inadequate benefits in light of pervasive child poverty (Freiler and Cerny, 1998; National Council of Welfare, 2000).

Provincial Programs

Workers' Compensation (WC, 1914–)

Workers' Compensation is designed to make payments to and cover rehabilitation and medical costs for workers who have been injured on the job. In the case of workplace death, it also provides payments to an employee's survivors. It was first introduced in Ontario, and subsequently spread to other provinces. Assistance levels vary from province to province. Eligibility criteria are stricter now than in the past, and benefits have been reduced in scope. In Alberta, for example, benefits as of February 2001 are 90 percent of net income up to $50,100. In Ontario in 2002, an annual wage ceiling of $64,600 prevails. In other provinces benefits have been as low as 75 percent of net income, but the maximum net may have been more than, say, Ontario's wage ceiling (McGilly, 1998, 82). The program is funded by worker and employee contributions and is considered a form of Social Insurance.

Social Assistance (SA, various years)

Social Assistance, often called welfare, or public assistance, helps people in need who are not eligible for other benefits, and is one of the most important income security programs with which a social worker should be familiar. It is typically delivered to three broad categories of people: families with dependent children in need (often this is long-term need), individuals with disabilities (often this is long-term need), and individuals or families in short-term need. These three programs may have different names and may be administered out of different offices. The last category mentioned—intended for short-term assistance—is seen as an income program of last resort. Benefit payments help pay for food, shelter, fuel, clothing, prescription drugs, and other health services. Since its introduction in 1998, some of the cost of welfare for families with children has been covered by the CCTB.

Eligibility rules and the amount of payment deviate from province to province, and where, in some provinces, municipalities have administered and/or partially funded programs. Especially in short-term need assistance, means tests tend to prevail. Applicants must be of a certain age, usually between 18 and 65, but some provinces have provisions for minors under the age of 18 and not living with a legal parent or guardian. Full-time students of postsecondary education, under certain circumstances, may be eligible for assistance in some provinces but not in others. Single parents must try to secure court-ordered maintenance support to which they are entitled. Those on strike are usually not eligible for assistance, nor are sponsored refugees, or sponsored family class immigrants during their period of sponsorship. In general, welfare is granted if a household's net assets are less than the cost of regularly recurring basic needs for food, shelter, and other necessities. Fixed and liquid assets are usually examined; most provinces exempt the value of a car, a principal residence, furniture, and clothing. In most provinces, other assets—cash, bonds, securities that are readily convertible to cash, the value of life insurance—are limited by household size and employability. Applicants are usually required to convert non-exempt fixed assets into liquid assets and deplete those assets before qualifying for welfare (National Council of Welfare, 2000).

Benefit rates fall well below low income cut-off (LICO) poverty lines, as indicated in Table 3.1. (Poverty lines are elaborated in Chapter 4.) Social Assistance definitions of eligibility, and benefit rates, have also tightened in recent years (National Council of Welfare, 2000). In 1995, during its first term in administration, for example, the Ontario Conservative provincial government slashed Social Assistance by a remarkable 21 percent. In some instances, workfare has also been introduced. Workfare requires recipients to undergo training programs and/or other forms of work-related activities, in return for benefits. The program is funded by federal and provincial moneys under the CHST, and in some instances partially by municipal governments.

TABLE 3.1   Social Assistance Nationwide, 1999

	Total Income	Poverty Line	Poverty Gap	Total Welfare Income As % of Poverty Line
Newfoundland				
Single Employable	$ 1,341	$14,727	−$13,386	9%
Disabled Person	$ 8,717	$14,727	−$ 6,010	59%
Single Parent, One Child	$13,924	$19,963	−$ 6,039	70%
Couple, Two Children	$16,317	$29,211	−$12,894	56%
Prince Edward Island				
Single Employable	$ 5,515	$14,386	−$ 8,871	38%
Disabled Person	$ 8,442	$14,386	−$ 5,944	59%
Single Parent, One Child	$11,670	$19,501	−$ 7,831	60%
Couple, Two Children	$17,799	$28,539	−$10,740	62%
Nova Scotia				
Single Employable	$ 4,573	$14,727	−$10,154	31%
Disabled Person	$ 8,809	$14,727	−$ 5,918	60%
Single Parent, One Child	$12,558	$19,963	−$ 7,405	63%
Couple, Two Children	$16,633	$29,211	−$12,578	57%
New Brunswick				
Single Employable	$ 3,367	$14,727	−$11,360	23%
Disabled Person	$ 6,899	$14,727	−$ 7,828	47%
Single Parent, One Child	$12,319	$19,963	−$ 7,644	62%
Couple, Two Children	$15,170	$29,211	−$14,041	52%
Quebec				
Single Employable	$ 6,223	$16,766	−$10,543	37%
Disabled Person	$ 8,951	$16,766	−$ 7,815	53%
Single Parent, One Child	$12,957	$22,726	−$ 9,769	57%
Couple, Two Children	$15,000	$33,262	−$18,262	45%
Ontario				
Single Employable	$ 6,822	$16,766	−$ 9,944	41%
Disabled Person	$11,759	$16,766	−$ 5,007	70%
Single Parent, One Child	$13,704	$22,726	−$ 9,022	60%
Couple, Two Children	$18,130	$33,262	−$15,132	55%
Manitoba				
Single Employable	$ 5,551	$16,766	−$11,215	33%
Disabled Person	$ 8,257	$16,766	−$ 8,509	49%
Single Parent, One Child	$11,328	$22,726	−$11,398	50%
Couple, Two Children	$16,705	$33,262	−$16,557	50%
Saskatchewan				
Single Employable	$ 5,739	$14,727	−$ 8,988	39%
Disabled Person	$ 8,385	$14,727	−$ 6,342	57%
Single Parent, One Child	$11,877	$19,963	−$ 8,086	59%
Couple, Two Children	$17,590	$29,211	−$11,621	60%

TABLE 3.1   Social Assistance Nationwide, 1999 (continued)

	Total Income	Poverty Line	Poverty Gap	Total Welfare Income As % of Poverty Line
Alberta				
Single Employable	$ 5,023	$16,766	−$11,743	30%
Disabled Person	$ 7,061	$16,766	−$ 9,705	42%
Single Parent, One Child	$11,375	$22,726	−$11,351	50%
Couple, Two Children	$17,919	$33,262	−$15,343	54%
British Columbia				
Single Employable	$ 6,330	$16,766	−$10,436	38%
Disabled Person	$ 9,593	$16,766	−$ 7,173	57%
Single Parent, One Child	$13,661	$22,726	−$ 9,065	60%
Couple, Two Children	$17,830	$33,262	−$15,432	54%

Source: Adapted from National Council of Welfare (2000). *Welfare Incomes 1999*. Catalogue No. H68-27/1999E. Reproduced with the permission of the Minister of Public Works and Government Services Canada, 2002.

As the Caledon Institute of Social Policy points out, it may be wiser to approach Social Assistance as a human resource strategy issue rather than as workfare (Torjman, 1996a). Workfare implies compulsory labour and mandatory participation in designated activities. A human resource strategy, on the other hand, is voluntary. Both, ideally, are collaborative with numerous stakeholders—industries, educators, social welfare, and justice. Both also are supposed to provide a range of options including job search, academic upgrading and skills training, and employment creation, but some argue that workfare emphasizes these less. A human resource strategy "also ensures" more explicitly "that appropriate supports are in place—notably, high-quality, affordable child care and transportation subsidies—so that recipients can move off welfare" (Torjman, 1996a, 1). Finally, and perhaps most importantly, a human resource strategy promotes, rather than destroys, human dignity and well-being.

Some provincial governments have sought to revise their Social Assistance programs previously targeted for children and families, and align these with the federal CCTB. British Columbia was the first to consider a federally-provincially integrated child benefits system payable to low-income families with children (Battle and Mendelson, 1997, 2). Other provinces have followed suit. Earnings supplement programs for working poor families are also available in several provinces.

Provincial Top-ups for the Elderly (various years)

The combined OAS + GIS supplements are low enough to qualify most elderly couples in most provinces for Social Assistance. To avoid having the elderly as SA recipients, some provincially administered income supplemental programs have been introduced. Benefit rates vary from province to province, and are intended to raise incomes of recipients to roughly the income levels of public assistance recipients. Effective September 17, 2001, the Saskatchewan Income Plan provides a maximum of $90 per month to single claimants and $72.50 to married claimants (**www.gov.sk.ca/socserv/financial/SIPoverview.html**). The Ontario Guaranteed Annual Income System (GAINS) provides a maximum of $83 per month for a single claimant (**www.rev.gov.on.ca/images/irie-1934-all.pdf**). Some other provinces have no such equivalent programs. Provincial top-ups for the elderly are selective Social Assistance programs, funded jointly by federal and provincial moneys under the CHST.

Conclusion

Income security policies work best when they are collaboratively applied with other social and economic policies, and when they are successful at addressing categories of people who are most in need. The disgraceful incidences of poverty among Aboriginal peoples, children, peoples with disabilities, and women, among other social groups, ought to compel more comprehensive and successful policy responses. Disability pensions within the CPP, for example, have been criticized for not allowing beneficiaries who can work irregularly or part-time to do so—unless they are willing to forfeit all benefits (Torjman, 1997a). Some likewise argue that Social Assistance programs should be designed to provide income top-ups to low-income labourers, and that social programs should provide special transportation, child care, and other supports necessary to full and vital functioning in and beyond the workplace (Torjman, 1996a 1996b, 1997, 1998a, 1998b, 1999).

So, too, might policies be delivered in ways that more sensitively appreciate diverse positionality on the basis of age, ethnicity, gender, geography, race, religion, and range of ability, among other parameters. A 1998 report demonstrates high instances of poverty among 30 percent of families that immigrated to Canada versus 13.2 percent that were native-born to this country, and begs further replication based on different data sets (Beiser, Hou, Human, and Tousignant, 1998). The implications are considerable. People new to Canada may have little appreciation of, or experience with, a welfare state and may require especially skilful and competent social work assistance to gain access to income security programs.

These issues of diversity are examined in further detail in Chapter 6. But before discussing them, the following two chapters will look at some social, economic, and political consequences of social welfare (Chapter 4), as well as some broader contextual issues such as globalization, social movements, social inclusion, and social welfare retrenchment (Chapter 5).

Chapter 4

Ideological, Social, and Economic Influences

Chapter 1 points out that there are various definitions of social policy that influence how policies are conceived and carried out. As discussed in Chapter 2, history is important in determining how policies developed, and hence their current state (Chapter 3) and future prospects. This chapter builds further on what was developed in the preceding three chapters. It considers the ideological, social, and economic factors that influence social policy development in greater detail. After having read the chapter, the reader will have a better comprehension of how such dynamics influence social policies—and hence the lives of clients whom social workers serve. Likewise, the chapter will help readers appreciate why it is that social workers who are genuinely concerned about the people they work with are interested in such forces; and why, as a result, social workers, and the professional associations that represent them, ought to be continuously engaged in social advocacy leading toward social change.

Ideology and the Political Spectrum

Ideology refers to a shared way of thinking based upon a set of ideas that reflect the values, beliefs, attitudes, and experience of a particular person or group. Ideological beliefs focus on the nature of the ideal political system, the ideal economic order, and the ideal social goals. Ideology places a special emphasis on the role government should play in economic and social matters.

Ideology provides a way of interpreting problems and designing appropriate solutions. Ideological considerations are not the only factors that influence political decisions about social policy and social problems, but political parties attempt to shape social policy decisions from their ideological base. So, too, do individuals embrace particular ideologies. All social policy decisions influence the work performed by social workers. Social policy decisions affect the funding and delivery of social services, as well as who will receive what services.

In this section, we very briefly explore different ideological approaches to social policy, and then relate these approaches to how major Canadian political parties think about social policy. But before beginning either, we will cover a few core

FIGURE 4.1   Major Political Ideologies: The Political Spectrum

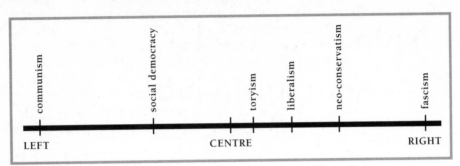

definitions that are key to ideology: communism, socialism, liberalism, toryism, neo-conservatism, and fascism (see Figure 4.1). There is tremendous diversity of views within each term. The following is nothing more than a short and necessarily non-comprehensive paraphrase of major attributes within each.

The six political ideologies presented in Figure 4.1 are ordered along a continuum from communism on the extreme political left to fascism on the extreme political right. It is important to remember that, as you read about these political ideologies, they do not necessarily represent the Canadian political parties that may bear the same name. The Liberal Party of Canada, as an example, has some aspects that are liberal in ideology and others that are not, as will be seen. Though political parties may have their foundations in certain ideological positions, each party has been uniquely shaped by historical, economic, and social forces as much as by ideological values and beliefs.

Because most political ideologies have something to say about the social unit of attention—the collective (society) or the individual—the following concepts are often used in ideological descriptions: individualism and collectivism, and egalitarianism and elitism:

➤ *Individualism* relates to political, social, and economic spheres; here the individual's freedom, worth, and self-determination are foremost.

➤ In *collectivism*, by way of contrast, the rights and welfare of the group or society are placed above that of any and all individuals.

➤ *Egalitarianism* pertains to the belief that all people should have equal political, social, and economic rights.

➤ *Elitism* sees society organized around interrelated but unequal functional groups, usually with those in the political or economic leadership group referred to as the elite. Elitism is a hierarchical rather than an egalitarian organizational view.

The central organizing principles of each political ideology will be discussed according to its stance on such dimensions as liberty or regulation, equality or hierarchically organized society, and individualism or collectivism.

Communism

A distinction between Marxist, radical, and communist perspectives is important; they should not be used interchangeably since each represents particular assumptions. As one author points out, "whereas Marxist social work is certainly radical, the reverse is not necessarily true" (Webb, 1981, 145). As elaborated in Chapter 7, radical social work emerged from a variety of theoretical traditions that also includes labelling theory and new criminology, among others (Webb, 1981, 145). Marxism, for purposes of this chapter, represents a variety of approaches that stem from Karl Marx; it is one part of the broader rubric of communist political ideology.

Although the term *communism* has roots extending back centuries, as a contemporary ideology, it owes much to the contributions of such nineteenth- and early twentieth-century thinkers as Karl Marx, Vladimir Ilyich Lenin, and Friedrich Engels. Communism often brings to mind the twentieth-century communist regimes of the Soviet Union, China, and Cuba (Krieger, 1993), and is a distinct version of socialism. It has become associated with both a political movement directed by the working class to establish an alternative to capitalist societies, and a societal ideal based upon strong egalitarian principles.

The focal point of communism is collectivism, that is, social ownership and control of lands as well as the *means of production* (the land, labour, and capital used by a society to produce material goods). State ownership and production is directed toward meeting human need rather than a "for profit" capitalist motivation. Under communism there is the assumption that citizens will experience themselves as co-owners of the means of production, acknowledge their true needs and the needs of fellow citizens, and work diligently to produce what is necessary to accomplish these ends (Krieger, 1993; Marchak, 1988). According to some communists, these aspects are to be organized under a dictatorship of the proletariat: for example, that period of history in which the Communist Party assumed political control without recourse to democratic elections, and brought about the advent of a classless, communist society in the former Soviet Union. In summary, the core ideological principles of communism are a highly communal and egalitarian social and economic order (Chappell, 1997).

The Communist Party of Canada was founded in 1921, preceded by various activities within trade unions, collectives, and former political organizations such as the Socialist Party of Canada (British Columbia, founded 1904). Until 1937, the Communist Party was illegal under the Canadian criminal code, and its members were persecuted. Party members took leadership positions in some trade unions, and have been elected to the federal (Fred Rose, 1943), and provincial (W.A. Kardash, Manitoba, 1941, A.A. MacLeod and J.B. Salsberg, Ontario, 1943) legislatures, as well as to many municipal councils. One of the Party's founders, Jacob Penner, served on Winnipeg City Council between 1931 and 1960; his son Roland became the province's attorney general in 1981. The Communist Party (Marxist-Leninist), founded in 1970, espouses similar ideology to the Community Party of Canada (Penner, 1992).

Social Democracy

Contemporary social democracy finds its roots in nineteenth-century Europe, which was strongly associated with labour activism and criticism of both capitalism and an unbridled free-market economy (Krieger, 1993). Social democrats believe that free-market economies cannot ensure the efficient and effective allocation of economic resources to meet the needs of all citizens. Most support the market economy model, but with some important state interventions; the degree of support for either may vary from one social democrat to the next. Social democrats often focus on economic issues, such as the ownership and regulation of basic or key economic resources. From this perspective, the state is responsible for planning, directing, and regulating economic sectors as well as providing social welfare services for those in need. In the Western world, socialism has most often become associated with social democrats as opposed to communists. Social democrats advocate free elections and democracy.

Unlike communism, in which a dictatorship of the proletariat without recourse to democratic elections may exist, social democrats limit the extent of state control to that determined by a democratic election process, and capitalism is tempered by a more egalitarian approach through government legislation and regulation (Chappell, 1997; Krieger, 1993). In summary, social democracy seeks collective and egalitarian means to moderate the effects of capitalist, free-market economic forces.

It is important to reiterate that these definitions are "ideal types," a conceptually precise term that may have divergent applications in real life. While the New Democratic Party (NDP) in Canada is seen as a major locus of our country's social democratic ideas, there are many social democrats who disagree with the NDP's approach to current social, political, and economic issues, perceiving them to be too right wing. These same criticisms may be applied to social democratic parties in other industrialized countries such as France, Germany, and Great Britain.

Toryism

In the eighteenth century, conservatism countered the "liberal" change of direction and the advent of egalitarian ideologies that threatened the status quo (Hoover, 1992). A "tory" conservative ideology contrasts with American brands of "liberal conservatism" by retaining British roots (Horowitz, 1970; Mishra, 1995). The characteristic Canadian attitude of deference to authority is seen as an expression of tory-elitism (Horowitz, 1970). Toryism also interprets its collectivist stance as an organic sense of society where a social and economic hierarchical structure contributes to the economic security and social stability of society (Mishra, 1995). This social "law and order" orientation contrasts with liberalism's individual liberty and freedom perspective. Marchak (1988) places toryism as slightly right of centre on the egalitarian-elitist and the individualist-collectivist dimensions, but left of the neo-conservative position on these dimensions. Historically, the term *tory* has been used to describe members of the Progressive Conservative Party of Canada. But, as we shall see, political parties change. Although some Conservatives are still described as tory, many Conservatives these days are in fact liberal in ideology.

Liberalism

The ideology of liberalism evolved in the eighteenth and nineteenth centuries as a change-oriented perspective that emphasized individual development in a social, political, and economic order unencumbered by government restraints (Krieger, 1993). Modern twentieth-century liberal doctrine for many liberals acknowledges the constraints of capitalism and the free-market economy in the unequal distribution of wealth and its attendant status and power (Chappell, 1997). This has led to a tempered liberal outlook with stronger humanistic values becoming more prominent. The liberal ideology is strongly individualistic, though its proponents claim it has sought to stave off the extremes of the left and the right by paying attention to developing policies that somewhat reduce economic and social inequalities (see Krieger, 1993 for a more extensive historical review). This has moved liberalism from a belief that individual differences accounted for economic and social inequalities to a recognition of the need for some government intervention to facilitate equality of opportunity (Marchak, 1988). The extent of this intervention would be less, as a rule, than what a social democrat might advocate. The Liberal Party of Canada, as will be seen, espouses values that are not to be confused with the ideology of liberalism described here. The terms *Liberal*, with a capital letter and describing the Canadian political party, and *liberal*, with a lower case letter and describing the ideology, are not the same concepts. Only *some* Liberals are liberal in ideology; others have social democratic leanings, and others may be considered neo-conservative.

Neo-conservatism

Neo-conservatives, like all conservatives, recognize the inequalities among people, but see these differences as more important than the similarities (Hoover, 1992). Neo-conservatism is a label used to distinguish conservatives on the "new right" who advocate less government and a more minimalist position toward social and economic affairs. Hoover (1993) would identify neo-conservatives as "individualist conservatives," sharing much in common with liberals. The more traditional or "red tory" conservatives tend to accept inequality less willingly, while neo-conservatives may more strongly revere freedom and personal initiative.

Fascism

Fascist political parties in the twentieth century rose to power between the two world wars in Europe, in Mussolini's Italy and Hitler's Germany. Payne (1992) describes fascism as opposed to almost all political ideologies of the time—communism, socialism, and liberalism. The strong, radical, nationalist stance of fascism arose out of several forces, among them an intense fear of communist and socialist ideology, and a racist assertion of nationality. Fascism gave rise to a one-party authoritarian state that maintained an active control of the economy, but without socialist ownership of the means of production. Like communism, fascism is inherently undemocratic. Once a fascist government comes to power, open elections are often banned. This ideology also places the interest of the nation or groups within a nation ahead of any particular class or individual. Fascists embrace a radical collectivist stance (i.e., a particular form of nationalism, often racially and/or ethnically based). They reject the egalitarian perspective of communism and socialism and maintain an elitist or class structure in society, *but* with the belief that the class structure should be subordinate to the social cohesion of the nationalist banner.

Mainstream Canadian Political Parties

There are numerous political parties in Canada, and many that do not have representatives in federal or provincial legislatures that represent theoretical concerns of interest. But for purposes of brevity, this section examines four divergent political ideologies as represented in mainstream Canadian political parties: neo-conservatism, toryism, liberalism, and social democracy. Common to all the major political parties of Canada are some basic values, such as the inherent right of citizens to self-determination, a belief in democracy, and a commitment to varyingly regulated forms of industrial capitalism—depending on the political ideology. Among our major political parties, and indeed within society, principles of egalitarianism appear to be weakening, as liberal tenets of individualism gain greater currency.

Confusion about the ideological orientation of political parties often arises from assuming a unilateral rather than a complex and divergent ideological base within the same party. Holding each party together and determining its social policy stance is a complex set of interactions between ideological, historical, economic, political, and social forces. For example, Turner and Turner (1995) characterize the Liberal and Progressive Conservative parties as governing by "brokerage" politics since the 1960s, whereby ideological tenets hold only a marginal place in decision-making processes and outcomes. More recently still, the ascendancy of neo-conservative and liberal ideologies calls into question whether brokerage politics continue to exist. In any event, in assessing the social policies set by governments, it must be remembered that ideologies tend to focus on several pivotal values, and from these postulate the society that would best foster those values (Marchak, 1988).

Liberal Party of Canada

The Liberals or "Grits" were part of the founding of Canada's political structure in 1867. Christian and Campbell (1990) characterize the Liberals as being represented by two ideological factions: business and welfare liberalism. These party factions are held together by the common traditional liberal values of liberty and individualism. Welfare liberalism places human rights above the economic rights of individuals. This element of liberalism is expressed in the willingness of government to impose taxation and other forms of economic regulation as well as to facilitate the development of social welfare programs. Business liberalism, on the other hand, interprets these as economic restraints to individual freedom. This faction of the Liberal Party is more attuned to minimizing government law making and regulation, especially in economic matters.

Any interpretation of Liberal social policy must begin by assessing which side of the business–welfare liberalism tension is in the ascendancy position within the party. For example, some Liberals, such as Jean Chrétien, have been characterized as being able to broker between the welfare and business liberal factions, thus halting the advance of a corporate-oriented, laissez-faire liberalism (Christian and Campbell, 1990). Others may perceive the Liberal Party as having sold out to international corporate interests, particularly in relation to Chrétien's perceived support of such transnational trade agreements as the North American Free Trade Agreement (NAFTA). When business liberalism dominates, social policy may be expected to be characterized by an accent on prohibitive costs, and thus limited access to and less emphasis on universal programs. Universal access and standards, in contrast, are sometimes stressed in social policy when welfare liberals speak for the party. At these times, emphasis on the costs of not providing these services dominates over concern about the financial costs of providing them.

Progressive Conservative Party

Conservatives have been referred to as "tories" since the time of Confederation and represent the British tory tradition. According to Christian and Campbell (1990) this Canadian party combines ideology similar to that of business liberalism with the tory values of hierarchical yet collectivist views of society. As with the Liberal Party, there is a tension between these two ideological aspects. Prime Minister John Diefenbaker's (prime minister 1957–1963) vision of a uniquely Canadian northern development policy to equalize economic opportunities was an example of toryism and a national vision that was juxtaposed against the Liberal business liberalism of the day (Christian and Campbell, 1990). Prime Minister Brian Mulroney (prime minister 1984–1993), on the other hand, was more representative of an ultra-business-liberalist, neo-conservative position on social policy, where free trade was a dominant force guiding political and social agendas. Most Progressive Conservatives today are far more liberal or neo-conservative than tory in ideology.

New Democratic Party

This social-democratic-oriented party had its origins in the Co-operative Commonwealth Federation (CCF) party established in the Great Depression of the 1930s among trade unions and farmer cooperatives. It was renamed the New Democratic Party (NDP) in 1961. The NDP has ideological roots in welfare liberalism and a reaction to the tory hierarchical view of society. A collectivist but egalitarian stance characterizes the Canadian socialism portrayed by the NDP. Legal and opportunity equality are major features of Canadian social democracy. Social policy proposed by the NDP tends to be universal, with broad access and a uniformity of distribution across Canada. To many party faithful, the costs of sustaining these social programs should be borne more prominently by corporate Canada.

Alliance Party of Canada

This party has a very short history within the Canadian political spectrum and seems to represent the reform of the conservative tradition. It was established in

1987 in Western Canada as the Reform Party, and became a national force in the 1993 general election, changing its name to the Alliance Party in 2000. This party is more akin to neo-conservatism and the American Republican Party than to toryism with its British roots. Social policy proposed by the Reform Party tends to be minimalist in nature. It is also selective, that is, provided according to a strict economic measuring stick—or, as proponents might claim, a living-within-our-means perspective for both individuals and governments. Reliance on self and families is favoured over social services provided by government. Thus, the Alliance Party would postulate a social agenda that restricts access and distribution of social programs financed by the public, and advocates privatization of many social programs, even at the expense of universality, because, it is claimed, selective and reduced programs can better control financial costs. A final point bears emphasis. As with this entire discussion, general principles have been emphasized. For example, while it is true, on balance, that Alliance Party advocates may prefer selective programs, some might also want to retain some universal programs.

Bloc Québécois Party

The Bloc Québécois, a federal political party electing its first leader in 1991, has had as its principal mandate the promotion of Quebec sovereignty. In 1993, the Bloc gained the second largest number of seats in the general election, and therefore became the Official Opposition (McMenemy, 1995). Although the Bloc has a very clear and precise political agenda, it has had support from diverse parts of Quebec society. For example, it is currently somewhat right of centre but has also had trade union support and other social democratic influences. The Bloc is also closely associated with the Parti Québécois, a provincial political party founded in 1968, and also devoted to the sovereignty of Quebec.

A final point on political parties bears emphasis. Political parties are elected at the provincial and federal levels to govern for a maximum of five years. Governments can be elected with a majority (half the members plus one) or a minority (less than half of the members plus one). When acting as a majority, a governing party can pass legislation regardless of opposition if all members of that party vote. For minority governing parties, any legislation can be defeated if all members of the opposition vote against it.

Theories of Social Welfare/The Welfare State

The previous section on ideology is a foundation for considering social welfare theory. This discussion is based on Mulvale's outline of six theoretical approaches to social welfare (2001, 15–29). The first, a social democratic perspective, assumes that the welfare state emerged out of democratic political pressures, be it via trade unions, political parties, or other social institutions; often these pressures are from the left end of the political spectrum (Struthers, 1994).

The second perspective, premised on Marxist thought, deems the welfare state an instrument of social control; for instance, it forestalls class insurrection. The welfare state serves the needs of capital accumulation—ensuring, for example, economic growth and relative peace with labour. It also serves the needs of the state: post-World War II economic growth financed a burgeoning welfare state, which in turn kept unemployment relatively low; political parties were elected in part on their ability to help facilitate these outcomes (Offe, 1984). Many Marxist thinkers see social welfare as having contradictory purposes in meeting the needs of the state and of capital. Some, in fact, accept right-wing arguments that some welfare programs create disincentives for work and diminish profit margins (Offe, 1984). Most see the post-World War II universal welfare state as decidedly a thing of the past. As elaborated in Chapter 2, economic growth in the 1970s faltered and governments abandoned the principles of intervening in the economy. Consequently, "two legs (high levels of employment and consumer demand, both premised on strong economic growth)" of the welfare state became wobbly; the third, the government's commitment to social welfare programs, was weakened as a result (Mulvale, 2001, 19).

A third perspective, based on feminist thought, sees the welfare state as having profoundly reinforced dependency of women and children on the bread-winner male. Women are fundamental actors in social welfare: as the clients, reformers, and state employees of the welfare state (Ursel, 1992). Yet the welfare state has been modest at best in meeting women's needs, and oppressive at worst in reproducing gender inequalities that arise within patriarchal structures. Income security programs, for instance, have been bifurcated into insurance-based entitlements for men, and needs-tested, stigmatizing programs for women. Many with these theoretical assumptions call for greater support for women in the workplace, the expansion of affordable day care, and the transformation of income security programs to reflect women's needs, among many other measures. These concerns are elaborated in Chapter 6.

A fourth perspective is an anti-racist critique of the welfare state. One writer describes the double process of disadvantage experienced by members of ethnoracial communities. Their less-advantaged positions on economic and social grounds make them more reliant on the welfare state. Yet the welfare state treats them "on systematically less favourable terms than members of the majority community" (Pierson, 1991, cited in Mulvale, 1991, 23). This perspective is also elucidated in Chapter 6.

Fifth, a green critique, sees the welfare state as "embedded in an industrial order" of economic growth that is no longer sustainable (Pierson, 1991, cited in Mulvale, 1991, 23). The welfare state, the critique asserts, is premised on an expanded economy that overproduces, depletes resources, and creates pollution. These concerns are elaborated in Chapter 5.

The final perspective calls for social welfare to make a shift from compensation to empowerment. Rather than emphasizing individual deficits, and providing some agreed-upon community standard, such as a poverty line, empowerment social welfare assumes that all require help in order to develop (Drover and Kerans, 1993 cited in Mulvale 1991, 26–27). Central to this view is how needs are interpreted and claims are made. As discussed in Chapter 5, on some level, these processes are mediated by an era of globalization, in which political and economic structures within and outside of Canada have a strong bearing on all aspects of social welfare.

Social Welfare as a Response to Need

Social welfare programs may be categorized as functioning in one of the following three ways (Macarov, 1995):

1. Intervention before a problem arises is perhaps the least-addressed function of social welfare, given that scarce resources are most often used to address existing cases of economic hardship.

2. Maintenance is provided for at-risk individuals or groups, such as families with children, who receive various tax credits in the hope that they will not slip into the poverty ranks.

3. Most commonly, social policy is directed at the amelioration of existing problems through such programs as Social Assistance. The quest for governments and social agencies is to develop clear indicators for identifying when personal economic troubles should fall within the realm of a social economic problem.

FIGURE 4.2   Maslow's Hierarchy of Needs

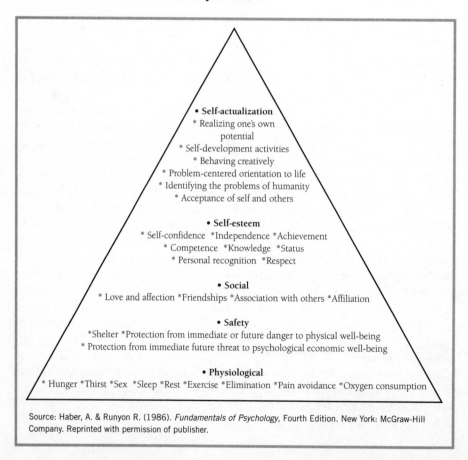

- **Self-actualization**
  * Realizing one's own potential
  * Self-development activities
  * Behaving creatively
  * Problem-centered orientation to life
  * Identifying the problems of humanity
  * Acceptance of self and others

- **Self-esteem**
  * Self-confidence *Independence *Achievement
  * Competence *Knowledge *Status
  * Personal recognition *Respect

- **Social**
  * Love and affection *Friendships *Association with others *Affiliation

- **Safety**
  *Shelter *Protection from immediate or future danger to physical well-being
  * Protection from immediate future threat to psychological economic well-being

- **Physiological**
  * Hunger *Thirst *Sex *Sleep *Rest *Exercise *Elimination *Pain avoidance *Oxygen consumption

Source: Haber, A. & Runyon R. (1986). *Fundamentals of Psychology*, Fourth Edition. New York: McGraw-Hill Company. Reprinted with permission of publisher.

There is a great deal of debate about how to define need worthy of societal intervention, as well as how to respond to identified need. It is important to remember that there is a direct relationship between how a social problem is defined and its perceived solution. In this section, we will consider how poverty is defined and the solutions that are implied by these definitions. This will involve distinguishing needs from wants, categorizing types of economic need, and examining how benchmarks for measuring economic need to be addressed by societal intervention are created.

Need versus Want

A four-part typology helps social workers to determine the exact nature of a particular human need. The types include felt needs, expressed needs, normative needs, and comparative needs (Chappell, 1997):

➤ *felt needs* are defined on a personal or subjective level;

➤ these become *expressed needs* when communicated to others;

➤ *normative needs* are determined by someone other than the individual by applying some benchmark or standard to the individual case; and

➤ *comparative needs* are determined by comparing one individual or group to another.

Establishing the benchmarks for normative needs and the boundaries of specific social groups, such as those living in poverty, are of major concern for the creators and administrators of social policy.

Theoretical and/or ideological perspectives influence how social policy planners determine the nature of a human need. Psychologist Abraham Maslow's *hierarchy of needs* theory (see Figure 4.2) is an excellent means of considering these distinctions (Maslow 1954; Macarov, 1995). This theory categorizes needs according to a hierarchy ranging from having (physiological needs), to loving (social needs), and finally to being (self-actualizing needs) (Macarov, 1995). Maslow defined the basic physiological needs (i.e., food, shelter, and clothing) as essential survival needs. Social policy is most often directed at this "having" aspect of need. Maslow's theory is based upon the principle of deficiency needs; that is, if a particular need is not being sufficiently met, then the person or group will seek to make up for this deficiency. This theory highlights a motivational element in meeting common human needs (adapted from Chappell, 1997).

Differential Human Needs

While Maslow's hierarchy distinguishes types of common needs, it does not address special conditions that create these specific needs. Macarov (1995) identified five categories of people with special needs:

1. the *incapable*, such as children;
2. the *unprepared*, such as recent immigrants to a new country and those who cannot read;
3. *disaster victims,* such as victims of war or environmental situations;
4. the *unconforming,* or those who do not abide by societal norms; and
5. the *unmotivated,* or people who lack the motivation to meet their own needs.

All five categories are essential to social policies.

Besides common human needs and special needs, some needs are created by society (Macarov, 1995). Institutionalized discrimination, along lines of race, gender, culture, or other areas of social diversity, may create obstacles to developing and implementing social policy. These include, but are not restricted to, lack of access to services, inadequate funding and representation in community-based programs, and ethnocentric values and practices in existing services and programs policy (Armitage, 1996; Henry, Tator, Mattis and Rees, 1995). These are examined in greater depth in Chapter 6.

Denying the impact of institutionalized discrimination affects how problems are defined and, therefore, the anticipated solutions. This may lead to an interpretation of needs based upon membership in the unconforming and/or the unmotivated categories mentioned earlier. In this way, social needs—for housing, income security, or other things—may be restricted or even denied under the weight of being evaluated as deserving or undeserving. As society changes, the social attention to needs may also change. Policy-makers decide how and when societal resources are directed at certain needs and when social norms dictate that social institutions other than social welfare (e.g., the individual, family, or informal social networks) should be directed at finding a solution.

Conceptualizing and Defining Poverty

The concept of poverty dates back to ancient times. *Poverty* is a state of deficiency in money or in the means of subsistence. Welfare state governments want to know how many citizens live in a state of poverty, and are not content to rely on subjective assessment. To this end, governments and organizations set *poverty lines* that measure the necessary amount of money for living at a determined *standard of living*. The "necessities, luxuries, and comforts" needed to sustain oneself or family at a determined level comprise a standard of living (Barker, 1991).

Defining poverty using a poverty line is based upon measuring the difference between *what is* and *what should be*. Poverty lines, as an indicator of an income level below which living would be seriously difficult, may be set at absolute or relative levels. Absolute and relative definitions of poverty are based upon destitution and disparity models, respectively. *Absolute need* definitions of poverty answer the question of what the bare minimum (destitution) level is in order for an individual or family to survive. On the other hand, *relative need* definitions are based on social values, rather than absolute needs, and start with a prevailing standard of living and then deduce the level below this standard that is intolerable to society. Writing for the Canadian Council on Social Development, policy analysts Ross, Scott, and Smith (2000) listed an absolute poverty line at about $2,000 per person per annum (6). This amount is a mere survival rate that incorporates using local resources such as basic provincial health care, community shelters, food banks, and thrift shop clothing. Relative poverty lines are concerned with what should be— they establish the norm against which an individual or family can be compared. Ross, Scott, and Smith provide a number of working definitions of poverty as established by national and regional groups (2000).

Normative Basis of the Poverty Line

How do Canadians define poverty? Table 4.1 presents a summary of major indexes for defining a poverty line used in Canada (Ross, Scott, and Smith, 2000). As reflected in Table 4.1, Canadians cannot agree on a unitary definition of poverty. Statistics Canada's Low Income Cut-off (LICO) definition is the best known of these indicators. The LICO has been a standard since 1959 and is based on information from a survey of family spending patterns conducted by Statistics Canada. From the 1959 survey, it was determined that the average Canadian family spent 50 percent of its gross income on the essentials: food, shelter, and clothing. It was estimated that any family spending more than 50 percent on these essentials was living in constrained circumstances and any family spending more

TABLE 4.1   Measuring Poverty

2000-Based Poverty Lines	Cut-Off Income for Household of 4
Statistics Canada	$23,653 LICO (rural) to LICO $34 226 (city of 500,000+)
Statistics Canada	$25,984+ LIM
CCSD*	$33,912
Toronto SPC**	$44,668
Montreal Diet	$19,080 (basic needs)
Dispensary	$21,697 (minimum adequate standard)
Fraser Institute	$15, 681 (QC) to $19,754 (BC)
Provincial Social Assistance	$10,164 (NB) to $14,965 (PEI)

+ Note that family type is conceived as two adults and two children, or one adult and three children; this statistic is taken from Ross, Scott, and Smith, 2000, 19, based on 1997 Statistics Canada data adjusted to 2000 by use of increases in the consumer price index.

* CCSD = Canadian Council on Social Development;

** Toronto SPC = Metropolitan Toronto Social Planning Council.

Source: Based on Ross, D. P., Scott, K.J., & Smith, P.J. (2000). *The Canadian Fact Book on Poverty*. Ottawa: The Canadian Council on Social Development, pp. 13–33.

than 70 percent on essentials was designated as "low-income"—in essence creating a poverty line. In subsequent years, the poverty cut-off has been adjusted using the same formula (i.e., spending on essentials for the average Canadian family plus 20 percent). For example, the poverty line was set at 54.7 percent of gross family income for essential expenditures in 1992 based on the survey in that year. Since 1973, Statistics Canada has also distinguished among five different sizes of urban and rural communities—the larger the community, the higher the Low Income Cut-off for any family (Ross, Scott, and Smith, 2000, 14–15).

In 1990, Statistics Canada calculated a second poverty line based on median after-tax incomes rather than the average gross income. This measurement became known as the Low Income Measure, or LIM. The LIM is based not on the proportion of income spent on food, clothing, and shelter, but rather on income itself. It is calculated on the basis of one half of median gross (or after-tax) income, where median income is first adjusted for family size (that is, a one-person household earning $60,000 has significantly more disposable income than a four-person household earning $60,000). (Note that the median income represents the income that half of all income earners earn more than and half earn less than, while an average income represents the sum of all incomes divided by the number of income earners.) An after-tax index may be a truer standard than the commonly used gross or before-tax measures. Statistics Canada nonetheless continues to use its LICO measurement as the standard for assessing poverty. As Figure 4.3 makes clear, the LIM approach and the LICO provide different measurements. The LIM tends to reduce the number of people in poverty by two or three percentage points. But this reduction is not uniform across the country; in the Atlantic provinces and Saskatchewan it increases poverty rates while lowering them in other provinces (Ross, Scott, and Smith, 2000, 18–19).

Defining the Problem, Defining the Solution

In 1984, the Canadian Council on Social Development (CCSD) outlined the following four rationales for establishing poverty lines:

1. Poverty lines are needed to determine the number of people living in poverty. In Canada, the Statistics Canada LICO measurement is most frequently used to determine this figure.

2. Poverty indicators are used to inform and perhaps motivate those receiving and administering social service programs. This rationale is used to explain the minimal level at which Social Assistance payments are set in order to motivate people to view this financial program as temporary.

3. Setting the parameters of an accepted "market basket" (the amount of goods and services consumed by a family or individual over the course of a typical month) is another use of defined poverty lines. This market basket approach is used to develop only a few of the poverty indicators reviewed: the Metropolitan Toronto Social Planning Council budget guides and the Montreal Diet Dispensary budget guidelines of basic needs.

4. Poverty indices inform future social policy planners, especially with respect to setting income security levels.

The various poverty lines described above can be pegged across the political spectrum. The conservative right of the political spectrum is represented by the Fraser Institute and Montreal Diet Dispensary definitions of poverty. This position asserts that poverty levels using other standards are grossly exaggerated. The Toronto Social Planning Council figures represent the "left" or social democratic end of the political spectrum, or a more social-justice or equality focus, while Statistics Canada maintains poverty measures that are closer to the centre.

It should be stressed that the agreed-to definition of poverty is the one that Canadian society will accept. In the face of rising numbers of persons living in poverty, society ultimately has three options, none of which are mutually exclusive. Society can:

1. decide to leave more and more people behind;
2. find ways to distribute wealth more efficiently and equitably; or
3. hope to find ways for people to receive more income from their own efforts and work.

Likewise, it is essential to note some of the changing parameters of poverty in Canada. A 2001 study by the Organization for Economic Cooperation and Development (OECD) compares Canada's mixed record in combating poverty relative to those of 12 European countries and the United States (Figure 4.3). Likewise, according to recent Statistics Canada LICO data, poverty rates in Canada have fluctuated from 16.2 percent in 1973, to 14 percent in 1981, to 13.5 percent in 1989, rising to 17.5 percent in 1997 (Ross, Scott, and Smith, 2000, 47). Moreover, the poverty gap as measured by the LICO—how far below the LICO one's income falls—for all poor households nearly doubled between 1981 and 1997. Among the worst hit in this respect were poor working-age households, whose poverty gap increased by 113 percent between 1973 and 1997. Taking into account all household categories, there has been an increase in poverty among more than 1.3 million households since 1973. Here again, working-aged households have fared especially badly, experiencing significant increases in poverty rates during this period.

Seniors' households experienced a 16 percent drop in their poverty rate during this same period, 1973 to 1997. Many assert that income security programs discussed in Chapter 3, such as Old Age Security and the CPP/QPP, have been especially important in reducing poverty among seniors. But poverty among unattached elderly individuals remains high, at 45 percent in 1997. Within this cohort there is a profound gender bias, with 49 percent of unattached elderly females living in poverty versus 33.3 percent of elderly men—a reflection, in part, of the inequalities in workplace earnings that subsequently were translated into unequal pension rates upon retirement. Finally, it is important to emphasize that many elderly households have only barely been lifted above poverty levels, and, in fact, a significant proportion of the elderly fall into the category of nearly poor (Ross, Scott, and Smith, 2000, xix–xx, 47).

**FIGURE 4.3 Poverty in Canada Compared with Other OECD Countries—
Poverty as a Percentage of Population, 1993–95**

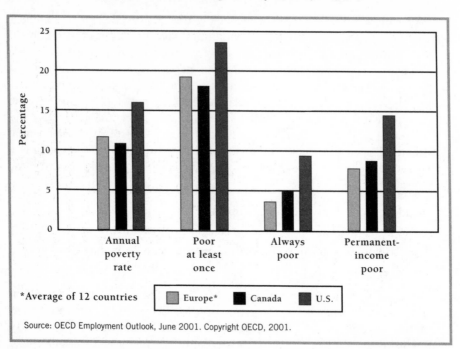

Source: OECD Employment Outlook, June 2001. Copyright OECD, 2001.

Young families are more likely to be poor than older families. What is more, poverty has increased dramatically among younger families. In 1981, 21.7 percent of young families (in which the oldest adult is under 25) were poor; by 1997 this had increased to 46 percent. In the next age cohort, those between 24 and 35 years of age, the poverty rate increased from 12 percent in 1981 to 19 percent in 1997.

On regional grounds, the face of poverty has likewise shifted. The percentage of all poor families in the Atlantic provinces was 8.8 percent in 1997, a drop from 12.3 percent in 1981. But in Alberta and British Columbia, the share of poor families increased from 14.8 percent to 20.9 percent in this same period. Much of Western Canada's increase in poverty occurred in the 1980s. In the 1990s, Ontario's share of poor families rose by more than 7 percent. Poverty rates across all categories—families and individuals—increased in many provinces in the 1990s. For example, Ontario had the lowest rate of family poverty at 8 percent in 1989, but this climbed to a startling 12.6 percent by 1997.

The child poverty rate increased from 14.9 percent in 1981 to 20 percent in 1997, representing 1.4 million children in the latter year. Although more than half of all children in poverty live in two-parent families, the proportion of poor children in lone-parent households has increased from 33 percent in 1981 to 43 percent in 1997. As noted in Figure 4.4, Canada's child poverty rates are higher than those of many other advanced industrialized countries.

FIGURE 4.4   Child Poverty in Canada Compared with Other Countries, Mid-1990s

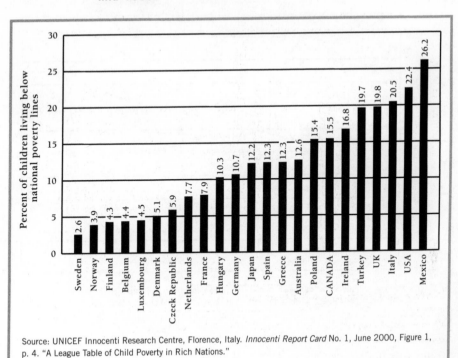

Source: UNICEF Innocenti Research Centre, Florence, Italy. *Innocenti Report Card* No. 1, June 2000, Figure 1, p. 4. "A League Table of Child Poverty in Rich Nations."

According to the 1996 census, 43 percent of all Aboriginal peoples, 36 percent of all Canadians of visible minority status, and 31 percent of Canadians with disabilities were poor in 1995. These rates are significantly higher than national averages of poverty (Ross, Scott, and Smith, 2000, xix–xxiv).

Durations of poverty differ. For roughly 60 percent of the poor, poverty is a temporary occurrence, unlikely to be repeated within a 10-year period. For 40 percent of the poor, poverty is "a more chronic problem," with longer spells of poverty and a greater likelihood of becoming poor again; "lone parent mothers are the most likely to fit into this 40-percent category" (Ross, Scott, and Smith, 2000, 119). There is considerable variability from one person to the next; taking aggregate statistics, the average poor person in Canada spends about five years poor—counting single and multiple experiences of poverty—while 5 percent remain poor for 10 years or more. Certain groups of people are more likely to experience longer spells of poverty: lone parents, people with disabilities, members of visible minority communities, recent immigrants, individuals with low levels of education, and unattached individuals. Also critical: the longer one is poor, the more difficult it is to escape (Ross, Scott, and Smith, 2000, xxiii).

Education remains an important factor in distinguishing the poor from the non-poor, as elaborated in Figures 4.5 and 4.6. Social policies that encourage people

FIGURE 4.5   Class Struggle

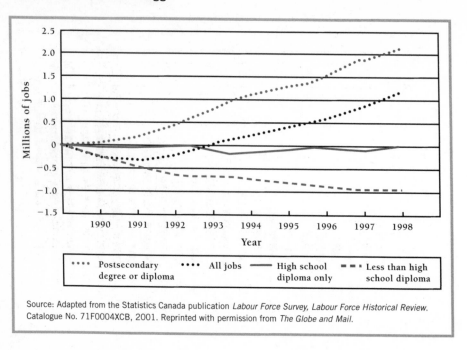

Source: Adapted from the Statistics Canada publication *Labour Force Survey, Labour Force Historical Review.* Catalogue No. 71F0004XCB, 2001. Reprinted with permission from *The Globe and Mail.*

to stay in school, as well as policies that encourage postdegree continuous learning, are potentially useful to assuage poverty.

Social Policy and Economic Policy

Chappell (1997) suggests that Canadian social and economic policies are related in three ways and reflect the Canadian experience of economic insecurity.

1. The state of the economy determines which social programs are needed. For example, in times of high unemployment the demand for social services such as Social Assistance, mental and physical health, and child welfare increases in many areas.

2. The pattern of social spending in recent years has been dependent not upon need but upon the government's economic priority of fiscal restraint in order to reduce deficit spending.

3. Some believe that social programs may discourage economic growth through such mechanisms as decreased spending power of individuals and an increased debt/deficit situation. This, however, is a highly debatable point. Indeed, several observers argue that social programs promote economic growth by putting more money into more hands (Battle, 1993; Mendelson, 1993).

FIGURE 4.6   Education¹ Makes a Difference

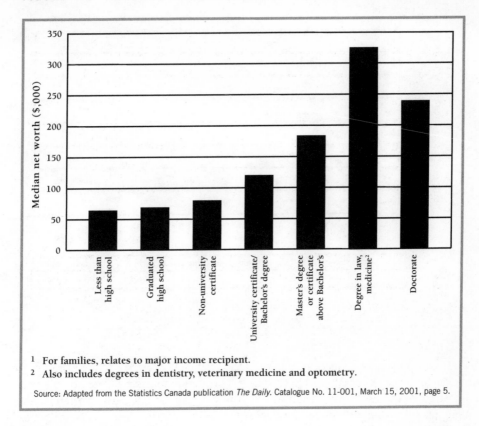

1 For families, relates to major income recipient.
2 Also includes degrees in dentistry, veterinary medicine and optometry.

Source: Adapted from the Statistics Canada publication *The Daily*. Catalogue No. 11-001, March 15, 2001, page 5.

Income Redistribution

The *Gini coefficient* (see Figure 4.7) is a means of comparing three types of income levels with each other and across time. In interpreting the Gini coefficient, 0 would indicate perfect equality of income where every Canadian would receive the same amount of money. A score of 1 would represent perfect inequality, where one person gets all the income and everyone else receives nothing. Both of these are ideal or theoretical scenarios that would probably never occur. The value of the Gini coefficient is that it provides the extreme parameters (0 and 1) between which we can make comparisons.

Figure 4.7 highlights the influence of income security programs and the tax system as tools of income redistribution. The highest line, and the one that shows the least equal income distribution, represents "earned income" prior to taxes. The next highest line, which reflects a state of greater equality, includes "earned income" as well as income derived from income security programs such as Social Assistance, the Canada Pension Plan, and Employment Insurance. This line in itself reveals the equalizing effect of income-security social policies. The third line, which tends to a greater state of income distribution, represents income *after taxes*, demonstrating the greater equalizing effects of the income tax system.

FIGURE 4.7   Income Distribution in Canada: The Gini Coefficient

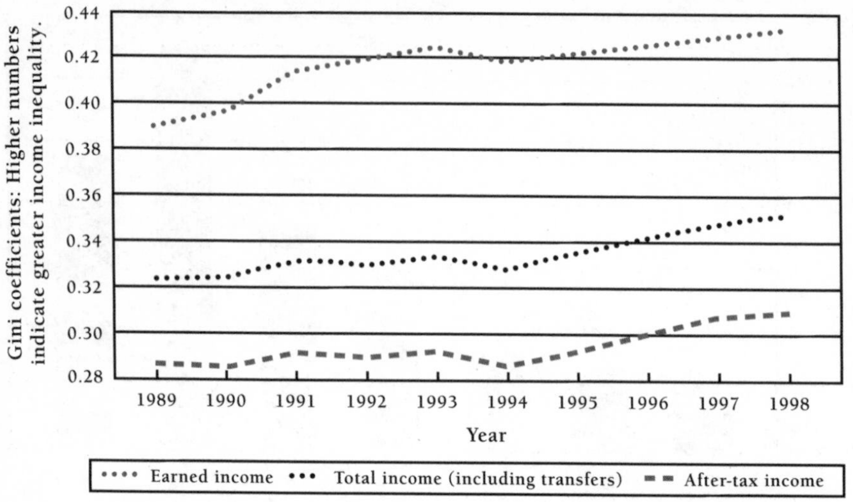

Source: Adapted from the Statistics Canada publication *Income After Tax, Distribution by Size in Canada*, Catalogue No. 13-210, and *Income in Canada*, Catalogue No. 75-202. Reprinted with permission from *The Globe and Mail*.

Having acknowledged the effects of the income tax system, scholars and policy analysts insist that many tax credits and tax deductions are utilized by the rich more than the poor, and benefit the rich more than the poor. Two writeoffs that favour well-to-do individuals are Registered Retirement Savings Plan (RRSP) contributions and child-care expenses. Far more high-income earners claim the RRSP than do low-income earners. Additionally, as one policy document remarks, "high-income Canadians are much more able than low- and middle- income Canadians to put money towards RRSPs, and, because tax assistance is provided in the form of a deduction, RRSP owners in the top bracket enjoy larger tax savings" (Torjman and Battle, 1995a, 5). Moreover and more generally, various tax breaks, to individuals and to corporations, drain billions of dollars from government budgets and thereby contribute to the retrenchment of social programs (Torjman and Battle, 1995a, 5; Guest, 1997, 188–189; Muszynski, 1987). RRSP exemptions, to cite one example, resulted in nearly $8 billion of foregone revenue to Ottawa in 2001 (Little, August 27, 2001, B2).

Paying Taxes

Death and taxes are claimed to be the two things in life that are unavoidable. Typically, Canadians are most aware of two types of taxes: personal income tax and consumption taxes, especially the Goods and Services Tax (GST) and Provincial Sales Tax (PST). Personal income tax represents about one-third of government revenue (Muszynski, 1987). Although the GST and PST are the most noticeable forms of consumption taxes, "sin taxes" on consumer items such as tobacco and

FIGURE 4.8   Income Tax Payment in Canada

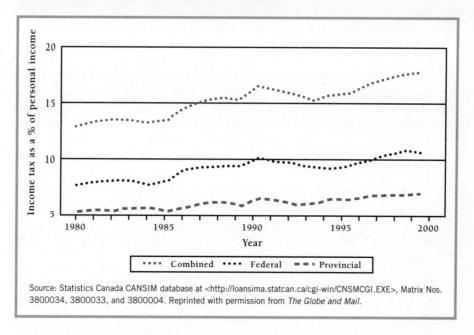

Source: Statistics Canada CANSIM database at <http://loansima.statcan.ca/cgi-win/CNSMCGI.EXE>, Matrix Nos. 3800034, 3800033, and 3800004. Reprinted with permission from *The Globe and Mail*.

alcohol have received increased public attention. Payroll taxes, business taxes, import taxes, property taxes, and resource taxes are other levies made upon the citizens of Canada. The federal government has the greatest power to impose taxes and collects about 60 percent of all tax revenues, while provincial and municipal governments collect 30 percent and 10 percent respectively (Muszynski, 1987). The proportion of our incomes going toward income taxes has increased over the past several decades, as elaborated in Figure 4.8.

Tax systems generally operate on either regressive or progressive principles (or on a combination of both). *Regressive tax systems* impose the same tax level on all citizens, which, in effect, imposes the greatest burden on those least able to pay (Muszynski, 1987). A provincial sales tax (PST) is a Canadian example of a regressive tax. It is levied on a particular good at the same percentage regardless of a person's income. Because they have less disposable income, persons with low incomes pay a greater portion of their incomes in PST payments than do those in higher-income brackets.

A *progressive tax system* bases the level of taxation upon a person's ability to pay, such that those with higher incomes pay proportionately higher taxes. A *regressive tax system*, in contrast, imposes the same tax level on all citizens—regardless of ability to pay. Our current income tax system demonstrates how many taxes contain elements of both the progressive and the regressive. It is somewhat progressive in so far as there are multiple tax brackets, with a progressive increase in the percentage of taxable income to be paid as one's income rises. In this sense it differentiates somewhat between those with less money (and in lower tax brackets) and those with more (and in higher brackets). But critics point out that it could be still *more* progressive, with richer people and corporations paying more. In this respect it has definite regressive elements. If well-to-do individuals and corporations paid more, it would be more progressive and less regressive.

A recently proposed option that is not based on this progressive principle is the concept of a "flat tax." For example, as of 2001 in Alberta, provincial income tax is no longer calculated as a percentage of federal tax payable. Rather, it is 11 percent of taxable income (hence a flat tax) above the personal exemption of $11,000 per year (hence a small progressive aspect in that people under the threshold are not responsible for the 11 percent payable). A flat tax brings a simplicity and efficiency to the current complex tax system with less emphasis on tax loopholes than the present system. But it tends to make the income tax system less progressive, and hence a less powerful instrument of income redistribution.

Some Consequences of the Welfare State

Paradoxes of intervening in the economic life of some Canadians have long been recognized. For example, financial assistance programs may sometimes decrease the incentive to paid work for some recipients; that is, they contain inherent labour force participation disincentives. Authors of this textbook, like other progressive observers, insist on the need for plentiful jobs offering meaningful employment and decent wages. More than any other factor, decent jobs would alleviate much of the problem of such labour force participation disincentives (Clarke, 1997). Additionally, in the absence of a full employment economy, some observers point to social policies themselves. Components of social welfare programs that tend to act as disincentives to paid work include:

➤ the decreased purchasing power of current "minimum wages;"
➤ health care benefits that exceed those of many employment situations;
➤ insufficient coverage for back-to-work expenses;
➤ high tax-back rates for earning exemptions; and
➤ lack of affordable, accessible child care (National Council on Welfare, 1993).

The National Council on Welfare (1993) suggests that cooperation between the federal and provincial governments in reversing some employment trends is imperative to finding solutions to this complex problem. Strategies suggested by this report include searching for ways to promote full employment, halting the trend toward short-term and part-time jobs without benefit packages, indexing minimum wages to match inflation, and recognizing the need for increased funding for child-care programs.

These practical aspects of disincentives are often joined by moral arguments for and against government financial assistance programs. For example, in a review of findings of a Royal Commission on Employment and Unemployment in Newfoundland, Banting (1993) outlined some of the moral disincentives of social programs such as Social Assistance and Employment Insurance (EI) suggested by the Commission. The disincentives included an undermining of the intrinsic value of work, of furthering education, of developing reliable work habits, and of taking responsibility.

Others stress that the demoralization of Canadians receiving welfare moneys can be addressed by mandatory workfare programs as a condition for receiving Social Assistance and EI services (Handler and Hasenfeld, 1991). Proponents of workfare suggest that it promotes the "moral merit of work" in a "failed system of subsidized poverty" (Sirico, 1997 July 27, E15). Self-respect, taking responsibility, the development of a "worker" identity, and the acquisition of work skills and work experience are among the moral benefits suggested by advocates of workfare programs. Such programs are based upon separating out the able-bodied recipients from those who are unable to work. To some, this division seems a throwback to the nineteenth-century Poor Laws and their delineation of the deserving and undeserving poor. These laws were heavily influenced by the moral overtones of the view that poverty was a state resulting from idleness and immoral behaviour.

Evans and colleagues (1995) present a threefold normative argument against workfare regulations. Among points they raise are issues of a "deserving" poor, increased self-respect, increased responsibility-taking, and active participation in one's own destiny.

1. To some proponents of workfare, workfare participants become the deserving poor, and those who do not participate are implied to be "lazy" and "irresponsible." As Evans et al. note, this attitude may act as a veil to hide insidious forms of institutional discrimination against those who, for reasons of family responsibility, sickness, or other contingencies, cannot work.

2. Proponents of workfare also claim that increased self-respect will come from work, any work. But as Evans et al. point out, one should question whether more self-respect comes from a job obtained through a workfare scheme versus a job earned by other means.

3. Some workfare proponents assume that income redistribution programs diminish the sense of social responsibility in Canadians who receive them. The argument for workfare often includes augmenting the link between rights and responsibilities. Workfare is sometimes promoted as a way to re-instil a sense of making a contribution to society. However, the authors question the argument that workfare is the answer to addressing the issue of enhancing social responsibility and active participation in one's own destiny. Indeed, one could argue that workfare diminishes a sense of social responsibility toward those individuals who experience temporary inability to work.

Many in the workfare debate recognize that this style of program regulation shifts the ideological base of the welfare state from the redistribution of income (i.e., social justice) to one of production activity as an individual responsibility (Evans, Jacobs, Noel and Reynolds, 1995). Sociologist C. Wright Mills (1963) suggests an inextricable link between the private troubles of an individual and the public issues of which they form a part. He believes that private troubles "have to do with an individual's character and with those limited areas of social life of which s/he is directly and personally aware." Public issues "have to do with matters that transcend these local environments of the individual and the limited range of his/her life. They have to do with the organization...of institutions of society" (Mills, 1963, 395–6). One can infer from Mills, and like-minded thinkers, that both society and the individual are implicated in the construction, definition, and solution of social problems. Thus, difficulties that some social work clients experience getting off income security programs represent, potentially, individual trouble *and* a public issue. To overlook the public issue component, as some liberal and neo-conservative thinkers do, is to miss the complexities and nuances of policy analysis.

Conclusion

As this chapter has discussed, a variety of ideological, economic, and social factors influence the nature of social policies, the contexts in which they were conceived and carried out, and the reasons why they change over time. The next chapter sheds light on important additional phenomena—globalization, the environmental movement, and social inclusion—which are now rightly seen as crucial considerations for social policies.

Chapter 5

Social Policy and Emerging Realities

The issues discussed in this book affect everyone: What level of entitlement is considered fair when determining benefit rates for such income security programs as Social Assistance? What should be the minimum number of weeks of paid employment to enable a claimant to obtain Employment Insurance benefits? How much money per capita should the state allocate to day-care programs? Should health-insurance programs be universal, selective, or a combination of both? These questions, and others like them, reflect societal values and determine the basic structures of social policies.

The answers vary from place to place, and over time. The welfare state of early twenty-first-century Canada is manifestly different from that of the early twentieth century.

As difficult as predictions into the future are to make, this chapter will consider the following five essential issues that we expect will continue to shape Canadian social policies well into the new millennium:

1. the environmental imperative;
2. globalization;
3. social welfare retrenchment;
4. changing conceptions of social welfare in relation to citizenship and social inclusion; and
5. the growing impact of social movements.

The Environmental Imperative

Rachel Carson's *The Silent Spring*, first published in 1962, was one of the earliest modern-day environmental treatises. Since then, an emergent environmental movement has sought to change social consciousness, and legislation, in the developed worlds, of which Canada is a part, and in the developing worlds of Asia, Central and South America, and elsewhere. *The 1995 Global Biodiversity Assessment*, a United Nations report, estimates that more than 30 000 plant and animal species now face possible extinction (Van Wormer, 1997, 646). Oceans cover almost three-quarters of the earth's surface, and contain 97 percent of the world's water. Sediments, oils, wastes, and a damaged ozone layer, among other phenomena, increasingly assault them. The annual tonnage of fish caught in the world's oceans has increased 1600 percent in the twentieth century, and yet the annual growth rates of many species have been falling since the 1970s (Sachs, Loske, and Linz, 1998, 74). The tragic decline and fall of a once-prolific cod fishery is well known to the Atlantic Provinces in Canada. In more global terms, today one-third of the world's tropical forests, one-quarter of its available fresh water, and one-quarter of its fish resources are gone (Sachs, 1999). To some extent, as Van Wormer and others argue, this is a problem of overpopulation, with a current global population of some 6 billion people, compared to 1 billion in 1850, and 2 billion in 1930. The United Nations, through its World Population Plan policy response, is initiating intensive family-planning programs to prevent unwanted pregnancy, coinciding with and bolstering similar programs in some developing countries (Van Wormer, 1997, 652).

But as relevant as overpopulation, and of particular significance to this textbook, is the fact that the current ecological crisis is a problem caused by the developed world. The wealthy 25 percent of humanity creates an ecological footprint—the extent of natural and geographic resources that it consumes—as large as the biologically productive part of the earth (Sachs, 1999). This footprint represents consumption of fossil fuels, agricultural production of food and other products, misuses of forests and water, human settlement, and so on. The consumption of fossil fuels alone, to briefly examine one example, illustrates the severity of the crisis. Carbon dioxide (CO_2) is released into the atmosphere through the burning of fossil fuels in cars and industries, by forest fires, and through other natural and human sources, causing a greenhouse effect in the atmosphere that is responsible for at least half of all sources of global warming (Sachs, Laske, and Linz, 1998, 29). The results are potentially calamitous: the possibility of the polar ice caps melting, resulting in the massive flooding of a considerable portion of the earth's land mass.

How can Canada respond? With today's world population of 6 billion, and levels of annual emission of CO_2 close to 29 billion tonnes, an "equal rights of emission" worldwide would assume 5 tonnes per head annually. But in Canada, current annual domestic production of CO_2 is equivalent to between 15 and 20 tonnes per head. Assume, as is the consensus among many demographers, current projections of a world population of 10 billion by 2050. In this scenario, our country would need to diminish CO_2 emissions by 80 percent over the next 50 years in order to achieve even the objective of equal utilization rights with other countries (Sachs, Laske, and Linz, 1998, 30).

Such a reduction would require a profoundly different approach to economic arrangements, sometimes called sustainability. Sustainability is an economic, political, and environmental world view that promotes present and future generations of stewardship of the physical world. Sustainable development, a resulting concept, "creates a process that ensures that natural resources are replenished, and that future generations continue to have the resources they need to meet their own needs" (Van

Wormer, 1987, 650). The 1987 Brundtland Report, commissioned by the United Nations (UN), was an important document in the evolution of this latter concept. In it, economic and environmental development issues are clearly linked. Also significant was the 1992 Rio de Janeiro Earth Summit, a UN conference that produced a 500-page document elaborating global partnerships that could achieve sustainability. Twenty thousand concerned citizens attended, outnumbering official representatives by more than two to one, and underscoring the importance of popular input into major environmental policies. Also significant was the presence of myriad non-governmental organizations (NGOs), such as Amnesty International, Greenpeace, and Friends of the Earth, as well as the world scientific community. Finally, innumerable treaties have also been signed over the past two decades, protecting the air and oceans from pollution and land from desertification (Van Wormer, 1997, 650–1). But continued rates of pollution far, far exceed their effect.

The 1974 "Group of 77" (now numbering more than 100) developing countries proposed to the UN General Assembly a new international economic order (NIEO) that would address North-South (the developed world and the developing world, respectively) inequalities. Thinking about sustainability in that context, Sachs and other environmentalists propose significant changes to the way in which ordinary Canadians think about, and act upon, patterns of consumption. Among many proposals are:

➤ sharing goods such as skis, cars, and other commodities that are not required on a daily basis;

➤ using and further developing public transportation infrastructures, rather than roads, highways, and other car-oriented patterns of movement;

➤ urban planning that revives notions of greater densities of population, greater built-in proximity between homes, schools, places of work, and entertainment and leisure (Sachs, Losek, and Linz, 1998, 123, 133); and

➤ reduction, reuse, and recycling of consumer products.

Several other low-cost strategies that could reduce Canadian greenhouse emissions by 50 percent over 30 years include use of increased insulation in houses, building machines with increased efficiency in the engineering of heating and cars, using more efficient, smaller power plants in place of larger-scale plants (Torrie, May 19, 2000).

Beyond these immediate courses of action, social policies have scarcely begun to integrate issues of social justice for people with the imperative of physical ecology. Indeed, many social welfare organizations have had only very loose connections with environmental NGOs. Greater collaboration might be useful. A March 1999 *Globe and Mail* headline declared "Canada the Promised Land" for criminal polluters. Since 1992, federal government environmental charges of corporate polluters have dropped 78 percent, and in provinces such as Ontario, by about 50 percent over a comparable period. "Fines are few, jail time non-existent" in comparison with American prosecutions, the article continues. Many environmentalists are concerned that Canadian governments are using "weak enforcement practices to attract investors" into the country (March 13, 1999, A8). According to one Canadian research report, Canada ranks among the worst five OECD nations on 17 indicators, including greenhouse gas emissions, air pollution, water consumption, energy consumption, energy efficiency, fertilizer consumption, and generation of hazardous and nuclear waste (**www.environmentalindicators.com**); *The Globe and Mail*, April 27, 2001, A15). A 2001 report by Canada's environment commissioner is likewise critical of the federal government's lack of resolve in cleaning up the Great Lakes basin, which holds 20 percent of the world's fresh water (**www.oag-bvg.ca/ environment**). Outbreaks of e. coli in water tables in several provinces has resulted in dozens of deaths and hundreds of illnesses; in 2001 there were 22 boil-water advisories in British Columbia and 260 in Newfoundland. In 2000, there were 13 in Alberta, 70 in Ontario, and 542 in Quebec (*The Globe and Mail*, May 5, 2001, A11). Among other concerns, the country's environment commissioner points out, are problems of unregulated livestock sewage and nitrogen in farm fertilizers contaminating water tables (*The Globe and Mail*, October 3, 2001, A11). Many observers are worried about government cutbacks to departments that monitor and ensure safe drinking water, which, it is argued, is part of the wider phenomenon of government retreat from the social milieu. Indeed, as the next section elaborates, there are similar concerns about the decreasing corporate support of the welfare state, and the commensurate retrenchment of many social programs—such as health and Employment Insurance, which require employer contributions.

Finally, some observers have emphasized the connection between social policy development and economic development. To the extent that sustainability challenges previous notions of economic growth, the attending basis upon which social policies are conceived may also need rethinking. Moreover, the crisis of worsening public and environmental health concerns is, to stress an important point, an international, and not just a Canadian phenomenon (Garret, 2000). Perhaps a necessary condition to that end is a new world view that equates spiritual growth and self-realization with stewardship of the earth (Lonergan and Richards, 1988; Schumacher, 1973, 54–57).

Globalization

Globalization refers to the current, and pervasive, trend of internationalized finance, ideology, and political arrangements. As a result of globalization, money is invested quickly and easily across national borders. Principles of transnational competition for lucrative markets and inexpensive labour are actively pursued. What is more, in the absence of powerfully constraining national legislation or intra-national structures, multinational corporations achieve growing sovereignty to pursue these objectives.

The Economic Context of Globalization

There are two aspects of globalization that need to be considered: economics and politics. Global economics is vastly different from any of the systems that preceded it. In the sixteenth, seventeenth, and eighteenth centuries, a system of mercantilism formed the basis upon which colonial powers sought out foreign empires and cultivated worldwide systems of primary extraction abroad and production at home. Late eighteenth-century England, nineteenth-century France, Canada, the United States, and other countries underwent an industrial revolution, coinciding with increased urbanization, steam manufacturing, coal extraction, and railway and other industrial infrastructures. As shown in Chapter 2, capitalism was further transformed in the 1930s, with the advent of an interventionist state and the post-World War II comprehensive welfare state. These structures started to unravel in the 1970s, and in the 1990s there emerged a very different basis for economic arrangements.

One of the most noticeable changes is the ascendancy of regionally based structures of economic blocs. The "new Europe" of the twenty-first century, in the form of the European Community (EC), emerged gradually after World War II but was forged with the 1985 Single European Act allowing for the free passage of goods, services, capital, and workers amongst the 12 member states, which included Denmark, France, Germany, the United Kingdom, and other West European powers. The Maastricht Treaty of 1992 created a European Union (EU), to include a single European currency, and the future development of joint foreign and defence policies (Gwyn, 1995, 28–9).

On this continent, a 1989 Free Trade Agreement (FTA) was struck between Canada and the United States, after four years of intense negotiations involving the governments of Brian Mulroney in Canada, and Ronald Reagan in the United States. Prior to the FTA, the United States accounted for three-quarters of all Canadian exports. In one sense, the agreement consolidated a cross-border system of trade that was manifestly freer than any between the member states of the EC (Gwyn, 1995, 38). In a second sense, the FTA, like the EC agreement, removed still further powers and policy-making capacities from otherwise sovereign governments. Previous instruments of economic nationalism are a thing of the past, be they the Foreign Investment Review Agency, which ceases to exist, or the Bank Act, which no longer precludes foreign-chartered banks from Canadian markets. In 1995, a leading American economist and visiting professor at the University of Toronto proposed a new North American Central Bank, similar to that planned for Europe, in which Canada would secure minority status and relinquish control over its currency and exchange rates. At that same conference, Thomas d'Aquino, head of the Ottawa-based special interest group, the Business Council on National Issues, echoed similar sentiments, advocating infrastructures to reflect the growing integration of the American and Canadian economies (Gwyn, 1995, 42, 45). By then, the Chrétien government had successfully renegotiated the FTA to include Mexico, under the North American Free Trade Agreement (NAFTA). Subsequently, a Free Trade Agreement of the Americas has been under negotiation that is intended to move the entire hemisphere toward completed trade talks by 2005, covering 34 countries, 800 million people, and a combined economic output of $11 trillion (US dollars). Also recently, prominent Canadian economists Thomas Courchene and Richard Harris advocated more intra-national dialogue leading toward a unified North American currency (1999), and a 2001 TD

Bank study sympathetic to monetary union with the United States was followed by speculation by the governor of the Bank of Canada that Canada might adopt the American dollar within 10 years (*Montreal Gazette*, May 7, 2001, A9). Finally, and perhaps most importantly, all trade pacts are "less about liberalizing trade than about liberalizing money to go wherever it wants to go by making investors feel as secure abroad as they are at home" (Gwyn, 1995, 68). This facet, as will be seen, has especially troubling implications.

The Political Context of Globalization

Politically, international relations have been profoundly transformed over the past decade. The Cold War, beginning with the cessation of World War II, came to an abrupt end with the series of collapsed Communist governments in the former Soviet bloc during the late 1980s and early 1990s. In the aftermath, the old antagonism between the United States and its allies (sometimes referred to as the West), and the Soviet Union and its allies (sometimes referred to as the East, or Soviet bloc), ceased to be *the* defining facet of global affairs. Commentators such as Fukuyama (1992) declared that liberal democracy had triumphed over communism; many others agreed, implying that the West had won the Cold War. Immediately following World War II, a conservative British politician declared "we are all socialists now," with reference to the relatively widespread consensus in favour of a universal welfare state and an interventionist government. Some might have chosen to use a new expression for the 1990s, as social democratic governments in France, Canada, and other countries were seen by some to have lost touch with their ideological roots, and as globalization proponents eagerly sought opportunities to transform eastern European societies into capitalist enclaves. (So, too, have other marketplaces—in Asia, in Central and South America—become heightened targets for international capitalism.)

But what really defines the current era of globalization, perhaps more than the end of a previous era of East-West ideological antagonism, is the ascendancy of, first, international structures of finance, and second, the resulting ideological assumptions that make the current era possible.

To address the first point, the sheer volume of money trading hands has increased exponentially. The following figures mainly identify trends over the past 15 years, but some of these patterns began as early as the 1970s. Figure 5.1 conveys the increase in Canadian assets abroad, particularly since the late 1980s, while other evidence indicates increases in the volume of trading of international currencies during that period. Meanwhile, as Figure 5.2 demonstrates, the proportion of households using the Internet—unheard of in mass consumption prior to the 1990s—is now very significant, as is the considerable reduction in costs of long distance phone calls, and the increased use of faxes and other media to reduce global distances. Finally, foreign direct investment—the amount of money invested outside of an individual country—increased fivefold worldwide over the course of the 1980s. By the early 1990s, the world's 300 largest multinational corporations—the major players in foreign direct investment—mobilized over a quarter of the world's total capital (Marfleet, 1998, 15). We have entered an era of *turbo-cap-*

FIGURE 5.1   Canada in the Global Economy

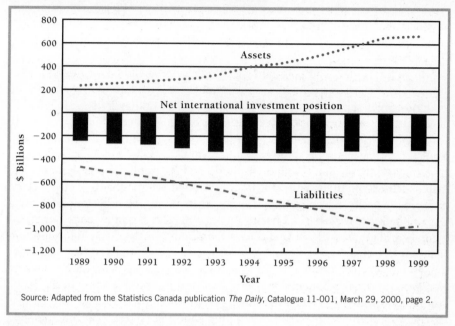

Source: Adapted from the Statistics Canada publication *The Daily*, Catalogue 11-001, March 29, 2000, page 2.

FIGURE 5.2   How Canadians Are Wired

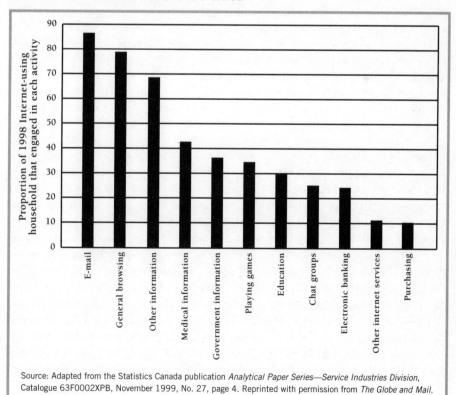

Source: Adapted from the Statistics Canada publication *Analytical Paper Series—Service Industries Division*, Catalogue 63F0002XPB, November 1999, No. 27, page 4. Reprinted with permission from *The Globe and Mail*.

italism, as one scholar describes it, where efficiency, insecurity, and uniformity prevail. Also prevalent—in a temporary way at least—is the generation of new wealth as older forms of practices, companies, and entire industries give way to the new (Luttwak, 1999). These forces create profound workplace changes, as discussed below.

To address the second point: the resulting changes in consciousness are nothing short of revolutionary. As one scholar points out, globalization "redefine[s] all the fundamental reference points of human society....And require[s] a modification of all existing paradigms" (Robinson, 1996 cited in Marfleet 1998, 2). Gone are the previous principles of a mixed economy, where governments of nation-states regulated capitalism. Indeed, most countervailing forces in a globalized world—governments, unions, public interest groups, and the public at large—are eluded. As journalist Richard Gwyn remarks, corporations' only remaining check is the marketplace itself. Nineteenth-century capitalism under the Industrial Revolution was unhindered by safety and health regulations, urban zoning codes, environmental regulations, and a strong trade union tradition, "and so could send ten-year-olds into coal mines." So, too, "transnational corporations" today "can make their products in a 'hands-off' plant in some underdeveloped country," where workplace and environmental standards may be profoundly lax (Gwyn, 1995, 98). Moreover, as Gwyn and others argue, the threat of transnational corporations moving production to plants in developing countries "tames governments, and workers of developed nation-states" such as Canada into reducing environmental, workplace, and social policy standards (Gwyn, 1995, 98). Recent interpretations of Chapter 11 of NAFTA have struck "down environmental and human-health protection measures" and have required "governments to pay out millions in compensation" (*Montreal Gazette*, April 28, 2001, B5). The very powers of the nation-state—the extent to which governments can exercise choices—have become highly contested. Canadian political economist Thomas Courchene argued, in his well-referenced 1994 report *Social Canada in the Millennium*, that we have two choices: either a radical but "made-in-Canada" social policy approach, or one that is devised with reference to international capital markets. Which will we choose?

Anarchist scholar Noam Chomsky has long criticized democracy in advanced industrial nations and the ability of corporate, political, and other leaders to divert attention away from true power within societal structures. As he wrote, "one fundamental goal of any well-crafted indoctrination program is to direct attention elsewhere, away from effective power, its roots, and the disguises it assumes" (1991, 303). On strictly ideological grounds, many advocates of globalization proffer its virtues: the promotion of new wealth and competition, and its implication that competition equates with human freedom. And yet all of these assumed virtues can be challenged. With governments, trade unions, and social policy legislation weakened by the forces of global capitalism, "corporations, above all transnational ones, [remain] free to reshape the world to suit their convenience" (Gwyn, 1995, 262). Unlike governments, corporations are not democratically answerable to a mass electorate, but accountable only to their shareholders, boards of directors, and to some extent the consumers who buy their products, as well as whatever forms of legislation remain to constrain them. The single operating principle of a corporation is accumulation. Stock market guru and multimillionaire George Soros sounded an important alarm in his 1997 article in *Atlantic Monthly* and 1998 follow-up book. "Market fundamentalism," he argues, "is a greater threat to an open society than any totalitarian ideology" (3). Like the communism of closed societies, Soros contends, the ardent belief that markets can solve all social, economic, and political questions has become hegemonic—all-powerful. The free flow of ideas, the bedrock of an open society, falls by the wayside.

Its proponents also construct globalization as unstoppable: beyond the control of any one person, government, or extra-governmental organization (Marfleet, 1998, 1). But, in 1997 and 1998, Maude Barlow and other Canadians demonstrated how effective the power of the people can be. Their e-mail and letter-writing campaigns, public forums, public debates, and articles in the media were important parts of an international effort that ultimately defeated the Multilateral Agreement on Investment (MAI). The MAI, a transnational document, would have given corporations even more latitude to pursue their interests in global expansion of markets and production with limited governmental constraints.

Social Welfare Retrenchment

A clear trend across Canada over the past decade has been the withdrawal of both federal and provincial governments from commitments to social welfare programs. This direction is expressed in political platforms and announcements of program cuts, along with public pronouncements that the welfare state has proven too expensive to the citizenry and is a cause of "dependency." Programs affecting even the most vulnerable populations are being cut, privatized, or redesigned to reduce usage and eligibility. Some familiar programs have been renamed to signify this shift. Unemployment Insurance, previously a hallmark of the social safety net, is now known as Employment Insurance. This new name, and indeed the entire program, is intended to emphasize the enhancement of employment opportunities, rather than the subsidization of unemployment. Stringent eligibility requirements have been introduced, and recent news reports show that successful claims are down dramatically, hitting women harder than men (*The Toronto Star*, March 3, 1999, A1).

No universal income support programs remain. The federal government, under the leadership of the Progressive Conservative Party, abolished the universal family allowance in 1993, introducing various targeted tax benefits to replace it. According to McGilly (1998), the last universal program, Quebec's Family Allowance, expired in 1997. Social Assistance programs have been renamed and restructured to focus on paid employment and to "target" those most in need. Health-care programs and services have suffered harsh cuts, and hospitals are being closed across the country. Although homelessness has become an increasingly visible problem in Canadian cities, the federal government has largely withdrawn from social housing commitments, notwithstanding the recent establishment of a ministerial portfolio to oversee homeless issues.

Various strategies are being used to justify this reduction in public resources for social welfare. One is the device of targeting resources to those presumed to be most in need, a strategy illustrated by the Canada Child Tax Benefit (CCTB). Through this policy, federal and provincial income security programs are integrated, creating a single benefit paid to all low-income families with dependent children. This program is the latest effort to replace universal family allowances with resources targeted to low-income families. It is promoted as a step toward alleviating poverty and equalizing benefits among low-income families (Battle and Mendelson, 1997). Rather than recognizing the needs of all low-income families, however, the plan focuses on benefits for the working poor as its first priority, leaving single mothers on assistance in essentially the same position of poverty they currently occupy.

As the Caledon Institute (1997) points out, this policy would effectively reorganize relations within the poorest class, creating a new gap in "fairness" favouring the working poor over those in receipt of assistance (Swift and Birmingham, 1999). Through the targeting strategy, the appearance of more efficient use of public funds is created, thus justifying the focus on a specific population as opposed to universal benefits. However, as Kitchen (1997) argues, the funds currently allocated to this program will not even begin to reduce poverty for the target group. For even a small reduction in poverty levels, billions more dollars would be required. While targeting may appear to represent a more efficient use of public resources, as well as a responsible way to reduce social spending, this strategy does not necessarily improve the lives or circumstances of the target group.

Another important approach designed to justify reduced public spending is an increased focus on job training and "social preparation" for employment, expressed in the idea of workfare. Workfare programs have taken on a wide variety of forms, but generally are characterized by requirements that employable recipients of Social Assistance either provide "approved" labour or participate in activities designed to increase their employment possibilities in return for benefits. Examples of participation requirements are job searches and active preparation for work, for instance in training and "upgrading" programs (Evans, et al., 1995). Penalties for failure to comply can include being cut off assistance or having benefits reduced. This scheme, which is being operated in some form in virtually all Canadian provinces at present (Evans, 1995), has deep roots in the tradition of the worthy and unworthy poor, and in the concept of less eligibility (Schragge, 1997).

Two recent books (Schragge, 1997; Evans et al., 1995) provide detailed descriptions of programs across the country. Researchers are critical of workfare programs in relation to their stated objectives. So far, workfare does not appear to improve employment prospects for most participants, reduce poverty, or remove the stigma of being on welfare.

Women are most affected by these programs. As in the case of the CCTB, it seems that workfare programs simply rearrange the order of lineup for income support (Schragge, 1997). Through workfare, Schragge argues, the unemployed remain tied to the labour market, are constantly compared to the employed, used as a threat against them, held in reserve for cheap labour, and "trained" and disciplined in relation to the labour market. Lightman (1997) concludes that workfare programs are part of a broader political strategy to dismantle government social programs, thereby reducing public responsibility for social services.

Changing Conceptions of Social Welfare in Relation to Citizenship and Social Inclusion

How are notions of social welfare changing in the face of the realities of globalizing economies and retrenching welfare states? Examination of this question involves exploration of the changing nature of citizenship.

Social Citizenship

Current trends in the field of economic and social welfare policy are seen by many to constitute an important change in the way social citizenship is perceived and experienced. The work of T. H. Marshall is widely acknowledged as the starting point for discussion of social citizenship. His 1949 essay, "Citizenship and Social Class," examines the meaning of citizenship, which he thought had developed in three stages. In the first stage, forged in the eighteenth century, civil rights were established, leading to property and legal rights, due process, etc. During the nineteenth century, the second stage, political rights emerged, involving the franchise and the right to hold office. In the twentieth century, social rights were extended, through which basic social and economic security was administered through the developing welfare state (Morrison, 1997). Many critiques of Marshall's work have been advanced over the past half-century, largely concerning the unevenness of access to the rights described for all but reasonably well-off white males. Nevertheless, the creation of the welfare state during the twentieth century has certainly involved the emergence of entitlements through social citizenship, although these entitlements were often more tenuous than is generally realized.

In Canada, the social rights of citizens have been protected to some extent through federal social programs. The Canada Assistance Plan (CAP), for instance, obligated provinces to provide for people in need, included prohibitions against workfare and discrimination, and required the development of appeals systems at the provincial level. When the Canada Health and Social Transfer (CHST) replaced CAP in 1996, the federal government ended its commitment to a social "floor," below which federal funding for provincially administered social programs would not be cut (Morrison, 1997). The repatriation of the Constitution and development of the 1982 Charter of Rights and Freedoms might seem to provide new protections, but in fact the Charter contains no explicit protections of social rights. Further, hopes for additional Charter protections via legal challenges now being mounted do not appear to hold much promise for protection of social rights. Some social advocates fear that a two-tiered system of citizenship is being advanced—one tier for those who depend on public resources and another (superior) system for those whose main relationships are with the marketplace.

Considerable concern about this shift in direction has been expressed. Pascal (1993) notes that the logical end point of such a shift is that even the most basic needs of able-bodied adults and their dependent children might eventually fail to constitute legitimate claims to entitlement. Schragge and Deniger (1997) conclude their discussion of workfare with a warning that these programs may herald an era of profound social change and inequality in which large sections of the population will be excluded from stable, meaningful, and reasonably paid employment, even as entitlements diminish. As Rioux (1997) suggests, the alternative is to insist on formulating and evaluating social programs in line not with efficiency principles or utilitarian criteria of "what works" but with principles of social justice—a "made-in-Canada" approach.

As noted earlier, a primary concern has been whether the national state itself, and therefore its ability to develop distinct social welfare policy, is under threat of demise. As trade zones and agreements proliferate and supersede national law and policy, we may well question to what extent national governments can control internal economic forces (Delaney, Brownlee and Selleck, 2001) and whether states can retain the capacity to provide basic welfare provisions for their citizens. Most social critics now recognize that powerful transnational corporate interests actually do not wish for the demise of the state, but rather for the reshaping of states to better support their profit-based interests. As Barlow (2001) argues, national governments still provide the security forces required to protect global economic interests. Lamarshe (1999) points out that the state is also needed to manage the problems of poverty, which intensify with globalization. This kind of state management, however, transforms the notion of "good governance" from ensuring equality, citizenship, rights, and benefits to the project of producing better consumers. The "citizen" in this scenario becomes less a rights-bearing individual and more a "functional citizen" whose goal is intended to be success in the new and changing global market.

Until recently, conversations about citizenship have assumed the existence of the welfare state, along with the justice system, as the grounds within which claims and entitlements were legitimized. Buzz Hargrove (1999), president of the Canadian Auto Workers, says the resources, stability, and power of the welfare state provided the conditions for unions to build strength and credibility during the mid-1900s. Bargaining gains and expansion of public services complemented and reinforced each other. The benefits of the "rights revolution" of the 1960s (Ignatieff, 2000) appeared to be thoroughly entrenched in the Canadian consciousness and embedded in social institutions.

Recent developments have brought this assumption into doubt. Of course, the September 11 attack on New York's World Trade Centre led directly to new federal legislation curtailing a variety of accepted civil and legal liberties in the name of security.

Well before that event, the reorganization and delegitimization of many traditional welfare state functions had produced analysis suggesting that citizenship rights, especially for the poor, were rapidly eroding (Little, 1999; Swift 2001). Marshall and many others believed that the welfare state laid the foundation for full social citizenship. Those who agree with this belief will decry the dismantling or diminution of welfare state structures. Others, however, argue that the welfare state, with its "false universalism" (Hansen, 1999), was never capable of developing either the conditions or the content of authentic citizenship because it does not recognize the unique differences among individuals. The claims of diverse groups for increased entitlements and recognition, discussed at more length in Chapter 6, reflect this problem. Further, social welfare does not encourage the associative ties implied by the idea of full citizenship. Social welfare serves, but it does not identify and it does not involve. It creates "clients," Hansen argues, not citizens.

In any case, recent examinations of welfare state activities point to a shift away from service to a function of assessing "risk" and mediating accountability for risk. Rose (1996) frames the goals of this new idea of the welfare state as those of calculating and managing risk for individuals deemed unable to exercise self-management. Certainly, widespread use of risk assessment tools has become standard practice in health, justice, and child welfare, to name a few domains of the welfare state. In this conception of welfare, even the service function, already in doubt as useful grounds for promoting citizenship, has diminished.

Recently, discussions of citizenship have been linked to the idea of "civil society" rather than to the welfare state. Various theorists conceptualize the idea of civil society differently. Marx, for instance, saw civil society as synonymous with bourgeois society (Hansen, 1999). Civil society in this view is the site of market transactions for personal, self-serving activity and therefore a space to be challenged and replaced. Hegel theorized civil society as a social space developed to address the tensions between individual autonomy and communal interests, a tension that Hansen suggests is reflected in the welfare state (1999). More frequently, contemporary activists equate civil society with "the third sector"—neither government nor market. Barlow (2001) specifically names "citizen's organizations" and research institutes as members of this third sector. Civitas, an organization concerned with civil society, explains this sector as one that emphasizes alternatives to government other than the commercial marketplace. Collectives, church and charitable organizations as well as informal supports and the family are included in Civitas' research agenda (**www.civitas.org.uk**). In this conceptualization, civil society involves the associational life of non-governmental organizations (NGOs).

This non-governmental, non-profit, associational sector, now commonly referred to as "civil society," is estimated to be the fastest growing sector of society, expanding at four times the rate of the economy, according to one political scientist (Barlow, 2001). This growth has no doubt been facilitated by the emergence of widespread Internet use, which has allowed activists and groups to make connections far beyond their own communities and countries. The Transparancy and Civil Society project, sponsored by the Carnegie Endowment for International Peace, points out that whereas these organizations in the past have been grounded either in particular countries or in international organizations, they now are very quickly transcending these boundaries to become coalitions of groups claiming the right to have input into wide-ranging decisions in both government and corporate arenas (**www.ceip.org/files/projects/tcs/tcs_home.ASP**). As this trend continues, both the nature of civil society and of citizenship are shifting, along with ideas about the nature and auspices of social welfare. Rebick (2000) describes in some detail the idea of "active citizenship," which entails the participation of individuals in more than voting rights, but also in political, social, economic, and cultural decision-making. Thus, while some social critics have been predicting the narrowing and even the demise of social citizenship, especially for vulnerable populations, others are now beginning to reconceptualize its possibilities with more breadth and depth. Reduced citizenship will surely mean a concomitantly reduced social welfare arena, and one much more likely to be shaped in support of economic interests. An expanded concept of citizenship, however, might result in forms of social welfare that are more responsive to diversity and social justice. In this potential scenario, the relationship of social welfare to civil society would have to be renegotiated to account for the needs of "active citizens."

Social Inclusion

In the last several decades, the issues of "belonging," implied in Hansen's critique of the welfare state, and of active citizen participation examined by Rebick, have become issues for Western nations with advanced welfare states, as various groups have identified themselves as "excluded" from society and its opportunities. Social exclusion and social inclusion have consequently become useful concepts in contemporary discussions of the meanings of citizenship.

The concept of social inclusion arises from discussions about its opposite: social exclusion. This term was first used in France in the 1970s to identify people unprotected by social insurance programs. Through the 1980s and '90s its usage expanded to include those left behind by the effects of globalizing economies. These discussions were generally undertaken with a goal of enhancing possibilities of social cohesion. In both Europe and North America, the notion of exclusion has begun to replace the discourse of poverty, because it captures not only the conditions of the poor but also the underlying social and economic processes leading to marginalization of many populations. In North America, the loss of social cohesion is also a concern (Jenson, 1998), as large segments of the population are penalized in the new economy.

As spelled out by Barata (2000), the advantages of moving toward the language of social exclusion and social inclusion over the old language of poverty lines, disadvantaged populations, and underclass, are several. The language of exclusion/inclusion 1) includes power relations in the analysis; 2) has the potential to incorporate many levels of experience, for instance health, quality of life, and rights; 3) involves "the social," implicating society in general as the focus of discussion rather than just "the poor;" and 4) stresses process over established outcomes, such as contentious "poverty lines."

Concerns and critiques of the language of exclusion include the obvious problem of deciding what it is that people are excluded from and what we are meant to be included within. If not used with care and precision, discussions of exclusion come to imply that the goal is conformity with the status quo, and a homogeneity of experience. In addition, critics warn that important analysis of poverty levels could be lost altogether in an imprecise discourse of exclusion.

Many theorists are working to sharpen and clarify meanings of exclusion, taking into account these critiques. Klasen (1998), for example, has identified four different sources of exclusion. One is economic exclusion, relating to the problems of unemployment and poverty captured in previous examinations of disadvantage. A second form of exclusion is social, based for instance on neighbourhood or family type. Exclusion by birth or background is another source, referring to such issues as disability. Finally, Klasen identifies sociopolitical exclusion, referring for instance to discrimination by race, culture, or gender.

The opposite of social exclusion is social inclusion, a term that is also coming into common usage in North American social policy discourse, and one that Freiler (2000) argues has the capacity to bridge social and economic policy. At least two Canadian policy research groups are currently focusing on social inclusion and its close cousin, social cohesion, as major discourses capable of challenging neoliberal policy directions and producing social welfare policy based on social justice goals. These are Laidlaw Foundation (**www.laidlawfdn.org**) and Canadian Policy Research Networks (**www.cprn.com**).

A major contributor to the international discussion of social inclusion is Amartya Sen (1992). Sen explores the notion of "capability enhancement" as a feature of inclusionary policies. In this case, capability means having access to resources necessary for the creation of a life one values. Sen identifies two levels of capability, basic and complex, each important in itself. Social welfare goals, now often framed in "risk" terminology, should, according to Sen, focus instead on enhancing basic capabilities such as food security and literacy, as well as complex capabilities such as civic participation. Capability may be enhanced by social, economic, cultural, and political structures. Analysis of social welfare and social policy then becomes an examination, not of risk and accountability, but of the way legislation and policy enhance or inhibit capacity building for individuals and identity groups.

Critics of the widespread use of social inclusion point out that this terminology can be used to support any political position. Silver (1994) has investigated this issue, identifying three ideological uses of this discourse: neo-liberal, social democratic, and social change. Her analysis shows that both British and North American usages of these terms are primarily neo-liberal. In Canada, *The Senate Report on Social Cohesion* (1999), for instance, developed strategies for inclusion that relied on neo-liberal terminology such as "investing in human capital" and "removing barriers to social and economic participation." These objectives signal workfare and other programs designed to enforce participation in a labour force that is increasingly insecure.

Used with specificity and caution, however, the ideas of social exclusion and social inclusion have produced useful tools for reconceptualizing social citizenship, and they are also helpful in considering how social welfare might be redesigned. Jenson's (1998) conceptual framework identifying dimensions of social cohesion provides an example. She shows five continua useful for analyzing inclusion:

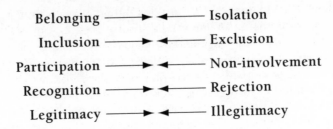

This framework identifies life possibilities and capabilities that allow individuals to become fully participating members of the society. The welfare state, as Hansen has pointed out, falls short on some of these dimensions; for instance in its capacity to legitimize its users and to involve its "clients" as active participants. The notion of inclusion may help to provide new language and analytical tools that enhance the possibility for recognizing what is needed for authentic citizenship for a diverse population.

Social Movements

In Chapter 4, current ideologies and their expression through political parties were outlined. At the present time, however, shifts in ideological stances and political party allegiances are taking place. These changes are to some extent effects of the accumulation of global capital as previously described. In 1993, the federal Progressive Conservative Party, in power for eight years, was decimated at the polls, retaining only two elected seats. In the same election, in which the Liberal Party regained power, the New Democratic Party (NDP) declined in the number of seats, the new Reform Party won almost enough seats to form the official opposition, and the Quebec-based separatist party Bloc Québécois won enough seats to become the official opposition. In two subsequent federal elections the ruling Liberal Party retained its majority. At present, with the Canadian Alliance (formerly Reform) in disarray over leadership and unable to "unite the right" by joining with the Progressive Conservative Party, there is no apparent electoral threat to the continued federal rule of the Liberals.

It is clear that neo-conservative ideology is the dominant political force of this and other Western nations. Even those parties not elected on neo-conservative platforms are developing policies not dissimilar to those of avowedly neo-conservative parties. Since the Liberals have been in power federally, policy directions developed by the previous Conservative government have continued in similar directions. Armitage (1996) notes that even the NDP is unwilling to increase social spending when in power provincially, and in fact social democratic parties around the Western world have for some time found themselves unable to promote their agenda effectively (Esping-Anderson, 1990).

At the left end of the spectrum, world events, including the breakup of the Soviet Union in the 1990s followed by revelations of extreme social dislocations in Eastern bloc countries, have dimmed enthusiasm for the Marxist/socialist vision.

Adherents of leftist ideas are also in a state of some disillusion and difficulty in the face of global market forces, which the public has been encouraged to think of as overwhelming and unstoppable (McQuaig, 1998).

At the same time, traditional "spaces" for public interchange and participation have diminished. Canadians are being coached to accept the neo-conservative beliefs that our social values and attachment to the social safety net need to be filtered through the realities of globalization and fiscal restraint (Armitage, 1996). Low voter turnout and the "withering" of public life, a trend elaborated in Chapter 1 (Aronowitz, 1992), illustrate withdrawal from civil participation of many people in Western democracies. McQuaig (1998) suggests that many people have become immobilized by a sense of impotence, believing that we must simply accept the changes that globalization brings.

The former strength of unions in challenging employers has been eroded over the past decade. With fewer benefits as the result of "flexible" jobs and fewer unions with less strength, members once again become more dependent on employers for personal income, security and benefits—a buyer's market (Hargrove, 1999). In this scenario, unions are faced with tough choices: to fight hard, using strike tactics, to retain what they have gained over decades of struggle, or to compromise in hopes of retaining some benefits and their union status. In a global market, transnational companies can move jobs to more profitable locations, so strikes may prove to be counterproductive. In its new partnership with business, the state is more likely to pass laws, as Ontario has recently done, that make union organizing much more difficult and union decertification much easier. The NDP is the traditional political partner of unions, although some of the large Canadian unions have been critical of the direction and leadership of the party for some time. At its most recent federal convention, the NDP struggled successfully to retain block voting rights for unions in its internal procedures, at the risk of alienating young, unaffiliated activists, many of whom see unions as themselves too rigidly bureaucratic to challenge the effects of globalization.

According to Armitage (1996), the values of fairness and security expressed in liberal ideology continue to represent the sentiments of most Canadians. In question, however, is how these values will be politically supported in the current neo-conservative climate. Some analysts suggest that our political future will become more polarized. In this projected scenario, traditional ideological subtleties and differences will dissolve into two loose coalitions: those defending the accumulation of capital and those opposing that direction. The emerging picture may mean that traditional elements of the right will form alliances to strengthen their political and economic control, and that they will be opposed by a coalition of various political parties and grassroots groups brought together by a common interest in social justice and a willingness to challenge the idea that there is any genuine benefit in developing a single capital pool (Laxer, 1995). Saul (1995) calls this the politics of "disinterest"—that is, political activity based not on personal gain but on a willingness to struggle for the common good.

What will this "social justice" coalition look like? Esping-Anderson (1990) speaks of a "red-green" alliance, involving traditional leftists and environmentalists and including rural elements along with urban dwellers. Aronowitz (1995) poses a coalition of new social movements concerned with ecology, feminism, racial freedom, and gay and lesbian freedom as a potentially "valid effort" to combat aspects of capitalist rule. Similarly, Laxer (1997) cites groups and organizations such as trade unions, feminists, child-care advocates, environmentalists, and antipoverty organizations as having the potential to oppose right-wing policies if they are willing to act in concert.

Esping-Anderson's vision involves politics outside Parliament, for he and others (Teeple, 1995) believe that the political parties of the past have either joined in advancing right-wing politics or have lost the ability within formal government structures to oppose the neo-conservative direction effectively. He concurs that it is virtually impossible for the left to form a government, since the working class does not constitute a majority (1995). In effect, the rise of the middle class has diluted socialist possibilities. However, a middle class hit with high unemployment and taxes coupled with a reduction in benefits from the welfare state such as health care and pensions, may itself now be shrinking and becoming more cynical about its future prospects, a development that could help to inspire new coalitions of interests. It is possible that the future will see some elements of the middle class in alliance with various marginalized groups against a small but wealthy and powerful ruling elite.

These observations about the shape and form of new alliances are largely based on familiar groups and movements using mostly traditional strategies to challenge the status quo. Participants and leaders are likely to be people with long service and ties to political parties, unions, and existing social movements such as feminism and the established environmental advocates. The collapse of communism in the early 1990s has to some extent shifted the political terrain of these movements, however, as popular opinion has reflected a belief that capitalism has "won" and class analysis therefore no longer has much relevance. Barker (1999) disagrees, suggesting instead that class analysis has become more complicated as a result of "cross-class influences" such as culture, religion, and organizational affiliations. The high end of the class structure has become more unified by the reward system of the new capitalism, Barker contends, while the lower end of the hierarchy has become divided and fragmented by competing loyalties such as culture, gender, and religion.

Tilly (1999) examines the new work of social movement organizers who must address competing loyalties and fragmented organizations. Tilly conceptualizes two major identity formations. One formation is "embedded identities," especially those based on culture and religion, that operate in and shape everyday life to a significant extent. The other is "detached identities," involving organizational affiliations not activated in everyday life but rather invoked selectively for particular reasons. The work of social movements often involves two processes in relation to the identities of participants: embedding detached identities into everyday life in order to increase loyalties of activists; and also working the other way, to generalize and detach embedded identities in order to blur divisions among participants and facilitate the development of alliances. The actual work of organizers, Tilly notes, involves "patching together provisional coalitions, suppressing risky tactics, negotiating…multiple agendas…and, above all, hiding backstage struggle from public view."

In executing these tasks, new groups of young social activists appear to have been exceptionally successful in the past few years. The new "youth" movements, so visible in Seattle and more recently in Quebec City, have their roots in at least two decades of changes in the way social movements operate, according to Barlow and Clarke (2001). First, the established social movements have been creating bonds across national borders, aided, of course, by rapidly spreading use of the Worldwide Web.

Second, the new coalitions have built on two decades of development of strategies, issues, and coalition-building by groups around the world focused on the effects of corporate globalization. Loss of farm land and food-production processes, free trade agreements, relaxed labour laws, poverty exacerbated by World Bank policies in developing countries, diminishing access to education, and corporate hegemony are some of the sources of discontent and organizing issues named by Barlow and Clarke.

In the past few years, these new social movements have experienced some spectacular successes. Widely covered public demonstrations at meetings of global corporate and national leaders have occurred, the most famous being the "Battle of Seattle," in November, 1999, where demonstrations embarrassed the host country and its President and caused the high-level meeting of the World Trade Organization to end in "failure." In 1998, massive public protests prevented a new world trade agreement, the Multilateral Agreement on Investment (MAI), from taking effect. This effort was conducted largely through the Internet, demonstrating to activists the value of this tool for creating "globalization from below" (Barlow and Clarke, 2001).

Tactics of these new social movements, like their membership, are fresh, fluid, and creative. Internet campaigns, street theatre, "flying groups" moving strategically to halt or disrupt formal meetings, widely distributed slogans, and conspicuous costumes have all been used at various times. Coalitions are loose, inclusive, and non-hierarchical, and energy appears high. While the new movement is characterized by agreement on the damage that unrestrained global trade will produce around the world, goals and long-term strategies for change among activist groups differ. Whether to work in any way with governments, corporate interests, and established non-governmental organizations or to remain independent as a means of avoiding "co-optation" is an important debate.

Naomi Klein begins her book, *No Logo*, with a quote that captures the hopes of the new social movement advocates: "You might not see things yet on the surface, but underground, it's already on fire." (Y. B. Manganwijaya, 1998). Since 1998, of course, some of this "fire" has risen to the surface in the form of massive demonstrations and protests against proponents of global capital around the world. Klein predicts the next major social movements will be in strong opposition to transnational corporations, especially those identified as "name brands."

Part of this growing resistance to current economic forces and trends relates to what Klein calls the "colonization of public space." Even mainstream media now report that certain spaces, such as classrooms, highways, washrooms, and taxis, might be characterized as "civic" spaces (*The Toronto Star*, January 7, 2002, B2). This issue relates to the discussion of "civil society." The site of the struggle is this political and social space. As corporations ensure their presence in civic spaces, the possibility of creating a "third sector force" in social and political life seems to diminish. One battleground involves young people, who are encouraged to "brand" themselves with logos and ads on the clothes they wear, the food they eat, and the events they attend.

Gramsci's notion of hegemony helps to explain the concern of social activists. Gramsci theorized that power by ruling elites is secured through two routes: overt force and ideology. By ideology he means not a body of thought as discussed in Chapter 4, but mechanisms and ways of thinking that influence people to conform to the status quo, even when it operates against their own interests. Ideology in this sense involves mass acceptance and internalization of the values of ruling classes, and regularly acting on those values. It is this process of accepting the necessity of buying the products advertised by large corporations that concern many of today's social advocates. As social space becomes invaded by advertising and the presence of products for sale, will the "third sector" remain politically viable? Will citizens of comfortable Western nations lose sight of the costs to inhabitants of developing countries of producing and selling these products? The protests of a significant number of young activists in the West are bringing to public attention the costs of this economic direction, both for developing countries and for ourselves. They are challenging corporate interests in an unexpected way. They are, as *Globe and Mail* columnist Michael Edwards says, "the mouse that roared" (January 3, 2002: A17).

How are the successes and failures of these social movements to be studied and judged? Giugni (1999) proposes examining both the "durability and direction" of change, focusing on policy shifts and short-term effects on the one hand, and institutional outcomes and longer-term effects on the other. Social movements, always aiming to change the status quo, face a contradiction. The possibility of success is greater if the goal is short-term policy change rather than durable, long-term structural change.

The findings of recent studies on social movement organizing (Barker, 1999) suggest that local politics and action or "street-level" democracy, by itself, is no match for the power of global forces. Such action must be connected to wider networks of information and to more broadly based organizations, as well as centres of power in government and elsewhere that have impacts on the local arena.

Conclusion

Historically, social policies have, to some extent, reflected the national will. Yet as this chapter infers, globalization influences the range of choices exercised by governments. As companies compete in an increasingly international marketplace, the demands upon governments to restrict the welfare state may grow. Some corporate leaders, for example, seek minimalist tax structures and minimal corporate contributions to income security, health insurance, and other forms of publicly administered programs. We in Canada are also subject to American political, cultural, and economic values (Grant, 1965, 1969). Given its growing presence, in part reinforced by the North America Free Trade Agreement, Canadian politicians, particularly those on the right, have looked to the United States for political precedents. Many policy analysts, in fact, are struck by the strongly American influences in contemporary Canadian social welfare retrenchment and workfare (Torjman, 1997, 1998b).

The influence of social movements, citizenship, and social inclusion, likewise, will have a strong bearing on future social welfare development. But, given the growing forces of globalization and North American political and economic integration, will the social policy choices Canadians make reflect what we agree as a society *should* be our destiny?

Chapter 6

Diversity and Social Policy

This chapter considers three questions. First, what is meant by "diversity"? Second, what are the relationships between diversity and social policy? And third, what is the "right" balance between recognition of the interests of specific groups and the needs of Canada's population as a whole? Three premises, in turn, guide the chapter.

One premise is that social workers need to avoid thinking too universally about social policy. "Minority" groups have often been treated differently in social policy terms. Different groups of people, for instance, received the franchise at different times, some very recently. In the early part of the twentieth century, women were not recognized as "persons," and lesbians and gay men are only now beginning to achieve access to benefits long since accorded other Canadians and permanent residents.

A second basic premise is that a major goal of Canadian social policy has always been the goal of equity. However, social policy that purports to be equitable and potentially universal is being challenged as too crude when universally applied, and as not reflecting the particularities of human experience. This is not a challenge to the idea of equality, but a recognition that the provision of the same services for all is not always appropriate or desired.

The third premise is that Canadian social policy has been built on principles drawn from European and especially British traditions. A focus on paid "work," and a concomitant notion of the "dependence" of those who are not breadwinners, are basic to our social policy framework. Basic principles also include the somewhat contradictory traditions of individual initiative and "the family" as the building blocks of society. The groups discussed in this chapter have in various ways challenged the relevance of these principles in contemporary times. The goals of these populations often do not fit well with tradition, and challenges to traditions, policies, and practices are the result.

What Is Meant by *Diversity*?

In everyday usage, *diversity* refers to characteristics of individuals such as race, culture, gender, and sexual orientation. These characteristics are those that especially affect access to opportunity and resources. Consequently, the term "minority group" has arisen, a term that does not necessarily reflect the size of the membership but the relative social and economic power of the group. In relation to social policy, the term *diversity* reflects the reality that different people in Canada occupy a different status and social location in relation to the state and its policies.

Previous chapters have discussed basic provisions of Canadian social policy. However, people's different physical, mental, emotional, and experiential attributes mean they have different needs and variable access to these general social provisions. Further, the recognition of diverse needs among the Canadian population has produced social policies specific to the issues of different groups. Social workers need to be aware not only of basic policy and welfare provisions but also of the related policies that reflect needs not addressed by these policies and/or that affect access to basic social provisions by specific groups.

Christensen (1995, 184) cites two British traditions that have influenced Canadian social policy. One is the tradition of the British Poor Laws, which continue to inform social welfare policy. The Poor Laws, as noted in Chapter 2, established the concepts of deserving and undeserving poor, concepts that apportion blame to individuals for their own problems. Poor Laws also implied differing gender expectations from the outset. A second tradition infused into social policy is the racist ideology of the nineteenth century, based on Social Darwinism (Christensen, 1985). This idea fostered belief in racial hierarchies that justified suppression and resource extraction from non-white populations. This ideology has shaped both immigration policy and majority-minority relations, and in turn has brought the need for anti-discriminatory policies and protections. Along the way, built into social policy of almost every kind has been "familism" (Williams, 1989), a concept implying that strong families will ensure a stable society. The traditional image, which still infuses our thought and policy, is that of the heterosexual nuclear family, with a male breadwinner, a female engaged in reproductive work, and children who are "in training" to become productive and reproductive members of society.

As Baker (1995) notes, Canada does not really have a set of coherent family policies. Rather, implicit assumptions and understandings about "the family" are infused into our laws and policies. Because there is no coherent family policy, there are some contradictions among policies and levels of government. Many policies have sought to define the family for purposes of benefit eligibility. Such definitions are currently subject to challenges from different quarters. Immigration policy, for instance, attempted in the early 1990s to enforce a very narrow definition of the family for purposes of sponsorship. This nuclear family model continues to be criticized by many cultural communities for whom the family is an extended kinship network, and the policy was eventually softened (but not rescinded). Some lesbian women and gay men are currently challenging the definition of family as exclusively heterosexual, a definition that has direct implications for workplace benefits. Older women are concerned about proposed new pension rules that might disallow some of their benefits by defining them not as individuals but as part of a traditional married pair. Single mothers have challenged the idea that having a "man in the house" constitutes a traditional family, which would deny them recognition of family status for eligibility purposes.

During the 1980s, various groups began to criticize the welfare state and its policies. "Interest groups," formed around cultural, racial, gender, and other "identities," have brought new demands and pressures for change and different directions in policy. In addition, the awareness of identity has brought challenges to policies previously assumed equitable and accessible to everyone. Changes in the constitutional structure of Canada in the early 1980s also had an impact on the way we think about social policy. Various controversies surrounding the Charter of Rights and Freedoms have brought new attention to the issue of rights. In turn, new rights have influenced policies and the way they are implemented (Canadian Council on Social Development, 1991), bringing attention to the identification and enforcement of anti-discriminatory policies.

Despite these advances, Lessard (1997) and Kallen (1995) argue, entrenchment of rights may also have the effect of entrenching existing relations of subordination. Kallen has shown that the Charter entrenches the rights of three different specific populations in the Constitution, and that different and hierarchical sets of rights have been developed to protect these groups. The group with the most rights protection is termed the "founding peoples," who are mainly of French and British extraction. Founding peoples are guaranteed positive rights that obligate the state in specified ways. Their rights are spelled out in some detail, involving, as an example, protection of Protestant and Catholic denominational educational rights. The second group is Aboriginal peoples, who are guaranteed collective rights under the Charter, but the rights guaranteed are "negative" ones, often involving non-interference rather than specific obligations of the state. The third group comprises other ethnic minorities, who are not specifically named, or *enumerated*, and who are protected only by negative, unspecified, and undefined rights. Furthermore, because certain minorities are enumerated in the Charter, and others are not, a hierarchy of rights has been established between these two groups.

History and Social Context of Diverse Populations in Canada

Canada's social policy was developed to redress specific inequalities, mainly those of class, income level and source, age, and family type. In general, state interventions were designed to mitigate poverty arising from problems with the market economy system (Williams, 1989). These policies generally related to the ability of an individual or family to access income and resources and were based on two principles: 1) ensuring that vulnerable populations did not fall below an established quality of life level, and 2) acting to effect some redistribution of wealth from those with sufficient resources to those in need. For several decades, the building blocks of social policy addressing these issues were considered sufficient and at times path-breaking. The health care system is an example.

In reality, social policy has never been "the same for all" in this country. Different social policies and limitations to access to resources have always existed for specific populations. In this section, several specific groups and policies that affect them are described. These are certainly not the only populations representing the diversity of Canadians but they do represent major groups around which social policy has been developed. It is important to keep in mind that these groups are not mutually exclusive. An individual may belong to one or more of these groups, and identify with other diversities as well. Nor are these groups homogeneous; many within-group differences and disagreements are apparent. This reality, not always overtly acknowledged in policy discussions, is one of the significant features of contemporary social policy development. Many social policy texts and discussions have assumed a universal "Canadian" who could access programs given certain eligibility requirements. In the postmodern era, however, this assumption is continually challenged. This chapter describes historical differences of various populations with a view to making visible their particular relationships to and claims upon the state. The discussion is intended to elaborate information presented in previous chapters, as well as to examine some challenges to the traditional foundations of Canadian social policy.

Ethnoracial Minorities

Often, when references to diversity are made, the focus is on racial and cultural groups. This may be because Canada's cultural and racial groups have been changing rapidly over the past several decades. It may also be because explicit social policies designed to address these shifts have been made. Certainly, Canada's population is changing. Early in the twentieth century, the majority of the Canadian population was white and of European descent. At present, no single ethnic group accounts for a majority of the Canadian population (McGilly, 1998, 5). Changes in immigration policy account for this shift. Until 1967, immigration to Canada was restricted to "preferred nations." The particular immigrants seeking and allowed entry varied somewhat, depending on world events and the needs of the country. However, they were overwhelmingly white Europeans, since Europe, and especially northern and western Europe, comprised the most preferred countries. British immigrants remained the largest single cultural group until World War II. Until this period, immigrants were differentiated largely by language, and regional concentrations of ethnocultural groups were prevalent (Christensen, 1995). In 1967, a new liberalized immigration policy came into force, one that focused not on source country—by then considered discriminatory—but on the characteristics of individual immigrants. During the 1970s and '80s, source countries of immigrants to Canada changed dramatically from European to Asian, African, South American, and Caribbean. The result has been a change in Canadian demographics, one of considerable interest to social workers. New arrivals now come from several dozen different source countries. Although difficult to determine from census data, it is estimated from 1996 census data that at least 11.2 percent of the Canadian population is non-white (Department of Canadian Heritage, 2000). The great majority of this population, 87 percent, have settled in Ontario, Quebec, and British Columbia (Department of Canadian Heritage, 2000). Especially in the major urban reception centres—Toronto, Montreal, and Vancouver—many different languages are spoken and a broad spectrum of cultural groups require services previously offered only in English and/or French.

As noted in Chapter 2, major policy responses to these population changes were announced in 1971, and again in 1988 legislation (An Act for the Preservation and Enhancement of Multiculturalism in Canada). The 1988 Act recognizes diversity as a basic characteristic of Canada and promotes participation of people of all origins in Canadian society. In spite of these apparently worthwhile goals, the policy has been under attack in recent years. People question whether the policy will result in a hierarchy of ethnic groups, isolation of communities of immigrants, and perhaps even intergroup dissension (Bissoondath, 1994). In any case, the legislation and policy provide an ideal espoused by many majority and minority Canadians rather than guarantees of equality. Legal protection of rights, however, was established in the Charter of Rights and Freedoms (1982), which is intended to guarantee cultural and racial pluralism and provide anti-discrimination mandates for social welfare law, policies, programs, and practices (Herberg and Herberg, 1995). The forerunners of this policy were laws following World War II mandating "fair" access to housing, education, and employment for minorities. In the 1960s, these laws evolved into more comprehensive federal and provincial human rights codes. Kallen's (1995) argument suggesting that even these guaranteed rights are stratified for various groups of Canadian citizens and residents, with immigrants near the bottom, serves as a reminder that equality under the law remains elusive.

Information from Statistics Canada shows that the number of people immigrating to Canada have varied over the second half of the twentieth century (see Figure 6.1).

The Statistics Canada definition of an immigrant is anyone who has ever immigrated into the country. By this broad definition, the percentage of immigrants to the Canadian-born population is not particularly high. Figure 6.2 shows this proportion remained stable at about 16 percent from the 1950s to the early 1990s, and

FIGURE 6.1 Annual Number of Immigrants Arriving in Canada, 1860–2000

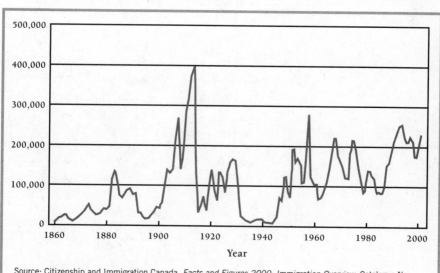

Source: Citizenship and Immigration Canada. *Facts and Figures 2000: Immigration Overview.* Catalogue No. MP43-333/2001E, August 2001. Reproduced with the permission of the Minister of Public Works and Government Services Canada, 2002.

**FIGURE 6.2   Number of Immigrants as a Percentage of the Population
of Canada, 1901–1991**

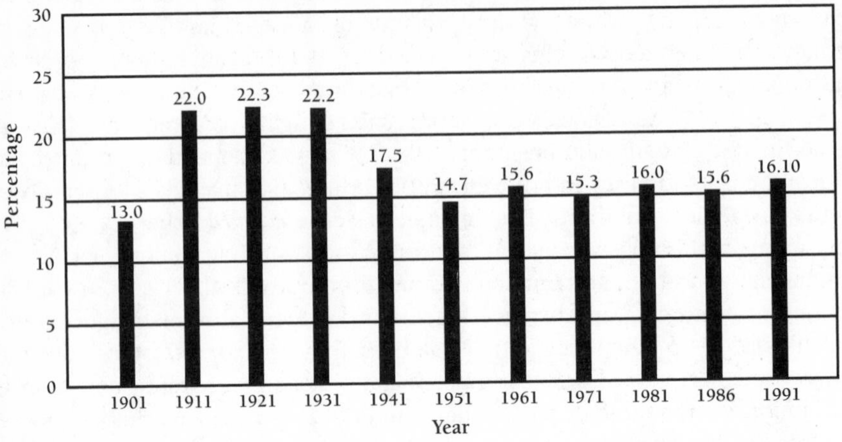

Source: Citizenship and Immigration Canada. Immigration Research Series—*Profiles:* "Total Immigration
Population." Reproduced with the permission of the Minister of Public Works and Government Services
Canada, 2002.

more recent data confirm the proportion remains about the same at 17 percent
(Department of Canadian Heritage, 2000).

The major recent immigration change is in source countries. In the 1950s more
than 80 percent of all immigrants arriving in Canada were from Europe, many from
Great Britain. In 1994 only 17 percent were European, while 64 percent of all arriving immigrants were from various Asian countries. In that year, 6 percent were
from Africa, and 4 percent each were from South America and the Caribbean. In
2000, only 2 percent of immigrants to Canada arrived from Great Britain. Asian
countries remained the greatest source of immigration, with the largest number,
36 664, arriving from China (Citizenship and Immigration Canada, 2001).

Another important change in immigration patterns is in the classes of immigrants now arriving. In the 1950s and '60s, the majority of arrivals were "family-
class" immigrants sponsored by relatives already established in the country. In
1994, 49 percent of new arrivals were "independent-class" immigrants. By 2000,
independent immigrants were 67 percent of the total 197 129 immigrants arriving
in Canada. These are the applicants demonstrating the requisite skills, education,
work history, or money to enable entry into the country. That same year only
about 31 percent of immigrants entered the country as family-class immigrants
sponsored by relatives, while about 2 percent arrived in a catch-all "other" category
that includes live-in caregivers, retirees, and several other small groups admitted
on "humanitarian grounds." In addition, 30 030 people arrived as refugees, some
sponsored by government, some privately, with 40 percent claiming refugee status
on arrival (Citizenship and Immigration Canada, 2001).

Currently, the majority of immigrants to Canada live in Ontario (55 percent) followed by 17 percent in British Columbia, 14 percent in Quebec, and 9 percent in Alberta (Statistics Canada, **cicnet.ci.gc.ca/english/pub/anrep99e.html# legislative**). Historically and at present, immigrant settlement is an urban phenomenon, with Toronto and Vancouver receiving the largest numbers of immigrants.

Anderson and Marr (1987) acknowledge the importance of the new wave of immigrants as the "third force" in Canadian politics not only because of their numbers but because many recent immigrants come from different cultural backgrounds and languages than either of the two "founding groups" and therefore bring different social policy issues to the fore. Also, many new immigrants and refugees over the past three decades are people of colour. While immigrants do not constitute a large percentage of the total Canadian population, many settle in urban areas and are substantially changing the racial composition of cities. It is estimated, for example, that within the first few years of the new millennium, people of colour will make up the majority of Toronto's population. These demographic changes not only put pressure on service organizations to adapt to different kinds of needs, but also call into question the policy frameworks that have traditionally guided service development and delivery. In past decades, social workers often worked as though cultural differences were a small side issue. That is, approaches to professional social work could be considered generalizable to all populations. This belief was given credibility by the fact that the clients they faced were often born in Canada, or were of European descent. Today's diversity of source countries providing immigrants to Canada makes this approach much more difficult to justify. In reality, of course, there have always been diversities that social workers might have noticed.

Because of the division of responsibilities between the federal and provincial governments in Canada, social welfare for newly arrived immigrants often falls between the cracks. The federal government sets policy that allows for classes and levels of immigration, and provides several settlement and adjustment programs from federal sources. The Adjustment Assistance Program, for instance, provides financial assistance for basic needs of poor immigrants on arrival. The Immigrant Settlement and Adaptation Program allows the federal government to contract services through voluntary agencies for basic settlement services such as translation and counselling. Changes in immigration policy have included specification of access to services.

There are currently three basic groups permitted entry into Canada: independent immigrants, family-class immigrants, and refugees. Each of these groups is positioned differently in relation to the state and its resources. Independent immigrants, sometimes called economic immigrants, are allowed into the country on the basis of financial assets and/or skills considered important to the country. The most recent changes in immigration qualifications for skilled workers place more emphasis on employment "flexibility" based on education and language skills than on specific occupations. These immigrants receive "permanent resident" status and have access to social programs along with Canadian citizens. Family-class immigrants, on the other hand, are permitted entry into the country on the basis of their relationship to a citizen or permanent resident already in the country. Entry of family members is contingent on a promise that the sponsoring relative will provide for the arriving family member(s) for 10 years following arrival. Arriving family members are therefore not eligible for programs and resources available to other residents. They cannot claim Canada pensions, for instance, and in many provinces they are not eligible for welfare, even if the sponsoring relative abdicates responsibility for them. These immigrants can, however, access health care through provincial auspices. These restrictions present some difficult problems for social workers, who may be attempting to assist people ineligible for services available to others.

Refugees present yet another situation. Members of this group enter the country through three different routes. A small number of refugees selected abroad enter the country with full participation rights. A range of basic programs, including housing and financial assistance, are available to government-sponsored refugees in their first year in Canada. Other refugees are sponsored from abroad by a group located in Canada that takes responsibility for supporting the individual for a set period of time. Groups must be prepared to supply basic needs such as housing and food, and agree to assist individual refugees to find employment and become self-sufficient. The third, and largest, group enters Canada without documentation with the hope of establishing a "credible claim" to stay in the country. Those who pass successfully through an initial screening become eligible for work permits and some provincial and municipal services, including health care.

Aboriginal Peoples

Aboriginal peoples, including those of mixed origin, generally constitute less than 4 percent of the country's population (McGilly, 1998, 7). However, they are often over-represented as clients in the service sector. Of relevance to social work and social policy is the fact that many different First Nations groups exist; for instance, there are 10 major cultural and linguistic groups speaking 58 dialects (Shewell and Spagnut, 1995). Also, different Aboriginal peoples stand in different relationships to the Canadian state. The term *Indian* can refer both to status Indians, who are registered by the federal government, and to non-status Indians, who are not registered. Inuit are Aboriginal people who are culturally and legally distinct from Indian peoples and who are not considered to be registered Indians. Métis people are those whose heritage is mixed Aboriginal and non-Aboriginal. Métis do not have rights under the Indian Act. It is generally acknowledged that most of Canada's Aboriginal peoples live in difficult and often impoverished conditions and that they have for many decades experienced severe structural inequities. This reality is the result of events of the past as well as continued relations between First Nations and the Canadian state. Before contact with Europeans, Aboriginal peoples generally lived in small communities, and although there are significant variations among groups, many operated on principles that all members of the community would share resources and have a valued role in the group (Mawhiney, 1995). Contact with Europeans, determined to dominate both Aboriginal peoples and their land, resulted in severe damage to and reorganization of Aboriginal cultural forms (Bourgeault, 1988).

The Indian Act of 1876, passed shortly after the British North America Act (1867), now known as the Constitution Act, 1982, marked the end of Indian self-government, which was replaced by federal control over the cultural, social, economic, and political activities of those defined in the Act as registered Indians. This definition was limited; those who fell outside this category became ineligible for the benefits of health, education, and social services provided in the Indian Act. The definition of status was, until recently, patrilineal; Indian women who married non-registered men lost their status. In February of 1985, legislation was brought to Parliament to establish more equality in the Act. The changes allowed bands in Canada to determine their own eligibility criteria for band membership, and assured the protection of rights for those who are band members. The regaining of Aboriginal status will provide women who have married non-registered men access to federal programs as well as services off the reserves (Minor, 1995).

To the present time, Aboriginal peoples who come under the Indian Act access many programs and funding sources differently than other Canadians do. The Indian Act of 1876 in fact gave jurisdiction for Indians and their land to the federal government (Patterson, 1987), and both benefits and sanctions were administered by agents employed by Indian Affairs. Also regulated by the Indian Act were legal rights, inheritance, taxation, wills, and many other matters. Until 1960, the penalty for registered Indians who exercised their Canadian franchise was the loss of their status and rights under this Act. Unlike other citizens and residents of Canada, the health and welfare services received by registered Indians flow through the federal rather than through provincial governments, which otherwise claim these areas as their jurisdiction. Over time, exceptions to this rule have been worked out by intergovernmental arrangements (McGilly, 1998, 7).

These measures have had profound effects on Aboriginal peoples in Canada. Education, for example, which is provided provincially to others in Canada, was administered for registered Indians by the federal government. Residential schools were the required form of education for Aboriginal children between the late nineteenth and mid-twentieth centuries, with the result that many Aboriginal children were removed from their families at an early age and sent to boarding schools outside their own communities. Similarly, child welfare, a provincially administered service for others, was supposed to be delivered by the federal government to registered Indians. Since many children attended residential schools a large part of the year, little service was therefore provided (Johnston, 1983). In 1951, the Indian Act was revised to recognize provincial law as applying to First Nations (Mawhiney, 1995). Aboriginal children were increasingly encouraged to attend provincial schools and access provincial services. After 1951, child welfare services were increasingly extended to reserves, with the result that many children over the next several decades came into the care of child protection authorities (Johnston, 1983). Many of these children were adopted by families outside the province or even the country, and records of the whereabouts of many of these children disappeared. Others were raised in non-Indian care and became alienated from their own parents and communities. Today, most child welfare services on reserve are administered by Bands. In 1997–8, 79 First Nations Child and Family Service agencies were delivering services to 70 percent of on-reserve children. In 2002, it is expected that 91 percent of on-reserve populations will be receiving services from First Nations agencies (Indian and Northern Affairs, 2000).

Other services to Aboriginal peoples came primarily from the federal government after 1951; however, these services existed at a very low level, as revealed by the 1966 Hawthorn Report on the issue (Mawhiney, 1995). It was clear that the ideal of equality among different groups of people in Canada was not met in the case of Aboriginal peoples. In a 1969 White Paper, recommendations were made that Indian people receive services through the same channels and government agencies as other Canadians, but this proposal was rejected by Indian leaders and organizations because it seemed to imply the phasing out of rights guaranteed by the Indian Act. Currently, with the exception of child welfare, most provincial governments do not extend services to reserves. The funding and delivery of health, education, and welfare services to Indians on reserves is a federal responsibility. Via Section 91 [24] of the Constitution, the federal government is able to provide universal welfare benefits to registered Indians without encroaching on provincial powers. Access to services is at the Band level. Bands are empowered under Section 81 of the Indian Act to enact and administer by-laws. In addition, most bands have developed sufficient administrative structure and capacity to deliver federally funded programs and services (Shewell and Spagnut, 1995). There are wide variations in how these tasks are accomplished, but generally speaking, service delivery through the Bands has replaced administration by employees of the federal department of Indian Affairs and Northern Development (DIAND) across Canada.

In addition, the federal government, under the auspices of the Indian Act, funds the Social Development Policy and Programs, which administers three services. These are child welfare, adult care involving basic homemaker services to the chronically ill and elderly, and Social Assistance. The latter continues to be governed primarily by DIAND, a situation that symbolizes the continuing "dependent" relationship of First Nations peoples on the government of Canada. A high level of usage of this program as a sole source of support continues at the start of the twenty-first century. For registered Indians on reserves, the rate of usage is as much as three-and-a-half to four times greater than the national level (Shewell and Spagnut, 1995, 39–40). The Department itself reports that most Aboriginal people in Canada remain at or below the poverty line (Indian and Northern Affairs, 2000).

The overall policy of the federal government since the early 1800s has been assimilation of Aboriginal peoples into the general population. Many efforts to achieve this goal have been made, but Aboriginal peoples have been determined to avoid this outcome. Over the past three decades, Aboriginal organizations and leaders have pressed for increasing rights and self-government. Advances in this direction have been made, for instance, in control of education and child welfare in particular locations. The Constitution Act of 1982 recognizes Aboriginal rights, specifically identifying Indian, Inuit, and Métis peoples. The wording of the Act places Aboriginal peoples in a new relationship with both federal and provincial governments, a new phase in the long relationship between Canada and First Nations (Patterson, 1987).

Three main themes are currently being pursued in the political activities of First Nations peoples: 1) ending the paternalistic relationship that is the legacy of the Indian Act; 2) the devolution of social programs from federal and provincial auspices to First Nations' control; and 3) working for self-government (Shewell and Spagnut, 1995). The scope of self-government negotiations concerned with social welfare is inclusive—health, justice, education, housing, social security, child welfare, and social services are all "on the table." Control of child welfare has been of particular importance to First Nations peoples, in order to stem the outflow of their children from their own communities and also to control the socialization of their children (Taylor-Henley and Hudson, 1992). No doubt First Nations representatives will pursue full jurisdiction in this and other social policy areas in future talks. The Métis have argued for entitlement to Aboriginal rights. At times, the federal government has recognized the existence of Métis claims. A federal cabinet committee on Métis and non-status Indians has been established to investigate claims and issues proposed by them. However, at present, the federal government views servicing these groups as a provincial responsibility (Frideres, 1998).

Women

Social work has traditionally focused on women as clients, and the field is dominated by women as workers. However, until the "second wave" of feminism in the 1970s, many social workers were not aware of the special interests of women as a group. Of course, this is no longer the case. We work with women more often than men because women are disadvantaged in relation to social welfare and face different kinds of life tasks than men, tasks that often involve dependants as well as themselves. As a result of these differences, various policies addressing women's particular needs have been promoted and in some cases adopted. Social workers need to be aware of these policies and the debates surrounding them in order to work effectively with both male and female populations.

Changing demography is a different issue with respect to gender than with some other minority groups. Females generally compose just over half of the total Canadian population. However, females tend to dominate in older age groups. In 1991, about 57 percent of the population over 65 were female (Statistics Canada).

Women have until recently been situated quite differently from men in relation to the law. Eichler (1987) notes that women were not considered to be "persons" under English Common Law. Following this tradition, Canada's Election Act contained a clause stating that "no woman, idiot, lunatic or criminal shall vote." Not until 1918 were Canadian women accorded the federal vote. In 1929 they were granted legal identity as "persons," and it remained to the 1982 Charter of Rights and Freedoms to guarantee women equality before the law.

Women have also been situated in relation to the paid labour force and its programs and benefits differently from men. The arrangements of industrial capitalism led to separation of the public from the private worlds of labour in the early part of the twentieth century. While men came increasingly to occupy the public and higher-status domain of paid work, women were consigned to the private world of unpaid and often invisible caring and household labour. Historically there has been meagre support for women who were not attached to a breadwinning male. While a succession of policies have addressed this situation, the separation of the public and private worlds continues to have repercussions for women (and men) today. As Eichler (1987) notes, the husband as breadwinner was the statistical norm that prevailed until the 1980s. Further, the paid work that women do continues to reflect their caring responsibilities in the private domain (Baines, Evans, and Neysmith, 1998) along with lower social value and pay.

A report developed for the Canadian Research Institute for the Advancement of Women (CRIAW) by Morris (2000) confirms that women are the majority of the poor in Canada. This examination of poverty among different types of women demonstrates how membership in more than one disadvantaged group increases vulnerability. The report notes, for instance, that 41 percent of single women under 65 live in poverty. Women with disabilities are especially vulnerable to poverty. Those who are aged 35 to 54 earn only 55 percent of the earnings of men with disabilities in the same age range. Recent figures show that the average annual income for Aboriginal women is $11,900 compared to $17,400 for Aboriginal men. Visible minority women fare slightly better than Aboriginal women, with an annual income of $13,800. Employment does not necessarily improve these results. In fact, the CRIAW report states that 67 percent of minimum-wage earners in Canada are women, many of whom are single mothers responsible for the support of children.

There have also been substantial changes in the relationship of women to the paid labour force during the twentieth century. At the beginning of the century, women made up 13.3 percent of the total labour force. In 1995, women constituted 45.1 percent of the labour force (Luxton and Reiter, 1997). Along with this change have come other changes in women's life paths. Women marry later and on average have their first baby at a later age. Availability of consumer goods has increased the possibility of spending less time doing domestic labour, thus freeing women to enter the paid labour force. At the same time, costs of basic needs have come to require increased paid labour to cover expenses. Women have often taken paid jobs to close the gap between expenses and income, but their earnings continue to lag behind those of men. In 1994, women still earned only 62.3 percent of men's earnings. The wage gap between women and men in full-time work narrowed in the past three decades. In 1967 women earned 58 percent of men's wages; in 1997 the ratio was 72 percent. For part-time work, women appear to be doing better, earning nearly 79 percent of the part-time male work force. According to Jackson and Robinson (2000), this narrowing gap was due only in part to rising earnings of women; other reasons are increased time worked by women and falling wages of men. Although women made strides in public sector labour force participation during the 1980s and early '90s, recent studies suggest erosion of "good jobs" for women in this arena. Armstrong's study (1996) for instance shows that many women are taking part-time jobs to replace full-time jobs lost, and that full-time jobs in what traditionally have been "women's" areas such as health, social services, and education are increasingly being taken by men.

As feminist scholars have been demonstrating for the past two decades, women do not access or benefit from social welfare policies in the same way that men do. Pateman (1992) has analyzed the income security system as two-tiered. In this scheme, the top tier provides benefits to people based on participation in the paid labour force. Canadian examples are the CPP/QPP, EI, and provincial workers' compensation programs. The second tier is available to the dependants of people in the first category. Canadian examples include provincially/municipally administered welfare assistance programs, or selective day-care programs. Women are much more likely to make claims on the state through family or dependency status than as "workers" or as public persons (Pateman, 1992, cited in Evans, 1997, 95). These second-tier policies that women are most likely to access deliver low benefit levels, have stringent eligibility requirements and means tests, and typically involve considerable scrutiny. Men are much more likely to access first-tier programs that generally carry less stigma than "insurance programs," provide higher benefits, and are accessed through administrative means (Evans, 1997). When women do access these programs, as they increasingly do because of greater labour-force participation, they still benefit less as a group because of lower pay and higher proportions of part-time work experienced by women than men. A large majority of men, for example, are eligible for 80 percent or more of the full benefits provided by the Canada Pension Plan, while half of all women receive less than 40 percent of the maximum (Evans, 1995).

Historically, there have been social policies specific to women, especially in their roles as mothers of dependent children. The provincially mounted "mothers' pension" program, initiated in Manitoba in 1916, is an example. This selective policy provided benefits to mothers only if they were raising children alone and were deemed "worthy." The universal Family Allowance (1940–1992), a federally financed and administered direct transfer to mothers for each child in her care on a monthly basis, was another example. Contemporary assistance policies are couched in gender-neutral terms. However, women continue to be the primary recipients of assistance claimed on the basis of providing care for young children. In fact, it was not until 1984 that single fathers were able to access assistance benefits on the same terms as single mothers. At the same time, Evans (1997) notes, single mothers are increasingly subjected to the same work requirements as married men and single women.

Over the past several decades, a range of policy initiatives dealing with the special concerns of women have been developed. Provincial policies funding women's shelters and other supports for victims of domestic violence are specific to women. Policies dealing with child care, pornography, sexual assault, sexual harassment, and sexual abuse (Eichler, 1987) are not necessarily confined to women but arose from women's concerns and experiences and are generally considered to apply to females much more often than to males. Equal pay legislation and policies are specifically aimed at reducing salary inequalities for women. These policies provide the legal framework to enforce equal pay for women who do the same work as men, or who do work of "equal value." A recent federal court decision to grant federal female employees back pay for past discrimination in wages demonstrates the potential importance of this direction for women. However, in Ontario, provincial policies supporting equal pay have been rescinded as too expensive. Some feminist scholars (Armstrong, 1997) are arguing that the legislation as written could result in increased inequalities among women, as settlements for higher-paid women reduce job options for others. Additionally, there are calls to redress policy directions that leave women in old age at a disadvantage in terms of pensions and benefits. Wages for housework and some form of pension credit for women whose labour has primarily been in the home are examples of suggested policy directions.

The federal government created an elaborate structure for incorporating women's issues into public policy. During the 1970s and '80s, this structure came to include a minister specifically responsible for the status of women, an Advisory Council on the Status of Women at "arm's length" from the government, and a Women's Program at the Secretary of State, which funded many women's organizations (Eichler, 1987). Recently, much of this infrastructure has been dismantled, although there continues to be a minister and an organizational structure for the Status of Women. In addition, provinces have their own organizational structures specific to women's issues and concerns. In the era of downsizing and downloading, women's groups are concerned that these structures and the funding for women's groups they have supported are diminishing.

Women's participation in the paid labour force increased dramatically during the twentieth century and especially in the past three or four decades. In spite of this, most recent studies suggest that women continue to perform most of the labour in the household, including child care. In addition, with recent downsizing of, and withdrawing funding from, many programs and services, women are increasingly asked to take up the slack in terms of care for vulnerable and dependent family members. For many years, women's organizations have lobbied for a national child-care policy that would support supervised, safe care for their children while they are in the paid labour force. Although repeatedly promised, as of now there is no such policy, a situation that continues to disadvantage women in the labour force.

Analysis of the globalizing economy by Mishra (1999) and others suggests that both men and women are being negatively repositioned in the labour force. Fewer "good" jobs and many more "bad" jobs characterize current solutions to changing labour-force demands. Flexibility, adaptability, and continual retraining are required of job applicants, and even the hope that the service sector would eventually replace manufacturing as a source of employment has dimmed. The phenomenon of "jobless growth" has intensified, putting the employment prospects of both men and women in doubt. These changes are rapid and far reaching, and social workers will need to inform themselves regularly about the gender implications of current labour-market trends.

Sexual Orientation

Not all groups in Canada have historically viewed same-sex relationships in negative terms. Some Aboriginal people, for instance, recognize the existence of people who combine aspects of both female and male. These "two-spirited" people are regarded as especially fortunate and associated with power and generosity. In contrast, European settlers, both English and French, adopted punitive positions toward same-sex relations. At times tolerance has been exhibited toward same-sex relationships by the founding peoples, for instance, in all-male situations of long duration such as lumbering or mining camps (O'Brien and Weir, 1995). The general Canadian climate toward homosexuality, however, has been one of hostility, with discrimination of many kinds evident in both public and private life.

Canada has long had a single national law on same-sex sexual activity: The Criminal Code. As recently as 1967, men engaging in sexual activity with other men were considered "dangerous sexual offenders" under the Code, and were subject to imprisonment. In 1969, provisions of the Code dealing with this issue were amended to decriminalize sexual behaviour between consenting adults.

Since the end of World War II, challenges to discrimination against gay, lesbian, and bisexual individuals have been increasingly raised at every level of government around the world, including the United Nations (Wintemute, 1995). Representatives of this population have been trying to establish a general principle that discrimination based on sexual orientation is inherently wrong. The adoption of such a principle would place the onus of responsibility on those who practice discrimination to demonstrate why such discrimination should be permitted. In Canada, two strategies can be used to establish this principle. One is the political strategy designed to create, change, or repeal laws in order to develop a non-discriminatory legislative framework. The second strategy is a legal one, carried out through courts and human rights tribunals designed to demonstrate that a particular instance of discrimination violates existing human rights legislation.

Through the 1970s and into the 1980s, a number of legal battles, some at the level of the Supreme Court of Canada, were fought concerning issues of discrimination against, or unequal treatment of, gay and lesbian individuals and groups. The advent of the Charter of Rights gave the Court the power to strike down laws depriving individuals of their rights. Section 15 of the Charter guarantees equal treatment under the law without discrimination. Although sexual orientation is not specifically enumerated in this section, court challenges have produced precedents confirming sexual orientation as grounds for protection under Section 15 (Young, 1994). The Charter of Rights and Freedoms has also helped to produce new debates, litigation, and directions concerning issues of sexual orientation (Kallen, 1995). For example, most provinces have enacted human rights legislation specifically prohibiting discrimination against lesbians and gay men. Also, legislation providing equality rights for this population with respect to workplace benefits has been proposed in some jurisdictions, including British Columbia and Ontario.

Both social policy and discourse tend to pose "the family" as separate and different from homosexuality, with the family symbolizing stability, responsibility, and happiness, and homosexuality representing a threat to this valued institution (O'Brien and Weir, 1995). Legal as well as social precedents define marriage inherently as involving opposite-sex couples, with at least the theoretical possibility of procreation. Advocates have mounted challenges to these traditional ideas about the family. From a social-policy perspective, a central issue is whether "the family" can or ought to include lesbian and gay couples. From a human rights standpoint, the issue is whether it is discriminatory to deny same-sex couples benefits and entitlements enjoyed by heterosexual couples. Inclusion in law on the same basis as heterosexual couples is referred to by Cossman (1996) as an assimilationist position. There are substantial differences among advocates, however, concerning whether assimilation is the most advantageous policy direction. Some advocates argue that a more beneficial position is to challenge and subvert traditional conceptions and definitions of the family rather than to fight for inclusion. This position, which Cossman calls anti-assimilationist, raises the issue of differences reflected in gay and lesbian relationships. Advocates of this view question whether acceptance of the traditional family definition would erase or devalue ways these relationships differ from heterosexual relationships.

Ontario's proposed Equality Rights Statute Law Amendment Act (1994) reflected an attempt to enshrine the assimilationist position in law. Following extensive analysis of current family law (Cossman, 1996), framers of Ontario's bill redefined *marital status* and *spouse* by removing any reference to "opposite sex." The effect would have been that rights and responsibilities of married couples, including common-law couples, would apply in the same way to same-sex couples. The bill was narrowly defeated in an "open" vote, reflecting the deep political and personal divisions the issue of spousal benefits to the partners of lesbians and gay men continues to produce at the policy level. British Columbia, on the other hand, has passed legislation (Bill 38, 1998) redefining "spouse" in the Pension (College) Act. The new definition includes "a person of the same gender who lived in a marriage-like relationship with that other person for the two-year period immediately preceding the relevant time." As of this writing, no other such legislation has been enacted (*The Globe and Mail*, October 24, 1998).

In practice, some pension and other benefits have been extended to members of this population in various provinces and by private employers. However, without provincial legislation allowing same-sex couples to make the same claims as heterosexual couples, the avenue of recourse remains at the level of courts and human rights tribunals. All provinces have some legislated provisions to protect the basic rights of lesbians and gay men. These may be embedded in other pieces of legislation, for instance relating to employment, but most often appear in provincial human rights legislation as one of the grounds upon which claims of discrimination can be made. Where sexual orientation is not mentioned, challenges to the legislation may be raised. A 1998 Supreme Court decision, for instance, concerning employment discrimination due to sexual orientation, ordered Alberta to include the words "sexual orientation" in its statute (Vriend v. Alta, 1998). As L'Heureux-Dube (2000) notes, this decision shows the importance of looking beyond the Charter in the search for protection of equality rights.

Other cases expected to be heard at the highest court levels are aimed at allowing same-sex couples the right to marry and/or to receive benefits accorded heterosexual married couples, for instance CPP, Social Assistance, child-care deductions (Wintemute, 1995), as well as the right to sponsor one's partner for immigration purposes, the right to spousal allowances under the Old Age Security Act, and coverage under medicare (Young, 1994). Holland was the first country to legalize same-sex marriage (Coolidge, 2001), and similar rights are sought in Canadian provinces. In a well-publicized decision, however, the British Columbia Supreme

Court has refused to grant same-sex couples the right to marry (*The Globe and Mail*, October 4, 2001). The Court rejected the claim that forbidding gay couples to marry constitutes discrimination under the Charter of Rights and Freedoms, instead basing its decision on the grounds that marriage is a "deep-rooted" social institution with the primary purpose of protecting the security of children.

A related, though seldom mentioned, aspect of this issue is tax policy, important since many of the benefits sought are subsidized by current tax arrangements. Tax expenditure analysis demonstrates that the tax system not only raises revenues but is also a spending program, involving deductions, credits, and exclusions (Young, 1994). This system is routinely used to subsidize pensions and other benefits. Couples considered as married are penalized in some ways and benefited in others by tax policy. Pensions are particularly crucial, since those benefits go only to a spouse. No wording in federal tax legislation requires a spouse to be of the opposite gender. Nevertheless, the Canada Customs and Revenue Agency currently treats partners of lesbians and gay men differently from heterosexual partners.

The Charter of Human Rights challenges being mounted by representatives of gay, lesbian, and bisexual people raise policy questions in several areas. One such question relates to the traditional formulation of what constitutes a family. A second is why minorities such as lesbians and gay men have not been more readily recognized by social policy experts. One of the hardest-hitting critiques of the field of social policy has been pursued by Fiona Williams (1989). She argues that social policies have always been intertwined with subordinations based on gender and race, but that these diversities have been hidden by the more universal categories of the social policy field, such as class and poverty. Certainly, those discriminated against on the basis of sexual orientation remain a marginal voice in social policy discourse, and the policy-based literature focused on them remains very small.

The third question is what constitutes social policy itself. Linda Gordon, writing from a feminist perspective, criticizes traditional approaches to social policy as being preoccupied with legislation and formal programs. Many writers in the field, she contends, do not understand that policy is constructed of practices as well as written legislation. This reality, as O'Brien (1998) notes, challenges traditional assumptions that the state is the primary site of power. Other critics suggest instead that state power is more fragmented and less coherent than the traditional field of social policy has assumed. On the other hand, it is important to note that much of the policy discourse related to sexual orientation, as well as policies themselves, are shaped through state-sponsored processes such as court challenges rather than through traditional processes of policy analysis and development. In the case of sexual orientation, in fact, court challenges currently appear to be the primary instrument for change. This may be problematic for many gay and lesbian people. Young's (1994) analysis, for instance, shows that winning benefit rights will not be equally beneficial for members of this population. Many of the Charter and rights challenges currently being mounted are linked to couples and will not benefit single persons. Since women, including lesbians, earn far less than men and are employed in fewer jobs with benefits, lesbians will not gain as much from legal battles for benefits as will gay men. With respect to the tax system, which privileges wealth, Young's analysis shows that low-income couples will not benefit from being redefined as a "family" for tax purposes. In other words, some of the current challenges, while rights-based and aimed at achieving equity in relation to heterosexual couples, will simultaneously reinforce other inequalities, including those based on class and gender. Countering these effects will require continued efforts through new policy development aimed at within-group equality. The Foundation for Equal Families (FEF), a coalition of concerned activists, has challenged legislation that does not incorporate same-sex spouses as equal to opposite-sex spouses as unconstitutional. The May 1999 Supreme Court decision to include same-sex relationships in the definition of common-law couples will doubtless have ongoing significance over the coming years.

Disablement

People with disabilities have at different times in history been seen as symbols of divine punishment, as sacred beings, and as members of the deserving poor (Roeher Institute, 1996). In ancient Greek philosophy, disability was viewed as a deficit to humanness. In Western liberal thinking, disability has constituted a reason for exclusion from society and civil life. Canada's first residential institution for people with intellectual disabilities opened in 1859 in Ontario. Over the following century institutional care dominated as the preferred form of service (Roeher Institute, 1996). The eugenics movement in the early part of the twentieth century, spawned partly by new technology, led to very punitive measures for people with both physical and intellectual disabilities, including institutionalization, sterilization, segregation, and medication (Stainton, 1994). Only within the past two decades have community-based services become the preferred service policy.

Vocabulary in the area of disablement has been confusing and has led to the misunderstanding of policy issues. The term *disability* itself covers a wide range of descriptors. Disabilities may be physical, intellectual, or emotional, and may be congenital or the result of life circumstances. Some disabilities are visible, and some, such as deafness, are invisible. An individual's disability status may change over time. Wide-ranging specifics of disability may be partly responsible for the fragmentation of social policy in this area. The 1980 publication of the International Classification of Impairments, Disabilities and Handicaps (ICIDH) by the World Health Organization was significant in clarifying terminology. This report identifies three dimensions of disablement. *Impairment* is defined in the report as an abnormality of physiological or anatomical structure or function. A *disability* is any limitation in ability to perform functions considered "normal" for a human being or required for a social role or occupation. A *handicap* is the resulting disadvantage. The term *disablement* refers to all three dimensions (Bickenbach, 1993).

Canada is signatory to a number of international laws guaranteeing protection for human rights generally, and rights for people with disabilities particularly. The Universal Declaration of Human Rights (UDHR, 1948) is based on three principles: freedom, equality, and dignity. A subsequent United Nations (UN) document, the International Bill of Human Rights (IBHR, 1978), articulates rights of access to the economic resources required for participation in social and economic life, participation in decisions affecting one's own life, and affirmation of the worth of each person. Two further relevant UN documents are the Declaration on the Rights of Mentally Retarded Persons (1971) and the Declaration on the Rights of Disabled Persons (1975). Although not legally binding, these documents provide a moral basis for the formation of national legislation and policy commitments to people with disabilities. They express the principles of care, economic security, guardianship when necessary, freedom from exploitation, and rights of consent to the full extent possible given individual circumstances.

Critics of these international instruments note that the framers represent Western philosophy and attention to the individual, largely ignoring collective interests and rights (Kallen, 1989). Nevertheless, it is clear that both national and international human rights movements have strongly influenced relations between people with disabilities and the state (Stainton, 1994). Significant support and publicity for disability issues resulted from the UN designation of 1981 as The International Year of Disabled Persons. Later, the International Decade of Disabled Persons was announced by the UN, leading to a sustained focus on issues of disability rights for a longer period of time. Part of the Canadian response to this attention was a report tabled in 1981 called *Obstacles*, written by a Special Committee on the Disabled and the Handicapped. In it, three aspirations by and for people with disabilities were articulated: 1) respect and dignity; 2) empowerment to participate in decisions regarding their own lives and futures; and 3) accommodations providing the *means* to participate. These goals are now at the forefront of efforts to shape and change social policy concerned with disablement.

Also in the early 1980s, the Canadian Charter of Rights and Freedoms was adopted. Section 15 of the Charter, which enumerates specific groups protected under the Charter, includes those with "mental or physical disability." Although Kallen (1989) notes that no right is beyond encroachment by state action, she also describes inclusion of disability in the Charter as a "monumental constitutional breakthrough." Previously, disability issues had not been seen as part of the struggle for equality rights, and Canada remains unique in its constitutional guarantees of equality for people with disabilities (Roeher Institute, 1996). Inclusion provides rights protection as well as the potential for specific legal challenges based on this section.

In addition, persons with disabilities are one of four designated groups specifically mentioned in Canada's Employment Equity Act of 1986. This legislation requires federally regulated employers to implement equity programs and report annually on their results. In 1987, the Standing Committee on Human Rights and the Status of Disabled Persons was established by the House of Commons, and in 1991 the federal government launched the five-year National Strategy for the Integration of Persons with Disabilities. Both initiatives have been instrumental in advocacy efforts.

In the 1990s, a number of reports issued at the federal level have provided more focus and commitment to policy relevant to disablement. The Federal-Provincial-Territorial Council on Social Policy Renewal in the mid-'90s considered this area a major focus. In 1996, the Scott Task Force, representing several federal departments, was charged with the task of defining the role of the federal government as it relates to the disability community. *In Unison: A Canadian Approach to Disability Issues*, a vision paper following up recommendations of the Scott report, was issued in 1998. This document includes principles for ensuring full citizenship, including removal of barriers to full civic participation, for the estimated 16 percent of Canadians (Valentine, 2001) living with disabilities.

Current policy concerning disablement is quite diverse, involving all three levels of government. Bickenbach (1993, 5) lists 14 distinct policy areas through which services related to disablement are considered and delivered:

1. biomedical services;
2. employment programs;
3. autonomy protection;
4. rehabilitation and institutional care;
5. independent living;
6. housing;
7. income security;
8. physical access;
9. compensation;
10. communications and access to information/education;
11. health and safety legislation;
12. research;
13. human rights; and
14. anti-discrimination.

A 1990 report issued by the House of Commons Standing Committee on Human Rights and the Status of Disabled Persons noted the fragmentation of policy concerning disability. The report, *A Consensus of Action: The Economic Integration of Disabled Persons*, demonstrated that policy in this arena is inconsistent, ambiguous, contradictory, and often merely an "add-on" to other social policy.

Bickenbach (1993) has attempted to clarify and critique past and present policy by outlining and exploring three main policy approaches to disablement. The highly individualistic biomedical model views people with disabilities as victims of personal misfortune. Solutions and supports are medically focused and are based on rehabilitation and palliation. The economic model, according to Bickenbach, is the dominant model for policy throughout the world. It focuses on work-based disability and the limits of a person's capacities to be productive in the labour force. People with disabilities are viewed as economic costs to be considered as part of economic policy. Recommended services concentrate on providing rehabilitation and/or compensation for loss of productivity. The third model, and one that is currently popular, is socio-economic. This model combines labelling theory with a civil-rights approach to disablement. People with disabilities are seen as oppressed, as victims of social injustice resulting from discrimination against them.

Disabilities are viewed as socially constructed, and infused into social systems that sustain disadvantages for this population. Bickenbach critiques each of these models as inadequate, proposing instead that a more comprehensive policy model must be developed. An adequate policy, he argues, must acknowledge the existence of differences and must establish a basis for social responsibility to redress inequalities based on those differences.

Prior to the 1970s, disability of any kind was generally viewed as illness or abnormality. Since that time, perceptions of disability have changed as a result of the advocacy efforts of Canadians with disabilities. Advocacy has been pursued in the form of three challenges to Canadian society and government (Valentine, 2001). One asserts the right of people with disabilities to organize autonomously, outside of the health care and policy sectors. The second asserts the right of disabled people to equal treatment as individuals with full citizenship. The third develops the argument that disability is a social construction, often more reflective of the fears and feelings of others than of the experiences of people with disabilities.

In Canada, as in the United States, a policy of deinstitutionalization has been in effect for more than two decades. Stroman (1989) identifies three dimensions to deinstitutionalization: the release of people from institutions; specific practices designed to prevent people from entering institutions; and modification of institutional practices to make them less institutional in character. A number of forces converged to create the movement away from institutional care:

➤ the growth of an advocacy movement, involving parents and organized associations;

➤ indictment and exposure of large institutions as dehumanizing and harmful;

➤ acceptance of the "normalization" principle—that people with disabilities can and should have access to normal living conditions;

➤ development of community-based services; and

➤ escalating costs of care in institutional settings.

Community services to supplement and replace institutional care have been initiated largely by local organizations, often with funding from federal or provincial governments. In this era of cutbacks, developing a sufficient funding base and service infrastructure, as well as the social commitment required, for the wide range of community-based services required for people with disabilities to participate to the fullest extent possible in public life has become a serious policy issue.

Increased attention to children with disabilities is currently being encouraged by community advocates. Recent research shows about 7.7 percent of Canadian children 0 to 19 have disabilities (Canadian Council on Social Development [CCSD], undated), and this percentage is expected to increase as medical technology helps to save the lives of more infants compromised at birth and in early childhood. Both CCSD and Valentine show that many of these children are multiply disadvantaged. For instance, children with disabilities are more likely than other children to live in poor families and in "problem" housing. Seventeen percent of children with disabilities rely on government support compared to 8 percent of children without disabilities. However, there is as yet no integrated and clear policy focus on this population. Valentine (2001) recommends three "enabling conditions" for improving services: adequate income, sufficient services for effective parenting to occur, and a supportive community environment.

Disability issues have recently fuelled high-profile media stories that demonstrate both policy goals and disagreements. The Latimer case (in which a Saskatchewan farmer killed his severely disabled daughter) and other similar cases demonstrate the contradictory perspectives of people with disabilities and their caregivers. Sometimes love and acceptance may prevail, and at other times fear and despair. The Latimer case and others like it also demonstrate substantial social disagreement about acceptable policy. Advocacy groups generally articulate the most important social policy goals as self-determination and equality. Self-determination for disabled people should mean the same thing it does for the non-disabled: the opportunity to participate in making decisions about matters that affect their lives and support in developing capacities enabling them to reach their goals. Equality means having the support (including special accommodations where necessary) needed to provide all people an equal claim on society's offerings (Roeher Institute, 1996). Stainton (1994) expresses two key sets of action required to meet these goals. One is *compensatory* action necessary to redress disadvantage. The second is *positive* action to ensure people with disabilities are able to exercise their rights.

Geography

A final area of diversity, which is of particular significance to Canada given its vast size, is geography. Historian Maurice Careless aptly describes the Canadian experience as a tension between metropolis and hinterland (1954). Externally, much of our history has been that of a colony, subject to the norms and will of a far-away political/economic system, be it Great Britain, or, more recently, the United States. Internally, powerful centres—economically, socially, and politically—have dominated those areas that are farther removed from such power (Careless, 1954). Toronto, and southern Ontario in general, has been the metropolis to a hinterland, resource-based Northern Ontario (Nelles, 1974). Central Canada may be seen to have been a metropolis to western provinces and to Atlantic Canada (Morton, 1969). But these hinterland areas, too, have their own complex networks of metropolis-hinterland relationships within them. St. John's, as an example, has been a metropolis to the rest of Newfoundland and Labrador; Calgary and Edmonton are metropolises to northern Alberta.

In social work, much literature has been imported from other countries, the United States in particular; and in social policy, as we have seen, many factors existing outside the country have influenced Canadian developments. Social policies and the way in which social policies are conceived have had other biases beyond these. They have been overwhelmingly urban in orientation, and have overlooked important differences relevant to rural, northern, and remote Canada (cf. Delaney and Brownlee, 1995; Brownlee, Delaney, and Zapf, 1996; Delaney, Brownlee, and Graham, 1997). As Zapf points out, in one social policy textbook published 20 years ago, "rural areas were dismissed as exhibiting 'all the same problems as their larger metropolitan counterpart'" (1999, 345), and more generally still, "few pages" within any social policy text delved into "Native issues" (1999, 346), among other areas of concern to the country's traditional hinterlands.

Canada's population dispersion patterns are striking. Only 1 percent of the population occupies the northern 80 percent of the country's land mass. And 90 percent of the population lives within 200 miles of the American border, with 6 out of 10 in a narrow, and largely urban, corridor between Quebec City and Windsor (Zapf, 1999, 348). In Canada's north, small, disparate communities numbering under 250 are scattered across a territory as large as Europe, with only a handful of these small settlements approaching 10 000 (Zapf, 1999, 348-349). In northern regions too, like their remote and rural counterparts, differential policy needs have been overlooked, and metropolis assumptions and metaphors have been system-atically—and inappropriately—applied. As Zapf remarks: "social policy and pro-gram planners have tended to view their own separate northern regions as variations of the south posing some service delivery problems" (1999, 349). Hinterland re-gions continue to be economically exploited, and when their natural resources are depleted, or no longer valued, problems of unemployment, poverty, and limited labour mobility are intensified. Social policies have tended to reinforce metropolis-hinterland power imbalances and inequalities, so much so that some authors refer to areas of northern and rural Canada as a domestic Third World (Carniol, 1987; Collier, 1993; Jull, 1986; Weller, 1984. Cited in Zapf, 1999, 349).

In order to devise, implement, and evaluate policies for such geographically diverse Canadian communities, Zapf borrows from anthropological literature a multiple-stage process of acculturation. A social worker beginning to work with a geographic community different from his or her own usually has assumptions and training that reflect and reinforce metropolis areas. At this stage, the worker sep-arates consciously and deliberately from the hinterland place of work and assumes a professional sense of distance as an outsider. Rural, remote, and northern com-munities, however, have social structures that tend to encourage workers to be more than mere repositories of technical and professional know-how. "Cut off from the supportive professional social circle of the southern urban centre (pro-fessors, supervisors, professional association), the new social worker begins to ex-perience the remote [or northern, or rural] community in an immediate sense, becoming aware of the values and experiences of the people who live there" (Zapf, 1999, 351). Ultimately, the worker may "enter into the meanings of the commu-nity," and the community may become "less a target group and more a home" (Zapf, 1999, 351). At this point, the worker begins to identify not as an outsider, but as an insider; and a sense of community and local identity helps to create and sustain a worker mind-set that will lead to advocating more geographically sensi-tive social policy practices. An anecdotal example of a proposed inappropriate policy, which originated in Toronto, would have seen foster home standards in Northern Ontario include indoor toilets, effectively precluding a good proportion of currently operating rural foster homes.

Soon after Confederation, the federal government began to implement economic policies and programs that affected regions of the country in different ways (Beaumier, G. 1998). However, it was not until the 1940s and 1950s that serious examination of the way policies affected different parts of the country were undertaken. The Rowell-Sirois Commission of 1940 marked the beginnings of the idea of equalization payments from richer to poorer provinces, based on recognition that uniform national tax rates did not provide equal services to all Canadians. The later Gordon Commission (1957) examined regional disparities further, especially those that persisted over time. A long-standing problem has been whether to define the issues in relation to provinces, regions, or subregions. Generally, provinces have been the identified unit of policy, since data are kept by province.

Since the 1960s the federal government has had regional development programs in some parts of the country. These were initially aimed at depressed rural regions, but the mandate was later broadened. A Department of Regional Economic Expansion (DREE), established in 1969, was integrated in 1982 into the Department of Regional Industrial Expansion (DRIE). DRIE was dismantled in 1988. Critics of these federal efforts have generally felt policies placed inappropriate emphasis on the manufacturing sector and on job creation to spur economic growth in rural areas rather than creating plans for sustainable economic development. DRIE was replaced by four regionally based agencies: Western Economic Diversification Canada (WEDC); Atlantic Canada Opportunities Agency (ACOA); Federal Office of Regional Development for Quebec (FORD-Q); Northern Ontario Program (FEDNOR). These agencies have attempted to promote local industries by way of a variety of financial supports to local firms and entrepreneurs, and also via previously established governmental programs. As one economist points out, regional development programs "encompass a broad range of policies, including grants, special depreciation allowances and loans to encourage the location of firms in designated areas. Federal departments and agencies have also entered into general development agreements with the provinces, which can include infrastructure programs, mineral exploration, industrial restructuring incentives, rural development schemes, etc." (Polese, 1998). The Cape Breton Development Corporation is a well-known example of a major undertaking in which DREE participated.

How Diversity Challenges Social Policy

Previous sections have dealt with policy relating to specific groups of people. However, social policy affecting the general population has also been challenged and changed by diversity issues. A primary example is child welfare policy, which has been challenged in all provinces by both Aboriginal and ethnoracial groups as culturally skewed by values of the "founding peoples" (Swift, 1997). These critiques have been supported by evidence of over-representation of Aboriginal children (Johnson, 1983; Hepworth, 1980) and black children (Hutchinson, et al., 1992) in the care system. The challenges raised by Aboriginal peoples have been especially stinging, implicating child welfare as playing a crucial role in the colonization and subordination of Aboriginal populations (Hudson and McKenzie, 1981; Armitage, 1993). Most provinces have responded by incorporating specific provisions relating to Aboriginal peoples and their particular political structures into child welfare legislation. Since the late 1980s, most provinces have added clauses requiring that services respect the cultural backgrounds of children served by the system. For social workers, these changes in the policy context mean that new and close attention must be paid to policy at both federal and provincial levels if clients are to be served adequately.

Traditionally, treating everyone alike or with like intentions has been a valued social goal in the service sector. Diversity raises the question of whether these are appropriate objectives. The extension of equal child welfare services onto reserves, for example, has produced unequal results in terms of children taken into care (Swift, 1995). And, as many feminists point out, there are assumptions of gender neutrality embedded in policies. In reality, the consequences of social policies have proven to be different for women than for men, and different in many cases for minorities as well. Issues concerning definitions of the "family" are especially at issue. Lesbians and gay men have challenged the meaning of the family as being necessarily heterosexual, and members of various cultures, especially non-European, do not necessarily see the family as nuclear.

A related challenge involves the relationship of labour to social policy. This issue is especially relevant to work traditionally done by women in the private household. The caring labour performed mostly by women is a crucial and assumed piece of Canada's social structure. Current examples include the return to "family care," which translates into invisible free care often given by women. In fact, without this unpaid and usually invisible labour, most of our social policies would not be at all workable. If this form of labour were compensated, even at minimum wage rates, the costs of social programs would substantially escalate. And as Eichler (1987) points out, until caring responsibility is equally shared—in actual practice—by men and women, social policy will necessarily be accessed by and will affect men and women quite differently, with potentially different policy outcomes.

At a fundamental level, diversity challenges the concepts, assumptions, and structure of the Canadian social policy framework, including conventional ideas of need. In the developing neo-conservative/liberal context, the idea of need is increasingly personalized and attached to individual problems and failings, in the tradition of the Poor Laws. An alternate and useful way to think about social policy and diversity is in relation to the concept of thick and thin needs, introduced by Fraser (1989) and elaborated by Kerans (1994). A "thin" need is characterized as "objective, universal, and abstract" (Kerans, 1994, 45). It is rooted either in human physiology or in obligations imposed on the individual by society. This concept of need has been crucial in the development of social welfare policy because, as Kerans points out, the idea of universal need carries the moral weight required to justify redistribution of resources. Most social policy shaping the welfare state has been based on a notion of "thin" needs. Programs flowing from this idea were socially supported because of the presumed universality of the needs they were intended to meet.

Of course, universality of need does not translate directly into universality of claims on the public purse. Western societies, as Kerans notes, assume the market as the "normal" route for need fulfilment (1994, 48). Claims on the state are legitimized through evidence showing that the special circumstances of individuals and families means that their needs cannot be met through this usual route. These circumstances typically include age, disability, caring responsibilities, job loss, and so forth. Nonetheless, a thin concept of need is an important assumption underlying social policy because it allows the possibility of claims by those in need. Thin needs as the basis for provision also enhance the possibility for justice and equity. An important characteristic of Canadian social policy is impersonal provision for socially legitimated needs. That is, it is not supposed to be patronage, or payoff, or promises of votes that justify provision. Rather, it is the universality of need that justifies resources distribution. The goal is to ensure "standard treatment of all individuals, regardless of their ethnic identity, class position or gender, as the basis for intervention with disadvantaged persons and populations" (Mawhiney, 1995, 223).

A problem with using thin or universal need as a basis for social provision, as Kerans notes, is that it is necessarily abstract. Thin need is an idea assumed to apply to all. Since it is not grounded in variations of real life, it cannot account for or express the multiplicity of experience and collective and individual differences that shape and give meaning to *need* in the everyday world. This reality has accounted for substantial dissatisfaction with social policies intended to address need as a universal experience. Bureaucratic procedures that objectify need for purposes of resource distribution (one size fits all) have become sources of frustration for both receivers and providers of social programs. In other words, the attempt to create policy that addresses universally experienced needs runs the risk of "universalizing" human experience in unacceptable ways. Also, social policy is not created by all people. Policy formulation in fact is dominated by white males. Policy has a tendency to represent the viewpoints of its authors, which may erroneously appear as "universal" ideas.

The idea of "thick" need represents an effort to interpret need within its particular cultural context. Diversity is central to this concept of need. In this conception, need is not objectified and measurable but rather is viewed as subjective. Its meaning is constructed by individuals or groups through their particular experiences. As Kerans notes, neither category of need is as clear as definitions presume, and neither can stand on its own as the basis for social policy. However, application of thick and thin ideas of need can help us explore the relationship between diversity and social policy. Challenges to the welfare state by diverse groups can be understood as insistence upon recognition of "thick" conceptions of need. That is, diverse groups are insisting upon their particular history and experience as factors in defining need and in satisfying it through social policy initiatives.

Conclusion

Caroline Andrew (1994) comments that the "old" view of social policy is based on concepts of dependence, class, and the state. Andrew uses as an example the concept of "the poor," a concept that glosses over who constitutes the poor and how particular groups come to be over-represented among the poor. The traditional conceptualization has been challenged recently from many directions, not least by the "multiple social identities" of women, racial and ethnic minorities, and others. Each of the populations presented in this chapter has a specific history and a set of policy issues particular to them. However, we must continually remind ourselves that these groups are neither mutually exclusive nor homogeneous. People with disabilities are either male or female, they are racial and cultural beings, they may be Aboriginal, they may be gay or lesbian. There are class and cultural differences and divisions among lesbians, among women, among Aboriginal peoples. As well, there are common issues of discrimination, of unpaid or devalued labour, of exclusion from decision processes shared by diverse minorities (Roeher Institute, 1996). There may be as many common interests among these groups as there are differences. Clearly, social policy of the future must be able to account for considerably more diversity and complexity than it has in the past. "Complication," as Andrew suggests, "is the only solution" (1994, 67).

Chapter 7

Social Policy and
Social Work Practice

Social work is about helping people. But the assistance a social worker provides—
be it to an individual, a family, a group, or a community—occurs in a social policy context. This chapter elaborates why, and how, social workers need to
understand social policy and policy processes. Without this understanding, we
argue, social workers can never be fully effective, and the help that they provide their
clients will never be fully satisfactory. This chapter also seeks to explain how the
relationship between social policy and social work processes has evolved in the literature. This facet is crucial to a final objective of the chapter: appreciating the
relationships between the practice skills of direct intervention and the skills of
social policy comprehension and analysis.

Why Study Social Policy?

Social policy students and practitioners in Canada may be more aware of relationships between policy and practice now than in past decades. An overall shift
in general policy from support for the welfare state to the dismantling of programs
and restricting of access to social services has brought awareness to social workers
of the ways policy affects direct practice. In the 1990s, social workers have seen the
effects of job loss and long-term unemployment, many have found themselves in
the position of refusing clients services previously offered, and we have all seen substantial withdrawal of funding and cutbacks. These events have made many social
workers acutely aware of relationships between social policy and direct practice.
Yet in schools of social work, and in social work literature, a sharp division often
remains between the ideas and skills of direct practice and those of social policy development and analysis. In this chapter, the focus is on exploring those relationships, with a view to examining policy-based knowledge and skills useful in
practising social work.

In spite of the recognized importance of social policy in direct practice, it
probably remains true that few students enter the field hoping to focus on social
policy itself. The majority of social work students in Canada traditionally have
been young women, many of whom express the goal of "helping others."

Acquaintance with social policy may appear a remote and dubious route to this goal. The social policy field has been dominated by men, who have tended to write and talk about this field in a somewhat abstract and impersonal manner. Perhaps one reason social work students so often avoid social policy is that it has indeed been too far removed from the ambiguous and messy "real life" experience of practice. Universalizing tendencies aggravate this problem, for students cannot easily recognize, in our abstract descriptions, the individuals and problems they work with in direct practice settings.

One of the unique features of social work is its focus not just on the individual, but on the individual in a wider context, be it within a family system, an organizational system (such as a workplace), a community, or a society; as well as the complex relationships between these broader structures and the individual. This emphasis on appreciating the individual in such broader contexts is sometimes called understanding "the person in environment"—a key skill that social workers must possess.

In the early years of social work, this "environment" clearly included social policies and the requirement to use, develop, and change them for the benefit of clients. Pioneers of social work such as Mary Richmond, Bertha Reynolds, and Jane Addams focused on both the personal and the social context in framing ideas about the new profession. As Wharf (1990) notes, agencies such as settlement houses, located in inner cities, provided appropriate settings for social workers to observe the effects of social policies on individuals, and also for social workers to apply their efforts simultaneously to individuals and to social causes. In fact, these early social workers became leaders because of their commitment to social causes. "They cared desperately about people, they had a vision of the good life and they were morally indignant about social evil" (Burns, quoted in Wharf, 1990, 16). These leaders considered social action, and the promotion of legislation that would alter the conditions of life for individuals they cared about, to be a natural part of their work. In 1915, Abraham Flexner, addressing a social work conference, issued a stinging indictment of this approach to social work. He urged social workers to enhance their own status as a profession by emulating the medical profession. Flexner said that if social work wanted to become a "real" profession, its members would have to develop a recognizeable technology as doctors have done, and would have to demonstrate this technology in their everyday practice with individuals where it could easily be seen.

As Popple and Leighninger (1998) argue, a focus on individuals and families has ever since been cast as the route to professional success. These authors cite Flexner's key work in the early part of the twentieth century as critical in the individualism that has pervaded social work through the rest of the century. Certainly, by the 1920s, casework had established itself as the "nuclear skill" of social work (Lubove, 1965). Supported by the curriculum of most schools of social work, the majority of social workers have since been directed toward and trained in interventions with individuals and families. This trend reached a peak in the psychoanalytic training of the 1950s. During the 1960s and early 1970s, a period of intense focus on social issues resulted in a shift in emphasis toward social action for many members of the profession.

However, social workers have continued to find pressing reasons to maintain their strongest focus on individuals. One reason is that individuals and families present themselves directly to us; they are immediately available as the focus of possible changes, whereas we know policies require long-term commitments to be changed. In the political climate that characterizes the beginning of the new millennium, we may even have become convinced that larger social change is beyond possibility. In *The Cult of Impotence*, McQuaig (1998) explores the notion that social forces affecting individuals are now too powerful and overwhelming to be changed. She argues the Canadian public has been fooled into believing that access to social programs and good jobs are now out of reach because of "globalization." Such disempowering myths no doubt reinforce for social workers the belief that the only useful point of intervention is at the individual level.

However, some recent changes in the Canadian political and economic context may bring new awareness to social workers of the importance of understanding and changing social policies. Downsizing, for instance, has eroded job security for social workers themselves. Cutbacks mean that some of the traditional casework jobs on which social work relied are disappearing. Cutbacks in related sectors, such as nursing, mean other professions may claim traditional areas of social work as their own. The substantial reduction in the size and number of institutions such as hospitals have meant clients previously counselled in institutional settings are now "in the community," requiring assistance with resources. Social workers must be intimately familiar with the relevant social policies and their related service provisions in order to be useful. Neo-conservative social agendas mean that a profession geared toward seeking social justice must become knowledgeable about and insistent upon policy development and change in order to work toward justice goals.

Theory: Understanding the Person in their Social Context

Over the century of its existence, social work has struggled to theorize connections between individuals and their environment. Generally credit is given to Mary Richmond as the first to theorize and extensively explore this relationship. In *The Long View* (1930) she expanded on the idea of casework:

....one perfectly good definition of social casework is the development of the character and welfare of the individual through adjustments effected between him (or her) and his social surroundings. Sometimes the surroundings need to be radically changed, sometimes the person needs to be, but more often a change, to be permanent, must be effected in both (577).

She recommended that caseworkers "consciously and deliberately" examine their work at the points of intersection with social movements, and strive to improve their work at these points. The casework movement, she thought, would inform the caseworker and in turn direct the workers toward the movement.

Sociologist C. Wright Mills' notions of private trouble and public issues, explored in Chapter 3, have also been crucial to the exploration of the personal and the social. A "trouble," he said, has to do with the self and the limited areas of social life with which a person is involved. "Issues," on the other hand, have to do with matters that transcend local involvement. An issue is a public matter, incapable of private resolution. In the conclusion to his important work *The Sociological Imagination* (1959), Mills offered this advice: "Do not study merely one small milieu after another; study the social structure in which milieux are organized.... Know that many personal troubles cannot be solved merely as troubles, but must be understood in terms of public issues....and know the human meaning of public issues must be revealed by relating them to private troubles" (224–6).

Feminists later explored this general terrain, elaborating on it and changing the emphasis to create the slogan "the personal is political." This notion, expanded since in models of feminist practice (Dominelli and McLeod, 1993), suggests the critical importance of understanding the nature of private troubles as intricately connected to the public and political worlds. Through feminist analysis, problems previously viewed as unique came to be seen as common and widespread (Gilroy, 1990). The arrangements of society, including social policy, are implicated in creating and maintaining problems experienced by individuals. These insights reveal, as Wharf (1990) observes, the reluctance of the Canadian state to establish policies to promote equality for various minorities, including women. Recently, the concept of "caring" has been employed to reveal this reluctance (Baines, et al., 1998). Analysis by feminists of the concept of caring shows how private issues of performing caring labour reflect the gendered expectations and hierarchies of the social world, including the organization of social work itself. A number of feminists (e.g., Leira, 1994) have focused on the welfare state, examining the ways social programs reinforce unpaid, undervalued caring expected of women in both the public and private realms. This approach shows the necessity of changing the fundamental structures through which social policy is shaped as a method of changing the daily realities of individual women.

Some social work theorists and writers have employed ideas from Marx and the later Critical School to explore the relationship between the person and the social environment. Marx and Engels (1846, trans. 1947) observed that the state is itself based upon the contradiction between public and private, and between general and particular interests. From this perspective, social work's original purpose was to mediate this contradiction, helping to soften the worst effects of public life on individuals and proposing remedial public policies. A Marxist perspective also theorizes the mutually constructing relations between society and individuals; in other words, the idea that people both create and are created by their social world. Writing about this idea from a social work perspective, Leonard (1975, 1984) has examined how ideological constructs are internalized by individuals and consequently shape personality. In the aggregate, the characteristics of individuals then come to justify public policy. This "dialectic" was an idea previously expressed by Berger (1966), who suggested that "man lives in society but society also lives in man" (cited in Bailey and Brake, 1975, 20). Internalized constructs tend to be those that support and recreate the status quo. Girls, for instance, are socialized to be caring and passive, qualities that, if internalized, ensure the continuation of unpaid caring labour upon which the economy depends. Given this idea, social work might do one of two things. According to Pearson (1975), social work might come to rest on a "false split" between society and individuals. On the other hand, social work has the opportunity to enhance the potential of people in both the private and social realms (Leonard, 1975).

Another, related view of the relationship between policy and practice is that social policy creates the world in which practice is accomplished. Rein (1983) points out that "....the things we think about and the ways we think about them, as well as the ways we act, are shaped by the institutional arrangements of the society we live in" (223). Of course, practice also contributes to policy. The activities of front-line workers are not merely neutral instruments of broad objectives. The activities themselves act to alter intentions (Rein, 1983, 40). "The lowest field officer," as Handler (1979) notes, interprets rules and guidelines for specific cases. This idea was taken up in considerable detail in Lipsky's book *Street Level Bureaucracy* (1980). Each encounter with a client, according to Lipsky, represents an instance of "policy delivery." These encounters have important effects in entrenching policy on the personal level. For instance, they help to socialize citizens to social expectations and rules. Through the creation of precedents, they also determine eligibility for the services created through policy. Lipsky focuses on the collective behaviour of staff in public service organizations, arguing that their practical behaviour actually *becomes* the policy they carry out. "Street-level" workers, according to Lipsky, actually make policy in two ways. First, they exercise discretion on an individual basis, which is an expression of policy. Second, in its aggregate form, this discretion then becomes agency policy.

Swift (1995) used the terrain of child welfare to explore the way social workers help to create social policy development through their casework practices, including agency records. She examined how the individual decisions of "anonymous" social workers become the raw material through which the concepts of child abuse and neglect are developed and legitimized. Simultaneously, their records provide evidence of the individual failings of the clientele. This idea had previously been explored by Rein (1983), who observed that service intervention can actually magnify problems, especially for vulnerable populations. The rich, he noted, are able to sort out problems, using their own private resources to do so. The poor, on the other hand, become subject to a "problem formulation process," which then legitimizes the organization of services and creates identifiable "targets" for social policy.

Among other important insights developed by Lipsky is the mediating influence of the organization in the dialectic between individual workers and the policy level. Perhaps one reason social workers often fail to see clearly the relationship between social policy and their own everyday work is that policy is filtered through organizational processes and practices. Agencies themselves also set policy, which is much more visible to front-line workers than macro-level policy is likely to be, but which may be viewed by social workers not as policy but merely as agency "rules." Lipsky shows the importance of the "mezzo" or organizational level in the processes of both enacting and making policy.

What most of these theoretical perspectives have in common is the idea that policy is not simply a top-down process carried out by the social worker in everyday practice. Rather, there is a dialectic (or interactive) relationship between policy and practice through which policy is not only carried out but created, maintained, and changed by social workers in their everyday practice.

Practice Models

An impressive literature has developed exploring the ways social work can integrate direct practice skills and policy skills to forge a more effective practice. These models are discussed separately, but in fact most share core values and ideas: the dialectic between practice and policy, the "social justice imperative" (Figuera-McDonough, 1993), and a belief that the intersection of direct practice and social policy is the natural terrain and most powerful field of endeavour for social work.

Systems and Ecological Approaches

Beginning in the 1960s, systems theory and its heir, ecological theory (focusing on the relationship between individuals and their social contexts), began to be used and promoted as a method of integrating direct practice with social (or as social work uses the term, "environmental") issues. Systems theory, building on the sociological writings of Talcott Parsons and other sociologists, explored the interactions between people and the systems they are enmeshed in. Applied to social work (Schwartz, 1974), systems theory was posed as a bridge between the individual and the environment. A systems approach called for a "generalist" social worker, comfortable working and intervening in the social environment as well as directly with the individual. Johnson (1986), for instance, describes the generalist approach as requiring social workers to determine which "system" is the appropriate unit of attention for the change effort. She lists 26 social work approaches that might be employed, from the individually focused to the models of social action and social planning. Since the 1980s, ecological theory, as espoused in the writings of Germain and Gitterman (1980) and Hartman and Laird (1983), has found favour among social work students and educators. It seems to capture the relationships between people and their immediate surroundings in a concrete way that social workers can visualize and work with. Both systems and ecological theories focus on helping people cope with and develop within a social context. Although both approaches are intended to create a balance in social work activity between the two spheres, in practice it is direct work with individuals and families that is usually emphasized in recommendations of knowledge and skill development.

Certainly, both models have been critiqued. A serious criticism has been the assumption that once a need for social change is identified, it is easy to achieve it. As Wharf notes (1990), Canadian society has proven quite tolerant of the ongoing existence of major social inequities, including child poverty, racism, and violence against women. A related criticism is that these approaches fail to conceptualize power and power relations adequately. As a result, the knowledge and skill base evolving from systems and ecological theory does not include analysis of power elites, power bases, or power processes common in Canadian society. This critique suggests that social workers hoping to challenge and change oppressive social policies using systems or ecological approaches are left without appropriate tools to carry out this work.

Radical Practice

Developing alongside systems and ecological models of practice have been a number of social work practice models specifically aimed at challenging social policies and structures. Significant contributions to this literature were made by Galper (1975) and Bailey and Brake (1975), outlining an approach to social work based on understanding the position and problems of oppressed people within the social and economic structures of their lives. Leonard's contribution (1975) describes the aims of radical practice as:

1. education, referring primarily to consciousness raising;
2. linking people with systems to serve their interests; and
3. building counter-systems.

Referring to Marxist thought and analysis, Leonard proposed the exploration of the "contradiction" as a primary method for radical practice. Through this exploration, both misinformation and missing information can be identified and supplied to help explain relations between public and private experience. Recognition of contradictions experienced in everyday practice can reveal to social workers the discrepancies between expressed aims of social policy and the actual experiences of their clients.

Only toward the end of the 1980s, according to Thompson (1993), did social work education begin to take seriously the impact of racial oppression and discrimination on clients and communities. Earlier "radical" texts focused primarily on class analysis and referred only slightly to issues of race (and even of gender, notwithstanding the substantial contribution of feminists). Most of the major published theorists of radical practice were themselves white males. Furthermore, much of this work was premised on classical Marxist analysis, which did not include race, gender, or other forms of "difference" in its scope.

Dominelli's work *Anti-Racist Practice* (1988) and Thompson's work, *Anti-Discriminatory Practice* (1993), both published in Great Britain, offer well-developed analyses of the relationships between oppression and social work practice. They also explore practice methods and propose the kinds of policy challenges social workers must deal with at the policy-practice intersection. Through anti-discriminatory practice, a move away from the individualistic approach to an approach that emphasizes "difference" is proposed. The focus is clearly on the impacts of policies that assume, entrench, or subtly allow racism and other forms of discrimination to be perpetrated; and on the impacts and experiences of discrimination on the individual and the group. Thompson (1993) argues that any model of social work practice that does not take account of oppression cannot be seen as good practice, regardless of whether standards are high in other respects. Social workers play the role of mediators between clients and the state and its apparatus. The practitioner, Thompson notes, may be encouraged through policy to provide either care or control, and to enhance either empowerment or the oppression of individual clients. This idea builds on one of Leonard's (1975), who noted that social systems and policies can be both oppressive and supportive: it is a crucial function of social work to enhance the possibilities of the latter and reduce the potential for the former.

Thompson (1993) identified the essential building blocks of radical practice as:

1. an understanding of the social and political contexts within which their clients' experiences occur;
2. the acknowledgment of the danger that their own practice could contribute to and reinforce oppression; and
3. the recognition and use of opportunities for the emancipation of clients from oppressive circumstances.

These three precepts also inform related models of practice that attempt to explore the relationships between policy and practice, including feminist practice, the structural approach, and anti-discriminatory practice.

Closely related to both radical and anti-discriminatory models is the structural model, developed through the initiatives of such scholars as Moreau (1989) and elaborated by Mullaly (1993). The structural approach pays systematic attention to race, class, and gender in the assessment of individual problems presented to social workers. The practitioner's tasks include helping clients to recognize the structural antecedents of their problems and the social changes that need to occur in these social structures.

The client-practitioner relationship is less focused on therapeutic processes than on consciousness raising and mutual social critique. Roles of the practitioner emphasize advocacy, mediation, and brokerage.

Community Development Models

Wharf (1984) points out that community settings provide a mid-range location for aggregating and acting on personal troubles. For several decades beginning in the 1960s, community organization and development were recognized in schools of social work as comparable in importance to casework and group work. Community work could involve helping communities to become more self-sufficient, social planning tasks, and, most prominently, social action components. For some years, however, the viability of the community development approach has been receding, perhaps largely because those granting funds do not value social action and the possibility of public policy challenges as many in the social work profession do. Caragata (1997) argues that the skills of community development and organization should not only be preserved and used, but they should be incorporated into all facets of social work. The principles of community development, she argues, can help to build bridges between the macro and micro areas of practice. They also help to raise consciousness of clients concerning social change by involving them explicitly in any effort to change social structures. Further, community organization is helpful in strengthening communities that are under stress as the result of neo-conservative political agendas.

Wharf (1990) distinguishes between the organization of geographic communities and the organization of interest or policy communities. While the former has perhaps lost visibility and commitment over the past two decades, the latter—organizing on the level of interest groups—has remained lively well into the

1990s. An example is Campaign 2000, an effort to pressure the federal government to make good on its United Nations commitment to end child poverty by the year 2000 (Hay, 1997). Through this campaign, organized largely by social work practitioners and academics, a national coalition involving individuals, schools of social work, and community groups gained funding, carried out research, and launched widespread lobbying efforts. The campaign has created a high profile for the issue of child poverty and has produced media and public support for the goal of changing social policy to provide more generously for poor children and their parents. Even Paul Martin, federal finance minister, has publicly espoused this goal (*The Toronto Star*, November 20, 1998). The goal is far from realized, but pressure has successfully been put on the federal government to re-examine policy options and create a different approach, one aspect of which is the Canada Child Tax Benefit. While the Benefit proposal is far from perfect (Swift and Birmingham, 1999), its development does demonstrate that social workers committed to improving the lives of vulnerable children can, collectively, help to reshape the policy agenda.

Closely related to community organization approaches to social work are "alliance" models of connecting practice and policy. This approach is captured in Bishop's work (1994) *Becoming an Ally*. Through this method, social workers are encouraged to ally themselves with social movements such as labour unions, the women's movement, poor people's organizations, First Nations groups, and various coalitions, providing supporting activity and expertise in attempting to address social change goals. Texts advocating this approach often address themselves not to professionals at all but to large groups of like-minded people such as "activists" (Bishop, 1994) or "women" (Ricciutelli, et al., 1998). Contributors to *Confronting the Cuts*, for instance, include popular organizers, people "struggling at basic levels of subsistence," and those working for social policy reform. In other words, alliance-building approaches ask social workers to move beyond the "elitist" professional sphere to work with a wide variety of people toward common goals. This approach is often, but not only, taken "after hours" by committed social workers who have strong community ties and interests in addition to their "day jobs." It asks social workers to contribute to a cause that uses both their professionally gained knowledge regarding the effects of policy on individuals, and their professional practice skills in organizing and in policy development. This approach specifically works toward coalition building, combining skills and experiences to develop a stronger challenge for change.

Everyday Relationships between Policy and Practice

In the everyday world of work, social workers specializing in direct practice may find themselves feeling cut off from social policy and analysis, whereas those in social policy development and analysis may feel cut off from issues of direct practice. Even, or perhaps especially, in social work education, these two fields of endeavour have been conceptualized and organized separately, and they often appear as distinct "silos" (Caragata, 1997; Lightman, 1982) or even bunkers to both students and practitioners. Typically, social work courses are cast as either direct practice or as social policy. In the world of work, the skills and tasks of policy and direct practice also tend to be organized in different spheres, so that practitioners do not see themselves as involved in policy development, and policy analysts do not come into frequent contact with the people who are most affected by their policy efforts. Schorr (1985) pointed out some time ago that social workers in fact "practise policy" in everyday practice as they choose instruments to employ in their interventions, make decisions influencing organizations, and attempt to change policy. However, many social workers and students remain unclear about how policy is practised and how practice reflects policy.

In the dogma of the field, social policy analysts have generally been characterized as "progressive" while direct practitioners frequently labour under the stigma of being the conservatizing agents of the profession. However, as Lecomte (1990) observes, "all methods of social work have the potential to be conservative or progressive" (45). Much theory, as we have seen, directs us to see and act on the ongoing connections between these two apparently separate endeavours. In this section, the tasks and skills needed for work in each arena are identified, and the potential complementarity between them is emphasized.

Policy Practice

Popple and Leighninger (1998) refer to social work as a "policy-based profession." They argue that over the past century, professions, including social work, have become firmly embedded in organizations and bureaucracies. They also suggest that social work, along with some other professions such as the law, base their authority on mastery of complex cultural traditions rather than on precise and specific techniques. These two characteristics of social work legitimize, and in fact require, social policy as a central feature of the profession. Following theoretical formulations outlined earlier in the chapter, Popple and Leighninger cite several ways that social policy, including policy at the organizational level, shape the tasks and foci of direct service to individuals and families. First, policy determines the major goals of service. This process is well illustrated in the current climate in widespread shifts in public policy away from universal and accessible social welfare services to a "leaner, meaner" model of reduced budgets and privatization of service delivery. Second, policy determines the characteristics of the clientele. For instance, policies may grant services on the basis of marital status, physical or mental abilities, age, immigration status, and so on. Examples of such eligibility requirements can be seen throughout previous chapters. At the mezzo level, eligibility may be further defined geographically, or in terms of religion or other characteristics. Third, policy may specify and restrict service options. For instance, abortion counselling services may be restricted on the basis of the age of the mother. Finally, policy can determine the theoretical or ideological focus of services. In Canada, for instance, multicultural policy underlies ideas of "inclusive" service provision, while human rights policies direct attention to such issues as who is hired to deliver services.

Popple and Leighninger identify policy at three levels—*macro*, *mezzo*, and *micro*. Macro-level policy includes legislation and regulations formulated at the federal, provincial, and municipal levels. These policies, many of which are outlined and described in previous chapters of this book, set the basic framework for the provision of services and benefits. Mezzo policy involves administrative guidelines, rules, protocols, and precedents that "direct and regularize" operations (Popple and Leighninger, 1998). These operations, in turn, mediate between macro policy and service delivery, translating policies into response systems. It is often at the mezzo level that social workers attempt to translate and reshape policy. A Canadian model examining the importance of the mezzo level has been developed by McKenzie (1997), who points out that it is at the organizational level that the connections between policy and practice take on real meaning. Micro policy describes the transactions that occur as social workers deliver services to particular individuals and groups. This is the level of potential discretion described by Lipsky (1980).

Taking a somewhat different tack, Jansson (1990) examines the practice component of social welfare policy. His approach is based on the belief that contemporary realities require social work practitioners to become conscious and active participants in the shaping of social policy. Jansson suggests that serving the needs of clients in a climate of increasing inequality requires social workers to become more proactive in policy development. His recommended approach is termed "policy practice," defined as "....the use of conceptual work, interventions, and value clarification to develop, enact, implement, and assess policies" (25). Skills required for "policy practice" include:

➤ conceptual skills, including data gathering, identification of policy options, comparisons of merits of various options, and drafting of proposals;

➤ political skills, including exploring feasibility, locating power resources, and developing political strategies;

➤ interactional skills, involving developing contacts, building networks, developing and using group processes, and creating individual relationships; and

➤ value clarification skills, including identifying moral and ethical considerations in both proposals and strategies and determining how these considerations will shape strategy.

Of course, these same skills may be and frequently are used in direct practice. For example, in working with a client who has been cut off assistance, a social worker will analyze the relevant policy to determine if the client meets eligibility requirements, employ political skills to locate allies with the power to support access, use interactional skills to tap into potential helping networks, and explore the moral considerations of potential courses of action. Jansson demonstrates that conscious application of these skills extends social work options by bringing knowledge of policy to bear on problem-solving efforts with a client.

Practice to Policy

A different yet ultimately similar approach has been taken by McInnis-Dittrich (1994), who begins with the traditional problem-solving skills of direct practice, showing how they can be used in policy development. Steps in this model include:

➤ assessment of the problem, including information gathering, problem identification, identification of resources and obstacles, and goal setting. Needs assessment may also be included in this process, involving the development of procedures to locate community services required to meet needs. In this phase, specific facts and figures are accumulated to answer specific questions about needs;

➤ exploration of alternatives, considering a wide range of possibilities and their potential consequences;

➤ development of an action plan and selection of alternatives;

➤ implementation—translating plans into specific tasks and allocating them to particular people; and

➤ evaluation of results.

A comparison of the recommendations of Jansson and McInnis-Dittrich reveals considerable overlap in the kinds of skills recommended for both direct practice and policy work. Both require conceptual and planning tasks, political and relational skills, and ethical considerations, although the language used may be somewhat different.

Use of Power

Central, although often implicit, to all discussions concerning the interplay between policy and practice is the issue of power. Traditionally, social workers have been taught not so much about power but about authority. McInnis-Dittrich defines authority as "the position in which an individual's right to exert power over others is recognized and supported by those who grant that power and those over whom the power is exerted" (28). Certainly, we accept the authority of supervisors (most of the time), of executive directors, and so on. However, this traditional definition suggests that the existing relations that vest authority in some people are perfectly reasonable, normal, and not to be challenged.

Typically, the social work functions of authority and helping are not necessarily mutually exclusive (Kadushin and Martin, 1988). However, social workers often have considerable difficulty negotiating these apparently opposing functions in their everyday work (Swift, 1995). Furthermore, the business of challenging existing policies and practices very likely will involve questions about appropriate authority, including the authority vested in organizational bureaucracies through which most mezzo policy is made. It seems that the idea of authority and the way it has been addressed in social work literature have not offered sufficient or clear guidance to social workers in working to relieve oppressive conditions. A direct focus on power may be more helpful. Recent attention to the work of Foucault has made many social workers and students aware of the complexity of the concept of power (1972). However, as a profession we have been reluctant to acknowledge its importance in our work.

Power, Jansson (1990) notes, is inevitable but hard to observe or define. In any relationship, however, power will be present, perhaps several kinds of power, and power held by each person will continually shift in the course of action. Jansson usefully identifies several kinds of power that may appear in "policy practice."

One kind is *person-to-person power*. Resources for this kind of power are expertise, coercion, reward, charisma, and authority. This form of power is perhaps most familiar to direct practitioners, since they engage in much person-to-person interaction and are made aware in education and training of the potential for misuse and abuse of personal power. In a client-worker relationship, the worker may be presumed more powerful most of the time, because he or she brings the mandates, policies, and resources of the organization and of macro-level policy to the encounter. However, clients find ways to exert power as well. Resistance, withholding, avoidance, withdrawal, aggression, and dishonesty are all strategies employed by clients to assert themselves in relations they consider to be to their disadvantage. Clients, individually and in groups, may also try to influence a social worker to become interested in an issue, or to take up a cause. Both kinds of power can provide social workers with information about social policies that impact on the people with whom we work.

Substantive power involves the actual content of policy proposals. Those who attempt to shape policy spend considerable time on the minute issues of arguments and evidence supporting one position or another, and in discrediting alternatives. Constantly at play in this work is the question of how particular content will be received by different parties and with what consequences. Attempts to make policy changes appear non-threatening, and the inclusion of provisos such as time limitations demonstrate how this type of power is deployed. Jansson identifies a third kind of power as "procedural," which is often overlooked in discussions of power exerted by social workers. The skills of chairing and participating in meetings are used by all social workers at some time or other. Procedural skills can help ensure that a topic reaches the floor for discussion, that challengers are satisfied or avoided, that barriers are bypassed, and that rules of order are used to advantage.

A related type of power identified by Jansson is *process power*, through which the tenor or scope of an issue is set. Social workers generally become familiar with and use complex and sophisticated means to develop and encourage a process favourable to their cause. Team-building skills, tact, emphasis on opportunities for key players, timing, and broadening or restricting participation are all strategies used to influence processes, and therefore the outcome of a cause.

Finally, Jansson identifies the *power of autonomy* as effective in influencing outcome. This refers to the ability to develop policies of one's own, at times in defiance of existing policies. Social workers have considerable latitude in some situations to display this kind of autonomy. In some situations, a group of social workers might discover and share a common issue, and prepare a proposal for dealing with the problem. A proposal might involve a grant to fund a programmatic response, a suggested change in organizational policy, or a larger movement to challenge macro policy. Social workers are also at times inventive in resisting unwanted policies, for instance by circumventing certain rules they consider damaging to clients, or meaningless recording requirements.

In direct social work practice, uneven power relations between worker and client are somewhat hidden by the concept of the "helping relationship." As radical social workers have warned, unacknowledged power can increase oppression for the client. Social workers who want to decrease oppressive experiences need to be aware of how power operates in various facets of social work. Moreau (1989) identified five kinds of power that can be learned, practised, and brought to bear in direct practice with clients. One kind is *expert power*, including access to information, resources, and networks of help. Another kind of power is *referent power*, meaning the ability to attract others to a cause. Third is the power of numbers. Direct social work provides many opportunities to gather data about individuals and their experiences. In the aggregate, these data can provide powerful support for a cause. Fourth is *legitimate power*, for instance, that which parole officers, welfare workers, and child protection workers have. Finally, Moreau speaks of *coercive power*, the power to reward or punish. This kind of power may be overused in mandated forms of social work, and underused when challenging oppressive policies. Social workers can become more knowledgeable about their own power, and put it to use in service of the client. Because many social workers are women, and because women are not generally socialized or encouraged to take and use power, this remains an arena for further exploration and skill development.

Empowerment has become almost a cliché in social work, to the point that some people will not use this word. However, there can be no doubt that significant contributions to professional work have been developed under the label of "empowerment." Quoting Rappaport, Wharf (1990, 158) defines empowerment as "the process by which people, organizations, and communities gain mastery over their lives." In an unpublished study written by a Master's student (Marno, 1997), empowerment was related to various political ideologies. Marno found that neo-conservative policies have eroded the concept of empowerment as employed in social work. She concluded, however, that social democratic and Marxist ideologies can produce a practice of empowerment that explores one of the major contradictions facing social work—that social work draws its funding and legitimization from the very sources that activists seek to challenge. It is perhaps this contradiction that prevents many social workers and students from fully developing and using their considerable skills in both practice and policy arenas. The next chapter therefore assists social workers in further linking the practice and policy arenas.

Conclusion

New visions for resolving contradictions between the policy and practice worlds are being developed by social workers. These proposals grow out of concerns about the post-institutional characteristics of the welfare state described in Chapter 2. A generally shared proposition is that social work has the potential to redirect social welfare from control to caring. Dominelli (1997), writing from a sociological perspective, suggests that social work can be profoundly revolutionary, challenging governments' current focus on economic priorities, and arguing for human needs as the organizing force in developing new forms of welfare. Leonard (1997) also speaks of human need as a crucial focus for social work in the future. He describes welfare as an emancipatory project, requiring not only cool analysis but the strength of moral outrage. Wharf and McKenzie (1998) say the task of building a more humane social environment will require that social workers "surrender the desire to control." They recommend we focus instead on an "inclusionary practice" as the most important reform in human services.

How would social workers begin to address such a goal? Wharf and McKenzie (1998) propose the development of genuine alliances between practitioners and service users as the key to tapping the power of both practice and policy strategies. Such alliances can, in the long term, be practical and effective in the policy-development process. Without the serious input of those who need and use services, they point out, social policies are doomed to be incomplete and inappropriate, at best. These authors also propose the development of "vertical-slice policy groups" as a mechanism for creating a more inclusive practice. These are groups that involve people at all levels of a policy process, including social workers and service users. To increase the potential for creating and changing social policy, Dominelli (1997) suggests that local issues be brought to national and international attention. A recent example is the appearance at the United Nations of Canadian social workers protesting that the country's rating as the "best place to live" ignores our escalating rates of child poverty. Dominelli further suggests social workers focus on making connections among different forms of oppression and helping to develop new paradigms that account for these connections. Leonard's (1997) proposal is "welfare building," involving the construction of new policies and practices promoting human welfare. This project, of course, would require the power and resources of the state. His suggested strategy is the development of a "confederation of diversities," designed to create a movement or even a political party with sufficient power to wrest needed resources from the state. Such a movement, he suggests, might involve feminists, trade unions, anti-racist groups, and the ecology movement, as these are some of the more active and solidified social movements in contemporary times.

These and other emerging proposals require work, knowledge, and skills at the micro, mezzo, and macro levels. Among the threads that tie these visions together is the insistence that social work move beyond the "silo" approach so that the potential power of the practice-policy relationship can be fully realized.

Chapter (8)

The Policy-making Process

This chapter discusses how social policy moves from ideas into action. The first part of the chapter deals with how world views shape unique perceptions about society, people, and people in society and about how these unique perceptions simplify reality to conform to each world view. In other words, not only does each world view correspond to a conforming social policy, they also prescribe how that social policy is converted into public policies, programs, and services. For example, a world view conforming to a neo-conservative ideology would welcome inequality as a mechanism to promote competition and stimulate individual initiative and would not be concerned with equality issues when formulating public policies, programs, and services. On the other hand, a world view conforming to a social democrat ideology would highly value equality and insist that public policies, programs, and services promote greater equality. Moreover, each of these world views would also prescribe who is to be involved in the policy-making process and how power and decision-making authority would be distributed.

The remainder of the chapter examines different approaches to the policy-making process, including comprehensive, incremental, and other approaches. It is important to remember that each model for policy-making has advocates who believe that their model best serves the people of Canada. Much like world views, each model for policy-making is based on notions that value to varying degrees issues regarding citizen participation, political and economic power, evaluation and feedback, and other related areas, which are discussed in Chapter 9.

The following four short stories are intended to convey in narrative form the notion of world views or social constructions of reality and how these affect how we see the world.

Story 1: Imagine you and a friend are walking down a country road on a beautiful autumn day. As you turn a corner, you spot a cluster of maple, oak, and elm trees sporting a magnificent array of fall colours. For a moment, you are enthralled by the beauty of these colours reflecting against the brilliant blue of the sky. You experience a sense of wonder at nature's glory and feel content. Then your friend says: "Look at those poor leaves. All spring and summer they work to provide nourishment for the tree. Then in the fall, the trees remove the chlorophyll, the leaves return to their natural colour, and are condemned to die. What a shame! Can you imagine anyone admiring a dying leaf?" You feel embarrassed and say nothing.

Story 2: It is the month of June and you are driving down the Trans-Canada Highway in northwestern Ontario. You see a beautiful lake surrounded by trees and wild grass, so you stop to take a picture at the roadside. As you exit your car, you are immediately attacked by hordes of blackflies. Fighting off the flies, you quickly take a picture and get back into your car. At home, you proudly display an enlargement of the picture that always attracts comments of how beautiful and peaceful it looks and how people wish they were there right now. You remember the blackflies.

Story 3: It is 1944 and the International Red Cross sends a delegation to visit Theresienstadt, a ghetto the Germans claim to be a paradise for Jews. Prior to the visit, the ghetto is a flurry of activity as fresh paint is applied, rooms refurbished, activity centres created, and the Jewish people clothed and cleaned. When the delegation arrives, children are playing, music from live bands fill the air, food is present, arts and crafts are on display, and the Jewish people themselves are friendly and open. The delegation members, even with some reservations, will speak highly of this ghetto and the Germans' treatment of these Jewish people. When the delegation leaves, all food, furnishings, and clothes are removed, and the Jewish people begin an exodus from this camp by cattle trains to the horrors of the death camps and eventual "final solution."

Story 4: It is 1998 and Canada is experiencing positive economic growth. New jobs are being created, and the federal government and many of the provinces are moving toward balanced and surplus budgets. Employment Insurance is experiencing a billion-dollar surplus and workfare is being introduced in some provinces to give the poor an opportunity to get back into the workforce. Companies and governments are becoming more efficient, and private interests are being encouraged to become involved in public-sector activities. Canada is a viable member of the North American Free Trade Agreement (NAFTA) and has been invited to join an international consortium through the Multilateral Agreement on Investment (MAI). The economic health of Canada is vastly improving as governments free the private sector to conduct business.

World Views and the Policy-making Process

What do these stories have in common? Each illustrates how world views or social constructions can frame our notions of "reality" and why it is sometimes easier to simply believe these stories than to try to confront "reality" as critical thinkers. The first story, about the dying leaves, shows how difficult it can be when our assumptions about reality are challenged. One such reality today is the issue of poverty. The neo-conservative domination of Canada's media has presented a constant negative image of the poor: women having children so they do not have to work; people cheating on welfare; unemployed people taking advantage of Employment Insurance premiums; young people going on welfare so they do not have to listen to their parents; lack of common sense among the poor; and so forth (Saul, 1995). This has created the impression that everyone is relatively well-off in our society and if they are not, it is probably due to a character flaw or bad life choices they have made. Yet, as the Senate Committee on Poverty (1971) stated a generation ago, "the time has come for a little common honesty. The poor, after all, are not, as some still pretend, poor of their own accord….They are casualties of the way we manage our economy and our society" (xxvii).

The second story, about the photo and the blackflies, relates to what it is like to view society from a distance. When one is removed from the helplessness and hopelessness, the poor-quality housing and food, the violence, the tensions, the frustrations, the pain and the emotional injury, it is easy to see why people choose to remain where they are and not to be responsible citizens. When one removes poverty, soup kitchens, hostels, street kids, low-paying, no-benefit part-time and casual jobs, pay inequity, and minority discrimination, Canada is doing very well in the global economy.

The story about the Jewish ghetto alludes to the social cosmetics and "spin" that can be placed on reality. In Ontario, the recent decision to introduce private sector "boot camps" for young offenders was carefully orchestrated—only the best candidates were chosen, the process carefully followed, and the results well publicized and even mentioned in the Throne Speech. Young offenders are presented as really bad people needing to be shamed and disciplined with a firm hand—often the very reality that has shaped these young people in the first instance. Positive publicity for boot camps is given prominence by newspapers essentially owned by those supporting conservative government reforms.

And the final story, about Canada's current economic growth, discusses how social policy analysts are constantly confronted by stories being perpetuated by those in positions of public and economic power. Through the clever use of rhetoric and propaganda, these groups perpetuate social myths that are designed to minimize criticism and maximize conformity (Saul, 1995). For example, companies are not firing large numbers of employees, they are "downsizing." Furthermore, they are not downsizing to increase profits, but to demonstrate "fiscal responsibility." The reality, of course, is that governments are not in the business of promoting equality and protecting the welfare of its citizens, but in the business of profit-making (surpluses). Just as the Gulf War brought us terms such as "sanitizing" to mean killing people, corporations are inventing euphemisms that make governments and public workers seem uncaring and uneconomical, and corporate models and corporate leaders a necessity for proper management of human resources where there is "a rush to use machinery—inanimate or human—while these are still at full value; before they suffer a depreciation" (Saul, 1995, 162). Moreover, Clarke (1997) asserts that the Business Council on National Issues and its allied corporations have heavily funded the Fraser Institute, the C. D. Howe Institute, and the Reform Party with the purpose of whipping up anti-government-interventionist sentiment. Not only have these organizations been successful in creating a negative image of government, but they have also been able to hide the fact that they play a powerful, behind-the-scenes role in determining public policy-making in Canada.

The policy-making process is manifold. On the one hand, a prevailing social construction implicitly describes the social policy-making process of the time by ascribing privilege and power to those it favours and ascribing a reduced or nominal role for those it does not favour. It answers such questions as: "To whom do politicians listen?" "How are people appointed on commissions and other bodies studying public and social policy?" "Is there a process for making social policies?" "Do some people have a greater say on which social policies will drive society?" The answer to these questions lies in understanding how social policy is made.

There are many people who are involved directly and indirectly in the policy-making process. Some of these people, such as members of the governing party, have the power to legislate policies into law. Others, such as business leaders, wealthy individuals and families, labour leaders, and well-known entertainment notables, may become involved as advocates for policies that best reflect their own interests or values. Still others, such as consumers, average citizens, or interested people, may become involved in the policy process as advocates for policy options that are relevant to the communities in which they live.

As noted at the beginning of the chapter, everyone who becomes involved in the policy-making process brings their own world views and life experiences into the policy debate. From a social work perspective, Wharf and McKenzie (1998) suggest that policy-makers have a professional responsibility in the policy-making process to ensure issues of social development and social justices are included. Citing Flynn (1992), they suggest that the acronym SCRAPs (sexism, classism, racism, ageism, and poverty) is an important reminder to policy-makers that many of society's victims of discrimination only receive scraps from most policy initiatives. Reamer (1993) recommends an additional tool to assist social workers to evaluate the impact of policy on citizens and that is by exploring how the concept of equality is being applied. Reamer suggests that equality has a range of definitions, which include:

➤ Absolute Equality exists where resources, such as wealth, property, and access to services are divided equally among all people (also known as equality of result).

➤ Equality of Opportunity is concerned with the opportunity individuals have to gain access to desired resources. This might also include remedial services to enhance opportunities to compete for scarce or limited resources.

In order to enhance equality and minimize inequality, Reamer proposes the following mechanisms:

➤ Maximum Policy simply seeks to maximize the minimum, that is, to raise minimum standards for items such as income, housing, health care, and education.

➤ The Ratio of Inequality approach seeks to increase the resources of those worse off in relation to those who are better off.

➤ Least Difference Policy seeks to reduce the range of inequality.

➤ Mini-max Principle seeks to reduce the advantage of those who are most privileged, that is, minimize the maximum (27).

Review "Are you a Number One" in Chapter 1. Advocates of social justice are essentially seeking a social order where the societal distribution of resources and rewards is as just as possible and where exploitive inequalities are removed. Again, examine your own reality within the existing social order and search for what policy solutions would benefit you in relation to the distribution of resources and rewards and exploitive inequalities. You may wish to identify existing policies that continue to promote inequalities in your own life. You may wish to break into groups and share your discoveries. Are their common themes? Are there common solutions? Do you or members of your group feel disempowered to remedy inequality in your lives?

In a similar vein, Gil (1998) suggests that social work's Code of Ethics requires all social workers to integrate a social justice approach to their practice setting regardless of the resistance they will receive at their workplaces. To further these positions on social justice and social work, Titmuss (1974) warns that because social policies are simply choices that direct government action toward given social ends, social policies may very well promote or create social injustice, discrimination, and oppression. For example, apartheid in South Africa was a social policy, as was segregation in several American states. It is important to question all policy initiatives. For example, are the current neo-conservative and liberal initiatives toward the poor, women, children, and the unemployed further promoting social injustices, discrimination, poverty, and oppression? After all, these same initiatives have resulted in workfare, limited insurance for unemployment, reduced benefits for welfare recipients, reduced support for women's and minority's programs, reduced support for all levels of education, and reduced health-care benefits

While cuts continue to be made to social welfare, there is evidence to suggest that a large portion of Canada's national debt is due more to tax breaks and loopholes for wealthy individuals and corporations, and to high interest rates, than to government spending (Turk and Wilson, 1996; McQuaig, 1993; Mimoto and Cross, 1991). Yet government spending is where the majority of cuts have been directed.

The world views of the rich and powerful certainly shape Canada's social policies and help determine who influences policy decisions and the policy-making process. Of major concern to social workers has been the constant decrease in government funding to support organizations that promote the interests of those who are not rich and powerful. This, of course, means that not everyone is in the same position to influence the policy-making process, and indeed, some people may be purposefully ignored. Being ignored as partners in the constitutional debates leading to the Charlottetown Accord was one of the complaints levelled by native groups. Many people on Social Assistance have been upset by the failure of some provincial governments to invite or to include their opinions, experience, and knowledge in the policy-making process. This is especially true of neo-conservative governments, whose view of the poor is hostile and dehumanizing. Advocates of the poor attempted to use both public protest and the court system in Ontario to stop the severe cuts to Social Assistance recipients being sponsored by Mike Harris's Conservative government, on the basis that these cuts infringed upon their human rights. These efforts failed and the cuts remained and even deepened. Yet when the medical profession and the legal profession were angered over anticipated cuts to their domain, the government backed down and granted concessions.

Given that so many people representing so many interests and world views are involved in the policy-making process at many different levels of power and influence, understanding the process is not easy. It can best be understood within a framework that incorporates models of policy-making, the role of political ideology and power, institutional structures supporting the policy-making process, and participation in the policy-making process. The policy-making process is constantly influenced by such factors as globalization; dominant political ideologies; institutional structures; public values; social and economic power holders; economic prosperity; degrees of social and economic equality and equity; quality of social, political, and civil rights; and the degree of public participation. These, therefore, are some of the important variables that must be considered when examining the various approaches to the social policy-making process.

Models of Social Policy-making

The Comprehensive Approach

When comparing the social policies of different countries, social indicators representing quality-of-life measures are often used. These social indicators reflect how public policies, social institutions, social programs, and social services work in each country and how they influence the various elements that make up a society of people. For example, countries may be compared to each other based on the quality and availability of educational institutions and of health (physical and mental) resources; child poverty; the social equality of women; social welfare spending as a percentage of gross national product; criminality and correctional resources; child welfare services; and income security levels, among others. As such, social indicators provide a comprehensive overview of each nation's social policies in practice, and in turn, allow nations to be ranked based on the various social indicators.

The following provides a summary of representative models of social policy. These summaries are helpful to review and revisit as you proceed through the chapter.

The Rational Model (Simon, 1957)

This decision-making model suggests the following:

a. identify and clarify a social problem;

b. identify and rank goals with respect to that problem;

c. develop various strategies that can remedy the problems (or achieve the goals);

d. carefully examine all possible consequences; and

e. decide on which policy best achieves government/organizational goals.

Because this model deals with societal-level issues, Wharf describes them as "grand issues," which are known only to the policy-makers and are confusing to the public.

The Incremental Model (Braybrooke and Lindblom, 1963)

This model suggests that the rational model fails because it cannot account for everything and therefore must be incomplete at design level. This model instead views policy-making as "muddling through" by making incremental adjustments to existing policies. Because incremental approaches are clearer to the public, Wharf (1992) refers to these as "ordinary issues."

The Mixed-Scanning Model (Etzioni, 1967)

This model suggests that the substantive (political or social) issues need to be addressed by rational decision-making; then adjustments need to be made to the policy in order to reflect unforeseen social realities and unintended consequences.

Rights Model of Social Policy (Marshall, 1965)

This model argues that the best way to ensure the welfare of citizens is to institute entitlements to the following three rights for all citizens: 1) civil rights that guarantee individual liberty and equality before the law; 2) political rights that ensure the right to vote and seek political office; and 3) social rights that ensure equal access and opportunities to all social institutions. By assuring people these rights, social policy advocates would rely on the legal system to monitor and correct any abuses of these rights.

Titmuss's Three Historical Models (1974)

1. The Residual Welfare Model of Social Policy
This model argues that the private market and the family are responsible for meeting an individual's needs. Only when these break down should social welfare institutions come into play. This model is favoured by the neo-conservatives and economists such as Friedman and Hayek.

2. The Industrial Achievement-Performance Model of Social Policy

This model argues that social needs should be met on the basis of merit, work performance, and productivity. Known as the "handmaiden model," it is favoured by positivists and other economic and psychological theorists who advocate incentives, effort, and reward.

3. The Institutional Redistributive Model of Social Policy

This model argues that social welfare is a major integrated institution in society, providing universal services outside the market based on the principle of need. It is based on a model incorporating systems of redistribution in command-over-resources-through-time. In other words, society must ensure that major income redistribution systems, such as income tax and regional distribution transfers, are moving constantly toward achieving equality.

Values Competition Model (Rein, 1974)

This model suggests that social policy is, above all, concerned with choice among competing values. From this perspective, society consists of people holding diverse values (world views) who are in competition with each other and, consequently, each other's values, in an effort to achieve maximum power. Values are so ingrained in every aspect of social, economic, and public policies that a major role of policy-makers is to learn how to control their own values and prejudices.

Social Justice and the Comprehensive Model of Social Policy (Gil, 1992, 1970)

This model suggests that social policies are guidelines for behaviour, evolved through societal processes, which specify and maintain or transform the structures, relations, values, and dynamics of a society's particular way of life. As such, comprehensive and rational social policies are viewed as the forces that govern societal life and, therefore, must be of great concern to social workers and other human-service personnel. From this perspective, social policies are not only concerned with life-sustaining activities which ensure minimum basic needs, but also with life-enhancing activities that stimulate our human potential.

The Value Criteria Model (Gallagher and Haskins, 1981; Wharf and Mackenzie, 1998)

This model suggests that after determining what the problem is and what policy alternative is available to address the problem, value criteria, informed by universal and selective values, and cost-benefit analysis must be used to evaluate each policy alternative. In short, the best policy is the one that maximally reflects these value criteria.

The Garbage Can Model (Kingdom, 1995)

This model suggests that the three types of policy processes—problems, solutions, and politics—operate individually and independently until a crisis occurs that requires all three to come together. Resolving the crisis is dependent on 1) how the public perceive the problem, 2) what the current political agenda is, and 3) who the participants are. Getting an issue on the policy agenda becomes a function of whether or not there is a crisis or situation that creates a need for the three processes to come together.

There are those who believe that social policy should work in a similar manner. According to this view, politicians and policy analysts should determine what each country's social policies should be and then put these policies into practice. Social policy is viewed as the aggregate of all social indicators and, therefore, as a statement about society's overall social values. This approach is called the comprehensive approach to policy-making because it begins with global objectives based on social values and then translates these policies into public policies, social institutions, social programs, and social services. The advantage of this highly centralized approach is that policy is equally applied to all parts of a country. For example, when the Canada Assistance Plan was enacted in the late 1960s, it meant that the federal government had the power to ensure that all Canadians received equal treatment under the act, or the province could lose federal funding. The same is true for medicare, which also ensures that all Canadians have equal access to health care. On the other hand, the recent creation of Employment Insurance signalled a limiting of benefits to the unemployed. The disadvantage of the comprehensive approach is that it affects everyone equally, and is less sensitive to Canada's social and regional diversities.

To understand the impact of comprehensive policy approaches, consider the following: the Canada Assistance Plan (1966) was repealed in 1995. The federal Liberal government, committed to balancing the budget and reducing the public debt, determined it was better to negotiate lump-sum transfers of money to provinces rather than actual cost transfers. The Canada Assistance Plan originally paid 50 cents for each 50 cents the provinces paid for programs that qualified under the act, including Social Assistance. Most importantly, the act allowed for assistance to be granted to people in need or likely to become in need, thus allowing for prevention services. When the Canada Assistance Plan was repealed, it was replaced by Canada Health and Social Transfer Regulations with the enabling legislation being the Federal-Provincial Fiscal Arrangements Act (1985, 1995). No longer would the federal government cost-share actual program costs, nor could the federal government enforce standards. Canada's poor were no longer protected; soup kitchens and flophouses re-emerged, and Canada had lost an act that provided public policy protection.

At the same time, the government did not substantively change The Health Act (1984) even though health costs were greatly increasing. The Health Act provided a number of protections for citizens by imposing restrictions on the provinces in order to deter any form of direct patient charges and to provide citizens of all provinces with access to health care regardless of ability to pay. Moreover, the core principles of universality, comprehensiveness, accessibility, portability, and public administration remained.

The political right remains committed to dismantling all universal programs and to re-instating needs- and means-based programs that require meeting eligibility criteria. The argument is that this approach assures that those most in need receive the benefits, while those who are better off do not. Given this logic, what is next for medicare, one of the last remaining universal programs in Canada, if this world view continues to dominate Canadian social policy? The provinces of Alberta and Ontario have both begun to challenge the Health Act and both have committed to privatizing some parts of health care. Moreover, most provinces have reduced medical and prescription services covered by medicare. What do you believe it will take to turn this process around? How empowered do you feel in being a part of the effort to redirect these policies? Comprehensive policies often have a "power-over" feel to them and solutions are often limited to "power-over" strategies. You may wish to examine these issues by exploring the concerns raised by Jackson and Sanger (1998); Blake, Bryden, and Strain (1997); Finlayson (1996); McQuaig (1995); Wein (1991); and Carniol (1987).

The comprehensive view of social policy suggests that a scientific, rational approach to social policy-making is not only feasible but desirable. Social policy is about accomplishing what is termed *net value achievement*. Net value achievement means that all of what society values is known and that the policy-making process is about ensuring that the rewards gained from those values, which are chosen by the policy-makers, more than compensate for any values that may have to be sacrificed. For example, a country may value stable economic growth to the point where it may choose to control inflation by increasing interest rates. These increased interest rates will result in higher borrowing costs, making it more expensive for companies to borrow money and to have large inventories. This process usually concludes with companies laying off staff and creating more unemployment. Therefore, although the country may value employment, it may value stable economic growth more and be prepared to sacrifice employment for stability. The choice about which values are to be sacrificed is often a function of the value preferences of those who have the power to determine social and public policies. Analyzing social and public policy-making from this perspective often focuses on issues of economic, social, and political power and how this power is used to influence value-based policy choices that serve the interests of those with power. In the above example, had the workers themselves been consulted, they might very well have preferred to sacrifice some economic stability in favour of maintaining or increasing employment levels.

Social and public policies are often about struggles between value preferences and how some values become dominant and why. Rein (1974) suggests that social policy is about choice between competing values. From his perspective (see Figure 8.1), the social policy process stresses the interaction between values (input), operating principles (conversion process), and outcomes (output). Because Rein's model provides a comprehensive view of the policy-making process, it will be examined in some detail.

Rein's Model

People who hold positions of political and/or social power have disproportionate influence on which values (input) are to be held as important. When the debate about values is limited to ideological and world views and not to the real world and the needs of those people who inhabit that world, then the social policy process suffers from what Rein calls *detached ideology*, that is, choices are made strictly in accordance with one's values regardless of the outcome and consequences to others. In other words, statements such as "It is important to reduce employment in order to control inflation;" "Adjustments to the safety net are required if Canada is to overcome its national debt;" or "Social services must be limited to what a country can afford" are validated by the people in power espousing one particular value (in this case, economic well-being) to justify reduced opportunities and services (i.e., reductions in another value) for the average Canadian (social well-being).

Consider the following trap that detached ideology creates. The political right believes in deregulation, decentralization, and free enterprise. This globalization orientation also allows business corporations freedom from government intervention, while advocating for minimal government programs and a balanced or surplus (profit) government budget. What options are available to advocates of this ideology when confronted with raising costs, such as those associated with medicare? The Canadian Institute for Health Information (**www.50more.com/50mnewsweb/news/1372.htm**) reports that the cost of drugs is the fastest-growing segment of health care in Canada and is now second only to hospital costs. Obviously, controlling health costs would seem to be a logical policy direction, but would this ideology allow this to happen? Or would reducing health costs associated with medicare be the continuing alternative, while drug costs continue to spiral?

Meet in groups to discuss the following: How important is balancing the federal/provincial/municipal budgets and what priority should be given to achieving this goal? What factors do you believe have driven Canada's determination to achieve balanced budgets and to permit globalization to direct Canadian social and economic policies? Who do these policies benefit the most? Are the poor and marginal income groups being asked to carry the major burden in reducing the public debt? Is it possible for any government to escape its own detached ideology? How much of the discussion you are having is being influenced by each participant's detached ideology?

The input for social policy design and analysis are the values and ideologies of dominant political and social powers. In Canada and all democratic societies, governments are elected by the people to lead the nation. Part of that leadership is the implementation of the "political platform," which states the vision the party has for the country or the province. This vision reflects the world views and ideologies that constitute the value base for that political party. In other words, different political parties, such as the Liberal Party, the Bloc Québécois, the Reform Party, the New

Democratic Party, and the Progressive Conservative Party, inform the public of what they will do if elected.

Once in power, a majority political party can pass legislation that creates new social policies and affects existing social policies. These policies, called public policies, are a purposive course of government action designed to deal with issues of public concern (Anderson, 1990). Berkowitz (1980) notes that social choices made in the policy process only rarely benefit the interests of all without being adversely consequential to some. What can limit this universality is the political influence held by various alliances and interest groups in Canada. These influential groups can represent such diverse sectors as the economic/business sector; special interest groups such as the elderly, women, or people with disabilities; or international monetary institutions.

As noted in Chapter 1, when social policy becomes public policy, it also becomes legitimate, universal, and controls the forces of coercion. For example, Canada recently underwent a debate about gun registration, with many people disagreeing with or wanting amendments to the proposed registration policy. However, once the policy became law in late 1998, gun registration became mandatory regardless of different opinions (legitimacy); it applied to everyone in Canada (universal); and the police were sanctioned to enforce the law (monopoly of coercion). On the other hand, physician-assisted suicide did not become legal in Canada and it is therefore illegal (illegitimate) for anyone to assist in suicide, regardless of one's personal beliefs, with prison or a criminal record awaiting any who chooses to do so (use of coercion). In Holland, where physician-assisted suicide is legal provided all criteria

FIGURE 8.1   Rein's Overview of the Policy-making Process

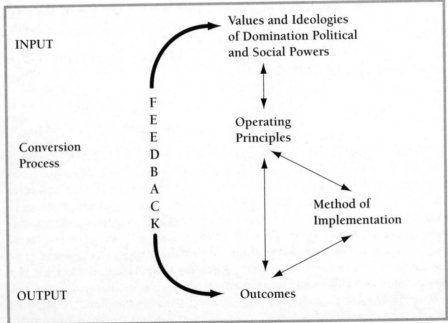

are met, it is legal for physicians to assist people with extremely painful terminal illnesses to commit suicide without having to worry about any social sanctions. Further discussion of this can be found in Chapter 9.

If a political party comes to power with a pro-business and anti-welfare state agenda, social workers can anticipate negative public policies regarding the poor and the disadvantaged. Wharf and Cossom (1987) warn of potential efforts to restrict the role of citizens in policy-making and policy decisions through *consociational democracy,* that is, "government of elite control designed to turn a democracy with a fragmented political culture into a stable democracy" (267). Marchak (1988) goes so far as to speculate the following: should the demands for the redistribution of power and wealth become public policy, the elites of Canada would break away from democracy and take power by force.

While these may seem like dire warnings, Saul (1995) identifies the modern corporate advocate as promoting economic objectives that are similar to those that were advocated by the early fascists in the early 1930s, namely:

1. to shift power directly to economic and social interest groups;
2. to push entrepreneurial initiatives in areas normally reserved for public bodies; and
3. to obliterate the boundaries between public and private interest—that is, to challenge the idea of the public interest (91).

A recent example of the use of power by Canada's economic elite is the 1989 Canada-United States free trade agreement, which eventually became the 1994 North American Free Trade Agreement (NAFTA). As Trudeau (1990) noted:

[T]he commendable goal of promoting freer trade has lead to a monstrous swindle under which the Canadian government has ceded to the United States of America a large slice of the country's sovereignty over its economy and natural resources in exchange for advantages we already had, or were going to obtain in a few years anyway through the normal operation of the GATT (385).

GATT is the General Agreement on Tariffs and Trade, which was adopted in January 1948. Not only did Canada give up a large measure of sovereignty, but thousands of Canadians lost their jobs as well.

Another major problem for social workers working with communities and with the poor is "social dumping," which occurs when corporations invest in countries with fewer labour rights and lower wages, thus driving down the wages and job security in Canada. The recent push to join the Multilateral Agreement on Investment (MAI) would have only served to enhance the rights of investing corporations and further weaken Canada's sovereignty (Clarke, 1997).

The *operating principles,* when combined with the methods of implementation, are the *throughput* or *conversion process.* Operating principles are "an attempt to integrate various social ideals with a practicable rule of application" (Rein, 1974, 297–298). These include universality, citizen participation, housing and in-kind benefit subsidies, earned access, equity, and other such principles that are held to be of value by society. Not all of these principles support a social work value system, and it is incumbent on social workers to carefully analyze and articulate the operating principles associated with social policy decisions and positions.

The *methods of implementation* consist of establishing various organizations, including social agencies, specifically designed or altered to provide the services prescribed by implemented social policies. For example, our social policies and public policies regarding children have resulted in a myriad of such social agencies as schools, Children's Aid Societies, Children's Mental Health Clinics, and Young Offender facilities. However, many of these agencies and the professionals within them can prescribe a particular value preference (children/youth should or should not be involved in agency policy-making, family is or is not the primary institution in a child's life, or children have or do not have the same human rights as adults) or practice methodology (psychotherapy, brief therapy, task-centred therapy, or community-based practice) as superior to all other values or practice methodologies. Therefore, when it comes to interpreting what a social policy is stating and how to carry out its operating principles, this prescribed value or practice methodology can in fact compromise the policy and operating principles to the extent that they become congruent with the prevailing value or practice methodologies. In effect, the agency or staff members could be doing the same thing but under a different name and could be acting in a manner that is counter-productive to the values and objectives of the new policy. This debate about the principles of implementation is known as *doctrinaire insulation* (Rein, 1974, 298). In Canada, other examples of doctrinaire insulation include situations where southern-based practice methodologies and specializations are applied directly to northern environments without adaptation and without citizen consensus, and public policies that do not account for the values and views of groups other than the policy-makers, such as women's groups, ethnic groups, religious groups, and gay groups (Delaney and Brownlee, 1995).

The output of social policy is its outcome. The importance of outcome centres on whether the outcome and the purpose of the social policy are congruent, and *in whose estimation*. Often social policy success is measured by social impact studies or by feedback from those whom the social policy was intended to benefit. However, the degree to which citizens are allowed not only to give feedback but to influence social policy is in itself a fundamental issue for social policy analysis.

Values, operating principles, and outcomes are viewed by Rein as being inseparable and in fact completely interrelated. Rein explains this interrelationship in the following manner:

Policies are in fact interdependent systems of: (1) the abstract values we cherish; (2) the operating principles which give these values form in specific programs and institutional arrangements judged acceptable for public support; (3) the outcomes of these programs which enable us to contrast ideals and reality; and (4) the often weak linkages among aims, means, and outcomes, and the feasible strategies of change this pattern suggests (298).

Rein's perspective of the social policy design and analysis process provides a method that allows social policies and public policies to be analyzed by social workers.

Gil's Model

Another social policy theorist who supports Rein's notions of value-driven social policy is David Gil (1998; 1992). From Gil's perspective, human beings and human development should form the basis from which social policy is determined. Gil believes that over human history, systemic inequalities have been introduced into societal practices that have resulted in social arrangements that benefit selected members of society and disadvantage the remaining members of society. He calls this process *patterned inequalities* and suggests that, over time, people do not even recognize the injustice or the inequalities created by certain groups claiming or taking power over social, political, and economic systems in society. The result is the creation of social institutions that serve to benefit the interests of the few, while dehumanizing, marginalizing, discriminating against, and/or oppressing the many. Gil believes that most societal violence stems from the damage these social institutions do to people.

Gil argues that social policy must serve to promote and enhance human development and potential and in doing so, serve as "guidelines for behaviour, evolved through societal processes, which specify and maintain or transform the structures, relations, values, and dynamics of a society's particular way of life" (Gil, 1992, 21–22). Gil offers a comprehensive, rational definition of social policy as a set of guiding principles that govern societal life, and therefore must be of great concern to social workers and other human service personnel. In effect, social policies should control all other public policies, excluding religion and foreign trade, but including economic policies.

From this perspective, social policy should reflect long-range visions of what a just and non-oppressive society would look like (Gil, 1998). This vision also stresses values and ideologies affirming equality, individuality, liberty, cooperation, community, and global solidarity rather than the currently prevailing values and ideologies that support inequality, individualism, selfishness, domination, competition, and disregard for community. For example, if Canada and other nations used the *Universal Declaration of Human Rights,* as adopted by the United Nations on December 10, 1948, as the centrepiece for all social policy, then all social policies would have to conform to this declaration in order to be established as public policies. Under the UN document, Canada committed to eradicate poverty and ensure basic human rights.

Gil's comprehensive view of the social policy-making process suggests that social policies should govern natural and human-created resources; all aspects of employment, including human issues; the production of life-sustaining and life-enhancing resources; social, political and civil rights; mechanisms for the distribution of rights and privileges; and mechanisms for the assignment of social status (Gil, 1992, 24–25). Therefore, all social problems are the result of a flawed social policy, and the policy, not the problem, needs to be redressed. As such, social policies are "potentially powerful instruments for planned, comprehensive, and systematic social change rather than reactive measures designed to ameliorate (in a fragmented fashion) undesirable circumstances" (Gil, 1970, 413). The primary domain of social policy is "all possible sets of human relationships and the quality of life or level of well-being in a given society" (415).

An important feature of Gil's approach to social policy is his insistence that social policies must not only address life-sustaining activities that ensure minimum basic needs, but also life-enhancing activities that promote and support human growth and potential. Social change theorist Paolo Freire (1968) argued that every person has an "ontological vocation," that is, each person is born with the desire to search for meaning in his or her life. Society that oppresses begins by thwarting this drive to maximize one's humanity. In this sense, Gil agrees with Freire that the ontological vocation for humans is to become more fully human and that social policy should be a mechanism to ensure that all humans have equal opportunity and equal access to society's resources to this end.

Swift (1995) suggests that existing social policies do in fact discriminate against the poor and in particular, poor women. In order to gain resources, mothers "must appear incompetent in order to qualify for the resources" (125) and, in effect, present themselves as failed mothers. And yet the alternative is to live in poverty with inadequate resources, with the result of many mothers being labelled "bad mothers" rather than people who have been failed by society. Similar criticisms of social policies, as they relate to other areas of social diversity, are outlined in Chapter 4.

For social workers, Gil's notion of social policy conforms to the profession's value and ethical base. Having social policy address the challenges and realities that make up the human condition is certainly an ideal to be espoused and sought. Making the interests of all people, their families, and their communities the first principle for societal governance places the emphasis on *the common good* rather than the *public* or *private interest*. As social welfare philosopher Frederic Reamer puts it, there is a substantive difference between the common good and the public interest, with commensurate implications to social policies. Social policies are decisions made from competing choices that reflect societal values regarding the quality and amount of life-sustaining and life-enhancing resources to which all citizens are entitled. As such, social policy is concerned with issues regarding the common good rather than the public interest. The common good refers to "that which constitutes the well-being of the community—its safety, the integrity of its basic institutions and practices, the preservation of its core values" and human end-states such as human flourishing and moral development. While originally referring to national security and prosperity goals, the public interest has now come to mean "a rational alliance of primarily self-interested individuals whose collective good is constituted by the collection or aggregation of private interests" (Reamer, 1993, 35). Thus, the public interest is promoted by enhancing an individual's pursuit of his or her own interests. It may be argued, moreover, that social workers, having a particular commitment to social justice for society's most marginalized, hold notions of the common good as sacrosanct.

Implementing Gil's approach would require a society to agree on what set of values should govern social policies, and achieving such consensus is highly unlikely. In societies where political, ideological, and economic power is in the hands of fewer and fewer people (Bishop, 1994), it is unlikely that this degree of social transformation will occur. For these powerful people, life enhancement is to be earned and society is responsible only to provide minimally life-sustaining activities, if that.

An Incremental Approach

Other social policy theorists do not take as comprehensive a view of social policy as Rein and Gil do. Wharf (1992) distinguishes between the *ordinary* and *grand* issues of social policy. Wharf defines *grand* issues as "those pertaining to the fundamental structure of political-economic life" (14), including distribution of income and wealth, political power, and corporate prerogatives. *Ordinary* issues of social policy include "the governance of child welfare services, deinstitutionalization and the development of community support programs, the struggle to raise social welfare rates in Ontario, and the debate about abortion politics in Nanaimo" (15). Wharf argues that *ordinary* issues should be of concern to social workers because these issues directly affect the lives of people, can be managed and redressed by community-based organizations, and are sometimes the unintended consequence of earlier reforms.

When dealing directly with the *ordinary* issues of social policy, social workers often employ the rational decision-making model that is used by the incrementalists. The incremental model views the social policy-maker as having to:

➤ define and rank governing values;

➤ specify objectives compatible with these values;

➤ identify all relevant options or means of achieving these objectives;

➤ calculate all the consequences of these options and compare them; and

➤ choose the option or combination of options that would maximize the values earlier defined as being important (Hogwood and Gunn, 1984, 46–47).

Wharf (1992) makes note of the "goal-directed-muddling-through" approach to the policy process (where goals emerge in a way that might not be clear at the outset of the intervention) that is used by community workers. This inductive approach allows the community worker to ensure that the people's interest is made known and that the policy process is "anchored in a philosophical position and a vision for change" (233). Because it allows a high degree of flexibility, practice wisdom, and discretion in pursuing objectives, Wharf believes it is an adaptive approach to policy-making. For most social workers who will only rarely be exposed to global social policy issues, being directed by the values and ethics of social work is often the only firm base they have in policy.

A criticism of this incremental approach is that social workers and other human service workers become too preoccupied with resolving local or immediate issues stemming from social policy and do not pay sufficient attention to the social issues that may be creating the problem in the first place. For example, when the new Employment Insurance program limited the time people were able to collect benefits, many regions with high seasonal unemployment organized against this policy. Unfortunately, the Liberal government that introduced these changes appears committed to globalization and to a right-wing policy agenda (Clarke, 1997). How then is the Liberal government's policy position best attacked? Will results be obtained from local (incremental) efforts to challenge this policy, or national (comprehensive) initiatives that challenge the policy direction this government is taking?

The Mixed-scanning Model

Etzioni (1968) argues there may be a method of reconciling the differences between a comprehensive policy-making process and an incremental policy-making process. The "mixed-scanning model" can bridge the gap between these two approaches. After a rational, comprehensive policy decision is made, adjustments to the policy are made incrementally, based on information gained from its implementation. By accounting for the need to make adjustments incrementally, policy-makers can give their attention to the greater issues without becoming bogged down in details (Hess, 1993).

In terms of understanding the sequencing of the policy-making process, Table 8.1 presents the following frameworks that address how policy is made.

The *policy agenda* refers to the need to identify problems in a priority manner and to make this known to those in policy-making positions, such as government officials. *Policy formulation* refers to the development of a clear and acceptable manner in which the problem can be resolved or at least addressed as a policy. *Policy adaptation* refers to the development of support and acceptance for the policy by such means as advocacy and accommodation. *Policy implementation* refers to the actual application of policy to the problem. *Policy evaluation* seeks to answer whether or not the policy worked.

Anderson's policy-making sequence is rational and easy to understand, but it fails to address who is benefiting from these policies and why policies are directed to their benefit (Mason, Talbott and Leavitt, 1993). While Wharf's sequencing of social policy appears similar to Anderson's, his approach is much more analytical and substantive, with a very clear community-organization perspective. Concern is expressed about which people are involved in the policy-initiation process;

TABLE 8.1   Sequencing the Policy-making Process

Anderson (1990)	Wharf (1992)	Wharf & McKenzie (1998)	Rein (1974)
Policy Agenda	Initiation	Problem Identification	Values
Policy Formulation	Formation	Identification of Value Criteria	Operating Principles
Policy Adaptation	Execution	Assessing Alternatives	Method of Implementation
Policy Implementation	Implementation	Feasibility Assessment	
Policy Evaluation	Evaluation	Recommendations	Outcomes

whether the problem the policy is addressing is correctly defined or whether it can be redefined; and whether sufficient resources, including people and funding, are available. Rein, like Wharf, recognizes that the policy-making process is not linear and that each stage is subject to problems and to political manipulation.

Wharf and McKenzie (1998) propose a social policy decision-making approach, the Value Criteria Model, which is inclusive—that is, it involves practitioners and those receiving services. The Value Criteria Model suggests that after defining the problem and the policy alternatives, value criteria (universal and selected values) and cost-benefit analysis should be used to evaluate each policy alternative. Policy decisions would have to maximize these value criteria with the clear support of all stakeholders in the policy process. Wharf and McKenzie also discuss the Garbage Can Model, which suggests that the three types of policy processes (problems, solutions, and politics) operate independently until a situation or crisis arises. Then all three processes come together. The resolution will depend on what the current public perception of the problem is, what a current political agenda may be, and/or who the participants are. If a particular issue does not get on the policy agenda, then it may have to wait until a new opportunity arises or it may be removed if it appears to be resolved. In other words, whenever there is a public concern, such as those being expressed over water quality in Ontario or farm subsidies in the western provinces, then all components come together. When the crisis is over, they separate again, only to be re-engaged when another crisis strikes. While these processes are separated, there is little opportunity for social change.

The importance of understanding the deductive, comprehensive approach is that it allows social workers to understand both the anticipated and unanticipated impacts of social policy, as well as potential or actual shifts in social policy in Canada. Understanding the social and public policy process allows advocacy strategies to benefit the person-environment fit of the people that social workers serve. As Pierce (1984) notes, "social workers also need to be able to identify policies that actually constitute a part of their practice world. If policy is to be used in generalist practice, its definition must come from the practice parameters and perspectives of line social workers" (4). However, the policy analyst should keep Wharf's (1990) cautions regarding four limitations associated with generalist practice models based on the ecological systems perspective. These are:

➤ The assumption that problems, once identified, will generate a demand for change, that is, change will occur and the problem will be solved.

➤ It ignores power and its distribution in Canada, that is, goodness-of-fit for the rich is good to excellent, while the goodness-of fit for the poor is bad to terrible. Who has the power and the will to change this—the rich who are benefiting?

➤ Social workers are not assigned responsibility by society to bring about change.

➤ It does not address the issue of auspices, that is, the fact that social workers work in agencies that are given their mandates by those holding political power. The social worker's efforts to change the system are limited by each agency's political and social agenda.

Controlling the Policy-making Process

If anything is apparent from the preceding discussion on policy-making approaches, it's the number of factors that can derail the policy-making process. In Canada, there are four major types of pressure groups involving social policy:

➤ business groups, including the Canadian Manufacturers' Association (CMA) and the Business Council on National Issues (BCNI);

➤ labour groups, including the National Labour Congress;

➤ professional groups, including the Canadian Association of Social Workers and the Canadian Association of Schools of Social Work; and

➤ advocacy groups including the Canadian Council of Social Development, the National Anti-Poverty Association, and the Canadian Welfare Council.

The most successful groups over the past few decades have been the business pressure groups that seek to create a context where all organizations, businesses, governments, and non-profit groups are structured on a corporate model. Corporate models essentially reflect a "power-over" (Bishop, 1994) approach promoting the value of competition, hierarchy, and separation. Separation here refers to a social vision where citizens are not responsible for each other but where groups of citizens may unite to promote their best interests against the best interests of others. Bishop suggests the end product of this type of "power-over" approach is a society infused with "sexism, racism, ageism, adultism, heterosexism, and ableism" (21). The question is simply this: what is needed to motivate people who are benefiting from the existing system (and who have the political, economic, and ideological power to maintain their advantage) to share their benefits with those less fortunate?

Consider the following example. Cancer patients in southern Ontario who had to travel to Northern Ontario or the United States for radiation treatment have their travel, hotel, and food expenses covered by Cancer Care Ontario. A Northern Ontario resident who travels to southern Ontario is not reimbursed equally. In one example reported in *The Globe and Mail* (June 11, 2000, A3), a cancer patient from Iroquois Falls travelling to Sudbury about a half dozen times received $109.89 in support payments. Cancer patients travelling to Northern Ontario from southern Ontario received approximately $5,000. The reason: Northern Ontario patients are covered by Northern Health Travel Grants and southern Ontario residents are covered by the generous Cancer Care Ontario. The same problem (radiation required), travelling in opposite directions for treatment, makes a difference of $4,900.

By limiting resources to those less well-off (such as the unemployed, the poor, the marginal income earners, and many postsecondary students) or in need of protection (such as abused children, battered women, and dependent elderly), an environment of competition exists where failure to secure funds can result in human hardship. For example, the simple tightening of Employment Insurance criteria has eliminated thousands of people who work in seasonal jobs from receiving benefits. Reducing Social Assistance and introducing tighter eligibility criteria has forced thousands of people off welfare. Reducing public housing projects ensures that thousands of people live in inadequate housing, which many cannot even afford. Reducing subsidies for women's shelters ensures that many women are left horrific options should they need to flee a dangerous home situation. These are all current examples of human deprivation and suffering in one of the world's richest countries—Canada. How can a nation such as Canada justify there being more food banks than McDonald's restaurants?

Social policy advocates, such as Banks and Mangan (1999) and Wharf (1992), have increasingly understood the need to engage the community in the policy-making process. By engaging the community, policy advocates can also link with existing community resources, such as local social and economic planning councils and citizen advocacy groups. These linkages not only ensure that the policy issues being discussed are relevant to the community, but that obstacles to policy development are also identified. Policy advocates are also in a position to translate new policy initiatives and existing public policies in terms that communities can understand, both with respect to what these policies are about and the potential impact to these communities.

Controlling the policy-making process is one of the major challenges facing policy advocates. Not only do political interest groups control the government public policy-making mechanisms, they also play a large role in the economic life of Canada and its communities. Advocates for progressive social policies based on social justice must put away their individual differences (avoiding separation) and unite as allies seeking the same end despite different self-interests. As Bishop (1994) notes, "Commitment to social justice means beginning a completely unknown journey—a journey that can unfold only one step at a time, with confusion and danger along the way" (124).

Conclusion

This chapter began by exploring how different world views shape unique perceptions about society, people, and people in society. The chapter also examined the power of world views to convert social policy into public policies, programs, and services and to prescribe who is to be involved in the policy-making process and how power and decision-making authority is to be distributed. Finally, different approaches to the policy-making process were discussed.

Every model of social policy-making has its supporters and distracters. Academic debate still flourishes around which model is most effective and which model is least effective. However, the tightening of control over the policy-making process in Canada by those with the most economic and political power signals a challenge to advocates for social justice to unite in a common cause—to let Canadians know "the other side of the story." Chapter 9 discusses issues associated with implementing social policies and strategies to bring social justice to the forefront of public policy in Canada.

Chapter 9

Implementing Social Policies

The goal for all advocates of a specific social policy is to shape the public landscape in a manner that reflects the values and objective of their policy position. This chapter discusses how this is accomplished. For example, when the Harris government was elected June 1995, the government began an unprecedented dismantling of pre-existing legislation and social programs in order to radically transform Ontario to conform to its vision. Dare (1997) details major changes made by the Harris government to include:

➤ disbanding the Workplace Health and Safety Agency (incorporated by Worker's Compensation) and eliminating worker input;

➤ limiting the Wage Protection Fund, which included wages, benefits, severance, and termination pay, to just wages and benefits;

➤ reinstating the "spouse-in-the-house" rule, where single women who are alleged to be living with a man are cut off welfare, and imposing a three-month wait for welfare if one quits their job;

➤ cancelling 390 co-op and non-profit housing projects;

➤ cancelling Jobs Ontario and closing 25 half-way houses for offenders;

➤ passing Bill 7, the Labour Relations Employment Statues Act, which dismantles all NDP law reforms;

➤ cutting welfare rates by 21.6 percent , Ministry of Health by $1.5 billion dollars, school boards by $1 billion dollars, and grants to municipalities by 48 percent over two years.

All of the above changes and many more happened in only five months. The list of changes for the first year would take many pages. The result of all of these changes is that the Province of Ontario has undergone a major social and economic shift—a shift that brought Ontario's public policies into line with the Harris government's vision of social and economic policies. Significant changes have also occurred in other provinces, such as Manitoba and Quebec, when new governments with strong policy positions were elected.

This chapter will explore how laws are made in Canada (both federally and provincially); what laws look like and their importance; the role of courts in the

policy-making process; how power and influence play a major role in policy selection; and the role of citizen participation in this process.

The Canadian Political System

Like the United States of America, Switzerland, and Australia, Canada is a federal
state. A federal state recognizes that having a federal government to promote the
best interests for the whole country is required to offset the diversity and chaos that
can be created by having each province seeking its own best interests. Canada has
two major forms of government—federal and provincial—built on a parliamentary
model with a constitutional monarchy. The British North America Act, 1867 (also
know as The Constitution Act, 1867), and currently, The Constitution Act, 1982,
establish the governance domains for both the federal and provincial governments.
While the territories—Nunavut, Northwest Territories, and the Yukon—are based
on similar parliamentary models as the provinces, they are headed by a
Commissioner rather than a Lieutenant Governor.

The federal parliament governs issues associated with Canada as a nation and
makes laws to support the peace, order, and good government of Canada, such as
international agreements and the right to levy taxes across the country. A provincial legislature is empowered to govern issues associated with the province, including hospitals (except marine hospitals); natural resources; municipal and
provincial institutions; property rights; marriages; social services; and the right
to levy taxes for provincial purposes.

> To learn more about the history of the Canadian parliamentary system of
> government, visit **www.parl.gc.ca/information/library/idb** on the Web or
> check out Landes, R. (1998), *The Canadian polity: A Comparative Introduction*,
> (5th Ed.). Scarborough: Pearson.)

At the federal level, Canada has a Governor General (representing the Queen
of England), a Senate, and a House of Commons. The members of the Canadian
Senate, called senators, are appointed by the Prime Minister. The members of the
House of Commons, known as members of Parliament (MPs), are elected from
across Canada and its territories. The executive authority for Canada is vested in
the Queen who is represented by the Governor General (the Lieutenant-Governor
in provinces). The Governor General governs through cabinet, which is headed by
the Prime Minister, who is the leader of the political party with a majority of seats
(or the largest minority party if no majority is elected as determined by the Governor
General). The cabinet, which is the Executive branch of government, consists of
MPs, known as Ministers, selected by the Prime Minister and assigned specific

ministries. These Ministers are responsible for all policy development within their ministerial portfolio and the promotion of these policies in cabinet. Obviously, a strong Minister will achieve greater success in moving policy to law or programs.

The Legislative Branch of government essentially consists of the House of Commons, including all parliamentary committees. Should the Governor General become incapacitated, the Chief Justice of the Canadian Supreme Court is appointed as Administrator of Canada and serves on behalf of the Governor General.

At the provincial level, there is a Lieutenant-Governor (representing the Queen of England) and a Legislative Assembly. The same process as the federal government exists, except that the head of the provincial cabinet is called a Premier. Members of the Legislative Assembly (also known as Provincial Parliament in some provinces) are known as members of the Legislative Assembly (MLA) or members of the Provincial Parliament (MPP).

Making Laws

The initiative to create a new law or reform an existing one can come from various routes. For example, strong public opinion, such as the current attitude toward terrorism, can influence Ministers, as can people lobbying for industry or other interest groups. As noted in the beginning of this chapter, a political platform for newly elected governments can also shape political opinion. The bureaucracy for each Ministry can also promote public policy initiatives based on their own operations, including program evaluations and need surveys.

> There are many routes from which laws can originate, but some routes are more effective than others. Explore this further by reading newspapers, magazines, and public opinion surveys and search for the answers to the following questions: Who is sponsoring the proposed new or reformed legislation? Who is likely to benefit from this legislative initiative? Who is likely to be negatively affected?

When there is a draft of the proposed legislation, called a bill, the Minister will introduce this to the House of Commons or Legislative Assembly. However, before it gets to this stage, the essential policy debate regarding this bill will have occurred in cabinet. The policy is then considered by appropriate committees of cabinet, including the Treasury Board (see: **www.canada.gc/howgoc/cab/ministry_e.html** for further information on the cabinet and its committees). Other constituents, such as the party's caucus (elected members of the ruling party), will also be involved in discussions, particularly for controversial or marginally supported bills.

In order for a bill to become law, it must be introduced to Parliament. Provincially, this is to the Legislative Assembly, and federally, either the House of

Commons or Senate. It must then pass three separate readings. Generally, bills are sent to committees composed of representatives from all parties, where some fine-tuning and minor amendments may occur.

There are two common types of bills. Public Bills are generally introduced by the appropriate Minister and are proposals that will impact the public as a whole. Private Bills usually concern individuals or local matters. However, there are also Private Members' Public Bills, Private Senators' Public Bills (federal only), Private Senators' Private Bills (federal only), and Senate Government Bills. To explore federal government bills, see: **www.parl.gc.ca/common/bills_about?Language+E&Parl+37&Ses=1**. At the provincial level, the Province of New Brunswick offers an excellent review of the provincial legislative process, which is located at: **www.gov.nb.ca/legis/billhtme.htm**.

Federally, once a bill passes three readings in the House of Commons, it then goes to the Senate, where the process is repeated. If it passes all three readings in Senate, it goes to the Governor General for royal assent. Once it passes all of these steps, it becomes law. Provincially, the bill becomes law once it passes its three readings in the provincial Legislative Assembly and receives royal assent by the Lieutenant Governor.

Each Department or Ministry in the federal and provincial government has statutes (acts), which empower these ministries and departments to do their business. For example, the Minister assigned to the Department of Family and Community Services in New Brunswick works under the following statutes: Charitable Donation of Food, Family Income Security, Health Services, Intercountry Adoption, Nursing Homes, Family Services (except Part 7), and Vocational Rehabilitation of Disabled Persons. As well, it operates under some sections of Change of Name, Education, Employment Standards, Hospital and reciprocal Enforcement of Maintenance Orders statutes. It is important for social policy advocates to know which acts govern which ministries or departments and to become familiar with those acts that affect their work.

The Internet provides ready access to provincial and federal ministries and departments. Most sites allow for downloading or printing acts and regulations associated with the different ministries. Try looking up ministries or departments that interest you and examining their enabling statutes. The sites are: **www.gov.nf.ca** (Newfoundland and Labrador); **www.gov.pe.ca** (Prince Edward Island); **www.gov.ns.ca** (Nova Scotia); **www.gov.nb.ca** (New Brunswick); **www.gouv.qc.ca** (Quebec); **www.gov.on.ca** (Ontario); **www.gov.mb.ca** (Manitoba); **www.gov.sk.ca** (Saskatchewan); **www2.gov.ab.ca/home** (Alberta); **www.gov.bc.ca** (British Columbia); **www.gov.nt.ca** (Northwest Territories); **www.gov.yk.ca** (Yukon); and **www.gov.nu.ca** (Nunavut).

Municipal governments located in cities, towns, villages, counties, districts, and metropolitan regions throughout Canada are established by the provincial legislatures. The powers accorded to municipalities are granted by the provincial and territorial legislatures. Officials, such as mayors, reeves, and councillors, are elected on a basis that the provincial legislature prescribes.

Municipal governments provide an array of services, including water supply, sewage and garbage disposal, roads, sidewalks, street lighting, building codes, parks, playgrounds, and libraries. Different provinces, such as Ontario, have granted municipalities a greater role in social welfare programs. For example, Ontario Works (1997) located workfare and Social Assistance in municipalities. Schools are generally looked after by school boards or commissions elected under provincial education acts.

As noted in Chapter 1, laws are powerful instruments that impact all Canadians. Whether or not a bill, or some component of it, is highly controversial, once it becomes law, all citizens must obey it or suffer some sanction, such as fines or even imprisonment. Certainly, issues such as capital punishment, abortion, and marriage definitions, are still in the public agenda for discussion, but laws exist that frame current behaviour options. Nevertheless, there are some options open to people who believe their rights are being infringed.

The Court Option

Canada has two levels of courts: federal and provincial. While the Constitution provides that most courts are created by provincial legislatures, judges from county courts up are appointed by the federal government (with the exception of probate courts in Nova Scotia and New Brunswick). The federal government in Canada, under the Judges Act (1952), appoints and pays for all federally appointed judges. However, removing judges is a different issue. Judges of the provincial supreme courts (Superior Court in Quebec), the Federal Court, and the Supreme Court of Canada may be removed by the Governor General only. This provides these courts with a great deal of independence from governing parties. Nevertheless, judges are appointed by a governing party and there is a tendency for parties to select judges who reflect their political ideology or orientation. A judge with a neo-conservative orientation may adjudicate differently on the same issue than a judge with a social democratic orientation.

People who believe their rights are being violated, or who wish to contend how a particular act is being interpreted, may address their grievances through the court system. What is important is that the ruling of the Supreme Court of Canada is final. This process is very expensive and time consuming, but is still an option for advocates of human and social rights to redress social injustices. For example, the Supreme Court has been asked to rule on such issues as the right of gay partners to receive the same employee benefits as the partners of heterosexual employees; the right of an individual to have physician-assisted suicide; and the right of citizens to practice active euthanasia.

Power and Ideology

Power has been defined by Etzioni (1975) as the ability to enforce compliance to authority and by Brager, Specht, and Torczyner (1987) as the potential for and the exercise of influence. Other theorists have viewed power in terms of its ability not only to create compliance, but to resist being made compliant (Gil, 1992). This ability to resist being made compliant is a critical issue for social work and all the helping professions. In terms of social policy, Wharf (1992) suggests that power is, in effect, the capacity to alter policies and decisions.

This capacity may be exercised through persuasion, rewards, or other means of securing compliance, but where these strategies fail, policy-makers can bring about change on a unilateral basis. Influence is viewed as an attempt to convince policy-makers of the need for change. Policy-makers have power, even though their ability to secure compliance may at times be slender because of the pitfalls of its implementation. On the other hand, social reform organizations possess varying degrees of influence, but not power (25–26).

In terms of political advocacy, Gil (1990) reminds social workers that they cannot be politically neutral if they value the social well-being of those they serve because their practice "either confronts or challenges established societal institutions or it conforms to them openly or tacitly" (20).

According to Woodsworth (1986), power, while operating on many levels, takes on many forms. Included among these are:

➤ big business and big government;

➤ management and bureaucracy;

➤ professional and interpersonal relationships;

➤ the Church; and

➤ professional, scientific, and technical leaders.

While acknowledging *pluralism* as a central concept in Canadian political life, Woodsworth notes that there is also an elite group in Canada that wields considerable power. *Pluralism* means that "there are many competing influences on the way people behave toward each other" (71). *Elitism* refers to the chosen or most carefully selected part of a group or society. Elitism in social policy terms implies that social and public policy do not reflect the demands of the people so much as they do the interests and values of the powerful few. Elitism views the masses as largely passive, apathetic, and poorly informed—a situation that allows the elite to manipulate mass sentiments by the use of power gained from monopolistic control of the boards of major corporations and financial institutions and by their overwhelming presence in government. This leads to a situation where the elite "develop policies to favour big business, and when in business they find ways of influencing public policy" (71):

Perhaps the central question for social workers is the extent to which the methods and goals of government and business (aimed at standardization and control) are accepted and continued by professionals in their ways of working with clients (70).

Galbraith (1983) suggests that power is derived from three sources: 1) personality (with leadership a major asset); 2) wealth or property (including disposable income); and 3) organization (viewed as most important). Wharf (1986) views politicians, bureaucrats, and pressure groups as having the most influence on policies, with provincial and federal cabinets being the most important units in the Canadian political system. In terms of pressure groups, Wharf notes that having well-organized groups with influential people who are known to those in power is essential for successful influencing. The Canadian Manufacturing Association, the International Bank, the Chamber of Commerce, the Canadian Medical Association, and the Canadian Bar Association are examples of business and professional groups. The National Council of Welfare, the National Anti-Poverty Organization, the Canadian National Institute for the Blind, and the Canadian Council on Social Development are all examples of pressure groups from the social welfare arena.

The influence of an ideology supported by powerful political and economic forces is enormous. Ideology is essentially a confirmed belief that a political and social order is correct. In effect, an ideology with political, economic, and sometimes religious clout becomes so dominant that other perspectives are viewed as dangerous or non-relevant. In effect, oppression and power-over thinking pervades the policy-making process. For example, Shragge (1997) suggests that the new political agenda of the 1990s promoted an ideology that not only "bashed the poor," but created a whole new ideology for the "underclasses." Not only have social programs been cut after being blamed for creating the public debt, but a meaner and dehumanized ideology has ascended into policy prominence, legitimating workfare as progressive policy development despite data that suggests it is repressive and counter-productive. The following quote exemplifies just how far neo-conservative ideology is prepared to blame the poor for their social conditions:

Social Work's reluctance to see that personal failings play a role in poverty is worse than unrealistic: it positively hurts the poor. Modern social workers have taken the position that environmental factors: the economy, racism, sexism, and so on, account for neediness, and sadly, many have preached this doctrine to their clients. By telling them that someone else is to blame for their fate. they encourage scapegoating and whining, and undermine the motivation to succeed (Payne, 1998, 109–110).

The goal of the oppressor's action is to maintain absolute control by planting fear and doubt in the minds of the oppressed, who are only rewarded for public docility and compliance. As Fromm (1967) notes, human freedom has historically been restricted by "the use of force on the part of the rulers...and, more importantly, the threat of starvation against all who are unwilling to accept the conditions of work and social existence that were imposed on them" (183).

Institutional Structures Supporting the Policy-making Process

The primary policy-making bodies in Canada are the federal, provincial, and territorial parliaments. All public policies stem from these bodies and the power granted to municipalities stems from the provincial and territorial governments. As discussed in Chapters 2 and 3, under the Canadian Constitution, provincial governments have historic jurisdiction over health, welfare, and education. Any federal government intrusion into these jurisdictions, such as occurred with Unemployment Insurance (1940, Section 91, 2A), Old Age Pensions (1951, Section 94A) and pensions extended to cover survivors, disability, and supplementary benefits (1964), require constitutional amendments. On the other hand, Family Allowances (1944) was contested (Angers versus Minister of National Revenue) and eventually allowed under the provision of "Peace, order, and good government" (Report for the Interprovincial Conference of Ministers Responsible for Social Services, 1980).

At both the federal and provincial levels, the two most important components of the policy-making process are the Prime Minister/Premier and the cabinet (Yelaja, 1987). The Prime Minister (federal) and the premiers (provincial) have the power to appoint cabinet members and to remove them as well. Each cabinet minister is given a specific area of government responsibility called a portfolio. This portfolio may be just one Ministry or Department of government, or it may include more than one. For example, Alberta has the Department of Family and Social Services; Ontario has the Ministry of Community and Social Services; New Brunswick has the Department of Health and Community Services; Prince Edward Island and the Northwest Territories have Departments of Health and Social Services; and Manitoba has both a Department of Health and a Department of Family Services.

Policy initiatives can come from these Departments themselves or from the Office of the Prime Minister/Premier. After being discussed by Cabinet committees, the eventual decision rests with cabinet. Once a policy is approved by cabinet, it is introduced to Parliament where it will be required to pass three readings in order to become law (as well as the Senate at the federal level). Each governing party is responsible for ensuring that its party members (known as backbenchers) who are not in cabinet vote in support of the proposed legislation. It is the responsibility of the "party whip" to ensure that all members of the governing party vote along party lines. Sometimes, when a piece of legislation has deep moral or social meaning, party members are free to vote according to their own conscience and not necessarily with the party's position.

The Charter of Rights and Freedoms (1982) is a major piece of social policy legislation that has the potential to ensure that citizens have the opportunity to challenge any legislation or amendments that might restrict, interfere, or impinge on those rights and freedoms claimed in the Charter. However, as Hess notes:

When interpreting complex and sometimes ambiguous sections of the Charter, the courts will inevitably play an increasing role in social policy, despite the fact that many people in Canada's judicial system have limited experience and understanding of social policy issues and the implication of their decisions on policies and programs (Hess, 1993, 45).

Citizen Participation

There are many means for citizens to participate in the social-policy-making process. Before exploring the different means of involvement, the issue of citizen participation needs to be explored. The role of citizens in the policy-making process is a major concern for social workers in terms of both social work's value base and code of ethics. People in a democratic country have a right to participate in issues affecting the public interest and the common good. However, there are problems in motivating people to participate.

Wharf and Cossom (1987) suggest that the *Principle of Affected Interest* is a major issue in promoting citizen participation. This principle states that everyone "who is affected by the decisions of a government should have a right to participate in that government" (271), especially in terms of the following three criteria:

➤ *Personal Choice* reflects the degree to which a person wants to be involved, especially in terms of how much people believe the policy will affect them. For example, university students may become involved in decisions to raise tuition but not feel affected or interested in decisions to raise the admission to local swimming pools.

➤ *Competence* suggests that some decisions are accepted because experts made them. As well, for issues of complexity, such as pollution and nuclear waste, a degree of knowledge is required in order to participate. People can be intimidated into not participating by complexities, such as the overuse of rules of order or presentations by technocrats.

➤ *Economy* suggests issues of efficiency, rationality, and preservation of scarce resources. In addition, economy refers to the time, energy, and money people may have to participate. For example, single mothers may not be able to attend meetings because they do not have bus fare or enough money to afford babysitters.

Another problem stems from Canada's political process. Canada's political system is based on the principle of representative democracy. Each political party in Canada is permitted to choose a candidate to represent that party in each federal/provincial electoral riding. In each riding, members of the party select from among a number of eligible candidates the person they wish to represent the party at the next election. Once an election is called, this member then runs against candidates selected by other parties in the same way. The winner is deemed to represent all those in the riding, including all members of other parties. Moreover, each member becomes a member of the party caucus and is expected (and even coerced) to vote along party lines. It is easy to see why people can feel alienated and powerless in getting their voices heard when the very system that is there to represent them is so removed from them as individuals. Moreover, it is difficult for an elected member of Parliament not to feel a sense of obligation to those who helped to win the election and to feel fewer obligations to those who were trying to defeat her or him.

There are a number of ways governments can involve citizens in the policy-making process. At the input or formative stage, governments can establish commissions with the mandate to explore a public issue in depth and to bring back a community-informed recommendation on actions the government should take. The Senate Committee on Poverty is an example of such a commission. This committee visited countless cities in Canada in the late 1960s and listened to thousands of delegations representing multiple interests. It prepared a final report including these recommendations that was made public.

Also at the input level, the government may appoint policy committees. The recent movement toward policy committees reflects the disparity of influence between "the haves" and "the have-nots." The core of policy committees consists of government, agency, and institutionalized interest group representatives who have an active and important role in the policy-making process (Hess, 1993). Other pressure groups that lack status or resources, such as academics and promotional groups, are given the status of "attentive public" and their contribution is limited to what they contribute to the public debate and the policy discussion.

This fact of unequal power and influence has led to the situation where the relative power of specific pressure groups can increase the predictability of what a policy outcome will be (Hage and Hollingsworth, 1977). Mishra (1995) notes that pressure or lobby groups "are associations of people with common interests which seek to influence public policy" (67–68). Pressure groups can either be interest groups that seek to enhance members' interests (chambers of commerce, rifle associations, trade and business associations) or promotional groups that "espouse a cause….or advocate on behalf of a particular group (the poor, the homeless, the disabled)" (68). Wharf (1986) recommends that any group wishing to influence public policy must be well organized and made up of influential people who are known by senior civil servants and politicians.

In other words, influencing public policy at the input stage is both strategic and expensive. Large corporations hire lobbyists who are often ex-politicians or ex-senior civil servants to advance their causes and to ensure public policies reflect their best interests. The poor, the injured, the unemployed, the sick, people with disabilities, and dependent groups cannot compete and are often dependent on the policy advocacy of others, such as The National Council on Welfare, National Anti-Poverty Association, the Canadian Council on Social Development, Canadian Association of Social Workers, and other promotional groups.

At the policy evaluation stage, citizen input is again sought. However, many of the problems that reduce citizen involvement at the input level also affect the evaluation level. There is sometimes an assumption that social policy makers reflect on their policy decisions because of the feedback generated by research. However, Grob (1992) and Galster (1996) suggest that this is not the case. Essentially, policy-makers are most receptive to research findings for ideological or pragmatic reasons and are most impressed when the research findings are easy to understand and to use. Timing is another important factor in that research becomes more attractive when there is a current, controversial public issue, and less attractive when there is no public controversy.

Unfortunately, there are very few built-in structures in Canada to ensure that citizens, both those directly affected by policy or those with an interest in policy, have the opportunity to be heard. Certainly, not voting for a party in the next election is one means of protest, but if one is a member of a minority group, it is of little consequence unless the majority understands the issues as seen by the minority.

Getting information to the public is another means of consciousness raising that can influence policy. However, in a country where the vast majority of media, such as television, newspapers, radio and magazines, are owned by the privileged few, it is unlikely that the minority and politically left views will be deemed newsworthy. Reports from an ally source such as the Fraser Institute, on the other hand, will be accepted without question or analysis. Those in power are able to maintain a "power-over" posture that maintains hierarchy (some rule, others follow), separation (we are not responsible for each other), and competition (the proving ground for competence and character) because those making decisions favour their own group, giving themselves increasing power.

These powers serve to sever those with limited power or no power from any substantive role in the policy-making process. It is essential that social workers and other human service professionals strive to open the channels for citizen involvement.

The Role of the Social Worker in the Policy-making Process

The call to use community as a basis for policy-making development is not new (Wharf, 1992) nor is the *strengths perspective,* which views the strengths and resources of people and their environment as the central focus of social work (Chapin, 1995). Together, they provide an excellent framework for conceptualizing societal needs in new ways, to allow a more inclusive approach to policy formulation, and a wider opportunity to develop more meaningful and realistic policy options. The personal, firsthand knowledge of the community's understanding of such terms as *respect, collaboration, caring, trust, sacredness, vision,* and *neighbourliness,* and how these terms translate into community needs, are examples of how knowledge of Canada's communities and their strengths and desires can play an important part in the formation and evaluation of Canada's public and social policies.

Obviously, the trust and value the community places in the social worker will play an important part in how well these resources are brought into play. Earning this trust without violating or compromising one's social work value and ethic base requires great skill and time. The knowledge that can be gained by virtue of this position of trust gives the social worker a unique ability to relate the policy-making process with social impacts, thus allowing the social worker to:

➤ objectively analyze the anticipated and unanticipated impacts of social and public policies on the communities they serve;

➤ examine the congruence between social policies and agency policies (their own and other agencies) and advocate for adjustments to align these policies;

➤ increase the community consciousness regarding existing social and economic policies and any potential consequences for these communities;

➤ organize community responses to social policies with negative consequences;

➤ develop coalitions between communities to enhance the response to negative social policies;

➤ ensure that those social policies that benefit communities are acknowledged;

➤ develop a research capacity of sufficient sophistication to allow information pertaining to the community to be collected; and

➤ develop mechanisms to ensure this research information is made available and acknowledged by policy-makers, even if lobby or pressure groups must be employed.

For many social workers, social policies often seem to be abstract concepts with little or no connection to social work practice. However, both policy advocation and policy practice are instrumental components of social work practice.

Conclusion

At a time when social programs and agencies are being downsized and even eliminated, it is paramount that social workers become involved in the policy-making process. As political and economic interest groups attempt to dominate Canada's policy-making process, the helping professions, especially those in the public sector, are being called upon to engage in collaborative partnerships with their client groups and their communities (Barter, 1996; Delaney and Brownlee, 1995; Graham and Barter, 1999) to fight for their inclusion as citizens who can partake in policy-making, and not just as citizens who are passively affected by social and public policies.

While there are and most probably will continue to be many different approaches to the policy-making process, it is important for social workers to advocate that citizen participation be enshrined as an essential element in all policy-making activities. Within the framework of social justice and equality, social workers can go a long way to ensuring that all voices are heard by policy-makers and that no voice is given preference over others. The objective is not to make social policy a matter of easy choices but of informed choices that benefit all the people of Canada.

Social work is being called upon to resist neo-conservative interpretations of social realities and to maintain its own vision and critical analysis to promote social and human justice. Social workers and human service professionals are being challenged to maintain their ideals in a storm of cynicism about people and human value. As Homan (1994) states: "Idealism is not to be confused with naiveté. Idealism is a purposeful, powerful belief....An idealist simply refuses to capitulate to a prodding dullness of spirit....Someone may say to you, 'You are an idealist.' Take it as a compliment." (32).

Appendix (A)

Social Welfare History Chronology, Canada

Prior to European colonization, Aboriginal peoples are in North America and have long-established traditions of social care.

1520s–1763: European settlement along the St. Lawrence River; establishment and growth of French colony in North America—New France. Formal European contact had preceded this date along the eastern coast of North America. European colonization in North America transforms Aboriginal communities across the continent. Colonization brings with it European social welfare institutions such as education, hospitals, and charity.

1759: The fall of New France leads to the 1763 Treaty of Paris and the creation of a British colony. British social welfare institutions, like their French counterparts, assume limited, local government (parish) responsibility for the poor and indigent. A residual approach to social welfare.

1867: The British North America Act establishes constitutional jurisdiction over provinces for health, social services, and education. Residual approach persists. There is an increase in the scope and number of voluntary charitable services during the latter half of the nineteenth century.

1876: The Indian Act establishes the Crown as a separate authority for services to Aboriginal peoples based on treaty obligations. The Act places Aboriginal peoples in a distinct legal category, as wards of the federal government, without the privileges of full citizenship.

1886: Early forms of Workers' Compensation legislation are introduced. Voluntary welfare organizations emerge over the early to mid-nineteenth century, with greater intensity at century's end. Highlights include the Toronto Children's Aid Society (1891), Red Cross (1896), and Victorian Order of Nurses (1897).

1914: The country's oldest social work school is established at the University of Toronto. Others follow at McGill University (1918) and the University of British Columbia (1928).

1914: Workers' Compensation is established in Ontario; other provinces follow.

1916: Mothers' Allowances, a selective program, is established in Manitoba; other provinces follow.

1914–18: World War I. Returning veterans provided retirement annuity insurance assistance (1920), settlement assistance (1927), and allowances (1930) to veterans, widows, or orphans with insufficient means.

1918: The vote is accorded to women federally; between 1916 and 1920, seven provinces also accord women the vote. Voluntary welfare organizations proliferate after World War I. They include the Toronto Family Service Agency (1914), Canadian Mental Health Association (1918), Canadian National Institute for the Blind (1918), Canadian Council on Social Development (1920), and Canadian Association of Social Workers (1926).

1927: Old Age Pension Act is introduced. It is federal, selective, and cost-shared with provinces.

1930s: The Great Depression. In 1933, the national unemployment rate is 25 percent. Municipal governments face difficulties paying for Unemployment Relief; many go bankrupt. An uploading of responsibilities to higher levels of government occurs.

1937: The Rowell-Sirois Commission on dominion-provincial relations is established, releasing its report in 1940. The report examines the economic and financial basis of Confederation. It advocates greater taxing provisions for the federal government; a national system of Unemployment Insurance and pensions; and revenue transfers to provinces.

1939–45: World War II—domestic conditions set the stage for the onset of a universal welfare state.

1940: Unemployment Insurance (1941–1996), a federal program resulting from constitutional amendment, is introduced.

1943: The Marsh Report, a wartime blueprint for a federal welfare state, is released.

1944: Family Allowances (1944–1992), a universal program, is introduced.

1951: The Old Age Security program becomes universal.

1956: The Hospital Insurance and Diagnostic Services Act sees the federal government agree to set up a plan in cooperation with the provinces, to provide hospital care for everyone.

1962: The Saskatchewan government of T.C. Douglas proposes the first medicare plan in North America (it had been announced in 1959 and was preceded by other initiatives from his government in 1947 covering hospital insurance). Medicare allows doctors to collect their fees only from the government.

1962:   The federal system of immigration selection begins to become more objective, yet individuals from European countries continue to be favoured in selection processes.

1966:   The Medical Care Act of the federal government extends health insurance to cover doctors' services. It is finally implemented in 1968 and it will take six years for all of the provinces to join.

1966:   The Canada Assistance Plan (CAP, 1966–96), a cost-sharing agreement between the federal government and the provinces to split fifty-fifty the costs of provincially delivered health, education, and social services, is introduced.

1966:   The Canada Pension Plan (CPP) and Quebec Pension Plan (QPP) are established. Intended to cover all working Canadians, the plans transfer income from workers to retired persons.

1966:   The Guaranteed Income Supplement (GIS), a supplement to Old Age Security for low-income earners, is introduced.

1967:   A points system is introduced to Canadian immigration in an effort to reduce the selection process's racial biases. Subsequent legislation further revises the immigration selection process.

1969:   The federal government's White Paper on Indian Affairs proposes the repeal of the Indian Act, the end of separate legal status for Aboriginal peoples, and conversion of reserve lands to private tenure. It is widely rejected by Aboriginal leaders, who begin a sustained campaign for separate constitutional and policy recognition.

1969:   Following the Royal Commission on Bilingualism and Biculturalism, the Official Languages Act is passed. This federal legislation recognizes English and French as official languages in the operations of all federal departments and agencies.

1971:   The federal government announces an official policy of multiculturalism. These principles are further elaborated in the 1988 Multiculturalism Act, among other policy documents.

1971:   The Unemployment Insurance program is considerably expanded in scope.

1971:   The Senate Committee on Poverty coincides with the creation of the National Council of Welfare and with more comprehensive publication of poverty data by Statistics Canada.

1973:   The Canadian Council on the Status of Women is established following the recommendations of a royal commission on the status of women.

1977:   The Established Programs Financing Act, signalling changes to funding arrangements of the CAP, is passed.

1977:   The Canada Human Rights Act is passed.

1982: The Charter of Rights and Freedoms, expanding previous legislation, provides individual rights and group rights to various communities in Canadian society.

1984: The federal government's Canada Health Act, outlining the conditions of universality—portability, public administration, comprehensiveness, and accessibility—is passed.

1989: Changes to the income tax system make Old Age Security effectively a selective program. Over the 1980s and 1990s, other programs are systematically eroded.

1992: Family Allowances are abolished and replaced with selective child tax benefits.

1996: Unemployment Insurance is replaced with Employment Insurance. Retrenchment of the terms/conditions of this program and others continue.

1996: CAP is replaced with the Canada Health and Social Transfer.

1998: The National Child Benefit (NCB), which provides income supplements to low-income families, is introduced. The Canada Child Tax Benefit, a federal program that is combined with provincial income security programs for children, is renamed.

1999: The federal government and the provinces join in a Social Union initiative to coordinate delivery of social and related programs.

2000: In response to a 1999 Supreme Court of Canada decision regarding same-sex couples, legislation defining spouses to be opposite or same sex for Canada Pension Plan, Old Age Security, and other income security programs, is introduced.

Appendix (B)

Selected World Wide Web Sites

Social Policy Research Institutions

Caledon Institute of Social Policy
http://www.caledoninst.org

Canadian Centre for Policy Alternatives
http://www.cprn.com/cprn.html

Canadian Council on Social Development
http://www.ccsd.ca

Canadian Institute for Advanced Research
http://www.ciar.ca

Canadian Policy Research Networks
http://www.cprn.org/main_e.html

Center for Research on Economic and Social Policy
http://www.arts.ubc.ca/cresp/links.htm

Center for the Study of Living Standards
http://www.csls.ca

Child and Family

Canadian Mortgage and Housing Corporation
http://www.cmhc-schl.gc.ca

Disability Web Links
http://www.disabilityweblinks.ca

Health Canada. Childhood and Youth
http://www.hc-sc.gc.ca/hppb/childhood-youth

Health Canada. Seniors Policies and Programs Database
http://www.sppd.gc.ca

Human Resources Development Canada. F/P/T
Working Groups on Child and Family Services
http://www.hrdc-drhc.gc.ca/socpol/cfs/cfs.shtml

In Unison 2000: Persons with Disabilities in Canada
http://www.socialunion.gc.ca/In_Unison2000/index.html

National Advisory Council on Aging
http://www.hc-sc.gc.ca/seniors-aines/seniors/english/naca/naca.htm

Policy Research Initiative
http://www.policyresearch.schoolnet.ca

Revenue Canada's Family Benefits
http://www.ccra-adrc.gc/ca/benefits/menu-e.html

Social Union
http://www.socialunion.gc.ca

Statistics Canada
http://www.statcan.ca

Vanier Institute for the Family
http://www.vifamily.ca

Health

Centre for Health Services and Policy Research
http://www.chspr.queensu.ca/

Canadian Health Network
http://www.cma.ca/cma/common/start.do?lang=2

Centre for Health Economics and Policy Analysis
http://www.chepa.org

Health Science Association of Alberta
http://www.hsaa.ca

Health Research Homepage (Calgary, AB)
http://www.calgary.ca/md/CAH/research/index.html

International Health Care Research Guide
http://www.ucalgary.ca/md/CAH/research/

Queen's Health Policy
http://www.chspr.queensu.ca/

Saskatchewan Population Health and Evaluation Research Unit
http://www.spheru.ca

Human Rights

Amnesty International
http://www.amnesty.org/

Canadian Human Rights Foundation
http://www.web.net/chrf-fcdp/

DIANA—An International Human Rights Database
http://www.law.uc.edu:81/Diana/

United Nations High Commissioner for Refugees
http://www.unhcr.ch/welcome.htm

International Policy

American Bureau of Labor Statistics
http://www.stats.bls.gov/

Center for Analysis of Social Inclusion
(London School of Economics)
http://www.sticerd.lse.ac.uk/case/

Economic and Social Research Council
http://www.tsa.uk.com/YCSC/index.html

Global Social Policy
http://www.stakes.fi/gaspp/GSPjournal/index.html

International Labor Organization
http://www.ilo.org

Organization for Economic Cooperation and Development
http://www.oecd.org

Social Policy Research Center (Australia)
http://www.sprc.unsw.edu.au

United Nations (Division for Social Policy and Development)
http://www.un.org/esa/socdev/index.html

U.S. Department of Labor
http://www.dol.gov

World Bank (Social Capital Web site)
http://www.worldbank.org/poverty/scapital/index.htm

Labour

Canadian Employment Research Forum
http://www.cerf.mcmaster.ca

Canadian Industrial Relations Association
http://www.cira-acri.ca

Canadian International Labor Network
http://www.labour.ciln.mcmaster.ca

Canadian Labour and Business Centre
http://www.clbc.ca

Canadian Labour Congress
http://www.clc-ctc.ca

Government of Canada
http://www.canada.gc.ca

Human Resources Development Canada; Social Policy
http://www.hdrc-drhc.gc.ca

Institute for Work and Health
http://www.iwh.on.ca/home.htm

Provincial and Territorial Governments
http://www.canada.gc.ca/othergov/prov_e.html

Statistics Canada
http://www.statcan.ca

Non-Governmental Organizations

Canadian Association of Family Resource Programs
http://www.frp.ca

Canadian Institute of Child Health
http://www.cich.ca

Canadian School Boards Association
http://www.cdnsba.org

Center for Families, Work and Well-Being, University of Guelph:
http://www.uoguelph.ca/cfww/index.html

Child and Family Canada
http://www.cfc-efc.ca

Childcare Policy Forum
http://www.childcarepolicy.org

Childcare Resource and Research Unit
http://www.childcarecanada.org

Child Welfare League
http://www.cwlc.ca

Child Welfare Resource Centre
http://www.childwelfare.ca

Gerontology Research Centre (Simon Fraser University):
http://www.harbour.sfu.ca/gero

Laidlaw Foundation
http://www.laidlawfdn.org

Research Resources for the Social Sciences
http://www.socsciresearch.com

Glossary

Aboriginal peoples: Native persons indigenous to Canada. Aboriginal communities consist of First Nations peoples (those Aboriginal peoples with treaty status), Métis (Aboriginal people who, following eighteenth- and nineteenth-century intermarriage of First Nations peoples with traders/settlers, founded distinct societies in Western Canada), and Inuit (Aboriginal peoples who live north of the tree line).

Alms: A historical term describing charity in cash or kind provided to the needy.

Block grant: A cash transfer provided by one level of government to another, the amount of the transfer being fixed independently of the purpose to which the funds are put. Also known as a general-purpose grant. Its opposite is a specific-purpose grant (see below).

Breadwinner male: A term coined by scholars to describe the social construction of men as the principal income earners. Notions of the breadwinner male have had mutually reinforcing relationships with some social programs, but have been challenged by feminist thinking and some contemporary social programs. See also *women's domesticity*.

Canada Health Act: Federal legislation enacted in 1984 that reaffirms five principles of our universal health care system: its universality, comprehensiveness, accessibility, portability, and public administration.

Capitalism: An economic system in which the production and distribution of goods and services are controlled through private ownership and open competition.

Canada Assistance Plan (CAP): Introduced in 1966, this program allowed provinces and the federal government to cost-share on a fifty-fifty basis education, health care, and social welfare services. Provinces administered these services and received federal moneys, subject to federal standards. The CAP gradually eroded during the latter part of the 1970s, 1980s, and 1990s, and was ultimately replaced in 1996 by the Canada Health and Social Transfer (CHST), with looser federal standards.

Canada Pension Plan/Quebec Pension Plan (CPP/QPP): Both pension plans were introduced in 1966. The Canada Pension Plan applies to all working Canadians except for those in Quebec, which has its own contributory pension plan, the QPP. Both are publicly administered and are based on employees' workplace contributions.

Canadian Constitution: A body of fundamental principles and established precedents on which the Canadian state operates, and which determine legislative and administrative responsibilities amongst the three levels of government: federal, provincial, and municipal. Named the British North America Act in 1867, it was renamed the Constitution Act, in 1982. Every law that is inconsistent with the Constitution is, to the extent of the inconsistency, of no force and effect.

Canadian Charter of Rights and Freedoms: The only Charter of Rights entrenched in the Canadian Constitution came into force in 1982.

Collectivism: A world view wherein the rights and welfare of the group or society are placed above those of the individual.

Comparative needs: Needs that are determined by comparing one individual or group to another.

Conditional grant: a transfer of money from one level of government to another, and tied directly to an expected type of service delivery. The Canada Assistance Plan (1966–96) is an example of a conditional grant. CAP provided federal transfers to provincial governments to cover the latter's delivery of health, education, and social services.

Consumer Price Index (CPI): An economic measurement consisting of a typical and predetermined "basket" of consumer items, from which analysts may measure and compare changes in inflation over time.

Debt: A cumulative, multiyear calculation based on the total amount of money that is owed.

Deficit: A yearly calculation based on annual operating costs. It occurs when spending exceeds revenue.

Detached ideology: Those political values that create policy choices that are made strictly in accordance with one's values, regardless of the outcome and consequences to others.

Dictatorship of the Proletariat: According to Marxist theory, the control of communist parties that begins immediately following a revolution. Marxist theory projects the dictatorship as ending with the development of a classless society.

Diversity: A concept that conveys differences between people on the basis of age, culture, ethnicity, gender, nationality, race, range of ability, religion, and sexual orientation, among other social factors.

Egalitarianism: A world view that values human equality politically, socially, and economically.

Elitism: A world view that sees society organized around groups that are unequal in power and resources.

Employment Insurance (EI): Formerly Unemployment Insurance (introduced 1940), this publicly administered, universal, employment-based contributory insurance program was initially intended to provide for the hazards of temporary unemployment, but has been expanded to include other reasons for temporary cessation of work, including maternal benefits. Renamed Employment Insurance in 1996.

Equalization payment: Also known as an unconditional grant, an equalization payment is a transfer of money from one level of government to another; no particular commitment by the recipient government to tie the grant to an expected type of expenditure is required. Its opposite is a conditional grant (see above).

Expressed needs: Needs that are communicated to others.

Family Allowance (FA): A universal program, introduced in 1944 and withdrawn in 1992, that provided mothers a monthly payment for each child under her care. In 1992, the universal FA program was replaced by a refundable, income-tested (i.e., selective) tax credit.

Federal system of government: In this type of system political power is divided between a national and provincial governments. Canada is a federal system. Most countries are unitary, meaning political power is centralized in one national level of government.

Felt needs: Needs that are defined on a personal or subjective level.

Fiscal capacity: A particular level of government's ability to change the total or composition of its revenues (e.g., taxes) or expenditures (e.g., a social program).

Globalization: A current, pervasive trend of international finance, ideology, and political arrangements. As a result of globalization, money is invested quickly and easily across national borders. Principles of transnational competition for lucrative markets and inexpensive labour are actively pursued. In the absence of powerfully constraining national legislation or intra-national structures, multinational corporations have growing sovereignty to pursue their objectives.

Grand issues of social policy: Those issues relating to the fundamental structures of political-economic life. Examples include distribution of income and wealth, political power, and corporate prerogatives. Grand issues are contrasted with ordinary issues of social policy.

Gross Domestic Product (GDP): A measurement of a country's economic productivity over time.

Horizontal imbalance: An unequal relationship in fiscal capacity between richer and poorer provinces.

Human rights: Those legal, social, and political entitlements that are justly claimed to belong to any individual in society. These include, but are not restricted to, the right to justice, equality of opportunity, and religious freedom.

Ideology: A pattern of ideas based on experiences, values, and beliefs, and profoundly influencing one's political views. Ideologies shape, organize, and justify a course of action, and are used to legitimize the power held by the active political party.

Individualism: A world view wherein freedom, worth, and self-determination are foremost attributed to the individual rather than a group.

Intergovernmental finance: The web of financial movement that links governments in a federal system.

Low Income Cut-Off (LICO): A relative measure of poverty and the standard poverty line (see below) used by the federal government since 1959. It is calculated based on information from a survey of family spending patterns conducted by Statistics Canada.

Means of Production: According to Marxist theory, the land, labour, and capital that are used by a society to produce material goods.

Normative needs: Needs that are determined by someone other than the individual by applying some benchmark or standard to the individual case.

Old Age Security (OAS): Introduced as a selective, means-tested program in 1927, Old Age Security was transformed into a universal program in 1952, providing all Canadian senior citizens a monthly income. The introduction in the late 1980s of income tax "claw-backs" for individuals and couples having or surpassing a particular net income has called into question whether OAS may truly be considered a universal program today.

Operating principles: The policy results that occur when various social ideals are integrated with a practicable rule of application.

Ordinary issues of social policy: Those policy issues that directly affect the lives of people in a community and the technical operating principles of direct social work intervention. These are often managed and redressed by community-based organizations, and are sometimes the unintended consequence of earlier reforms. Examples include how child welfare service organizations are structurally administered, or the deinstitutionalization and development of community support programs. Ordinary issues of social policy are contrasted with grand issues.

Poverty: A state of deficiency in money or in the means of subsistence.

Poverty gap: How far below a particular poverty line (such as the low income cut-off, or LICO, above) one's income falls. If the poverty line is $15,020/year, and one's income is $13,020, then the poverty gap would be $2,000.

Poverty line: A measure representing a minimal level of human need. An absolute poverty line presumes that there is some fairly objective means for determining the absolute minimum an individual or household requires for food, shelter, clothing, and any other physical necessity. A relative poverty line assumes that poverty is to be defined relative to prevailing community standards, as opposed to absolute criteria.

Power: In social policy, power refers to the capacity to alter policies and decisions.

Principle of affected interest: A principle of social policy relating to community or citizen participation, and affirming that anyone who is affected by the decisions of a government should have a right to participate in that government.

Proletariat: According to Marxist theory, the proletariat consists of individuals and families who are members of the working class, particularly manual and industrial labourers.

Public policies: Legislated Acts, regulations, and by-laws (including all associated policies in the ministerial, agency, and public arenas) at the federal, provincial, and municipal levels of government.

Selective programs: Social welfare programs implemented on the basis of assessed need. Eligibility for benefits is determined through means testing. Selective programs are distinct from universal programs.

Social assistance: An income security program that uses a "means" or "needs" test to determine eligibility.

Social insurance: An income security program in which eligibility for benefits is determined on the basis of a record of contribution and the occurrence of a foreseen contingency, such as injury, retirement, unemployment, or the death of an income-earning spouse.

Social policy: The statements of the selected social goals and objectives to which a group—be it professional, governmental, or private—is committed.

Social welfare: A complex network of personal relationships, institutions, policies, and services that a society creates in order to contribute to the well-being, or welfare, of its members.

Specific purpose grant: A cash transfer provided by one level of government to another. The amount of the transfer is tied to its intended purpose; an example would be a matched or shared-cost program. Its opposite is a block grant (see above).

Standard of living: A term denoting the necessities and luxuries required for living in a particular circumstance.

Sustainability: An economic, political, and environmental world view that promotes present and future generations of stewardship of the physical world.

Universal programs: Social welfare programs based on national and categorical membership. These programs are available to all persons regardless of need. They are distinct from selective programs.

Vertical imbalance: An unequal relationship in fiscal capacity between the federal and a provincial government.

Welfare state: A term coined by the Archbishop of Canterbury during World War II to describe those governments, such as Canada's, that were committing themselves to the use of resources and to the development of social policies for the collective well-being of all.

Women's caring: A term coined by scholars to describe the social construction of women as principal caregivers in family and social relationships.

Women's domesticity: A term coined by scholars to describe the social construction of women in the domestic or home realm—daughters, mothers, wives, or widows. This term contrasts with the gendered social construction that encouraged men to take on economic, political, and social activities outside of the home. See also *breadwinner male*.

World view: An outlook drawn from religious, political, social, and physical information about humans and the societies they create.

References

Adams, I., Cameron, W., Hill, B. & Penz, P. (1971). *The real poverty report*. Edmonton: Hurtig.

Allen, R. (1971). *The social passion. Religion and social reform in Canada, 1914–1928.* Toronto: University of Toronto Press.

Anderson, G., & Marr, W. (1987). Immigration and social policy. In Yelaga, S. (Ed.). *Canadian social policy* (Rev. ed., 88–114). Waterloo, ON: Wilfrid Laurier University Press.

Anderson, J. E. (1990). *Public policymaking*. Boston: Houghton Mifflin.

Andrew, C. (1994). Challenges for a new political economy. In A. Johnson, S. McBride, & P. Smith (Eds.). *Continuities and discontinuities: the political economy of social welfare and labour market policy in Canada* (62–75). Toronto: University of Toronto Press.

Armitage, A. (1993). Family and child welfare in first nation communities. In B. Wharf (Ed.). *Rethinking child welfare* (131–17). Toronto: McClelland and Stewart.

Armitage, A. (1996). *Social welfare in Canada revisited: facing up to the future.* (3rd ed.). Don Mills, ON: Oxford University Press.

Armstrong, P. (1996a). The feminization of the labour force: harmonizing down in a global economy. In I. Bakker, *Rethinking restructuring: gender and change in Canada.* Toronto: University of Toronto Press.

Armstrong, P. (1996b). *Wasting away: the undermining of Canadian health care.* Toronto: Oxford University Press.

Armstrong, P. (1997). The state and pay equity: Juggling similarity and difference, meaning and structures. In P. Evans, and G. Wekerle (Eds.). *Women and the Canadian welfare state: challenges and change* (247–265). Toronto: University of Toronto Press.

Aronowitz, S. (1992). *The politics of identity: class, culture, social movements.* New York: Routledge.

Artibese, A. F .J., & Stelter, G. A. (1985). Urbanization. *The Canadian encyclopedia* (Vol. 3, p. 1887). Edmonton: Hurtig.

Babbie, E. (1977). *Society by agreement.* Belmont, Cal: Wadsworth, 1977.

Babbie, E. (1986). *Observing ourselves: essays in social research.* Belmont, CA: Wadsworth.

Baines, C., Evans, P., & Neysmith, S. (1998). *Women's caring: Feminist perspectives on social welfare.* (2nd ed.). Toronto: Oxford. University Press.

Baker, M. (1995). *Canadian family policies: cross national comparisons.* Toronto: University of Toronto Press.

Banks, K. & Mangan, M. (1999). *The company of neighbours: revitalizing community through action-research.* Toronto: University of Toronto Press.

Banting, K. G. (1993). Ends and means in social policy: comments on the paper by Jonathan Kesselman. In E. B. Reynolds (Ed.), *Income security in Canada: Changing needs, changing means* (37–129). Montreal, QC: The Institute for Research on Public Policy.

Banting, K.G. (1985). Institutional conservatism: Federalism and pension reform. (48–74). In J.S. Ismael (Ed.). *Canadian social welfare policy: Federal and provincial dimensions.* Kingston/Montreal: McGill-Queen's University Press.

Barata, P. (2000). Social exclusion in Europe: survey of literature. Unpublished paper. Toronto: Laidlaw Foundation.

Barker, J. 1999. *Street-level democracy: political settings at the margins of global power.* Toronto: Between the Lines.

Barker, R. L. (1991). *The social work dictionary.* Washington, DC: National Association of Social Workers.

Barker, R. L. (1995). *Social work dictionary.* (5th ed.). Washington, DC: NASW. *Blackwell Encyclopaedia of Political Science.* (1991). London: Butler & Tanner Ltd.

Barlow, M. and Clarke, T. 2001. *Global showdown: how the new activists are fighting global corporate rule.* Toronto: Stoddart.

Barter, K. (1996). Collaboration: A framework for northern practice. In R. Delaney, K. Brownlee & K. M. Zapf.

Battle, K. (1995). *Government fights growing gap between rich and poor.* Ottawa: Caledon Institute of Social Policy.

Battle, K. (1998). *No taxation without indexation.* Ottawa: Caledon Institute of Social Policy.

Battle, K. (1999). *Poverty eases slightly.* Ottawa: Caledon Institute of Social Policy.

Battle, K. (2001). *Relentless incrementalism: deconstructing and reconstructing Canadian income security policy.* Ottawa: Caledon Institute of Social Policy.

Battle, K. (1997a). *Targeted tax relief.* Ottawa: Caledon Institute of Social Policy.

Battle, K. (1997b). *The national child benefit: best thing since Medicare or new poor law?* Ottawa: Caledon Institute of Social Policy.

Battle, K., & Mendelson, M. (1997). *Child benefit reform in Canada: an evaluative framework and future directions.* Ottawa: Caledon Institute of Social Policy.

Battle, K., & Torjman, S. (1993a). *Federal social programs: Setting the record straight.* Ottawa: Caledon Institute of Social Policy.

Battle, K., & Torjman, S. (1993b). *Opening the books on social spending.* Ottawa: Caledon Institute of Social Policy.

Battle, K., & Torjman, S. (1995). *How finance reformed social policy.* Ottawa: Caledon Institute of Social Policy.

Beiser, M., Hou, F., Human, I., & Tousignant, M. (1998). *Growing up Canadian—a study of new immigrant children.* Ottawa: Human Resources Canada.

Berkowitz, I. (1980). Social choice and policy formulation: problems and considerations in the construction of the public interest. *Journal of Sociology and Social Welfare,* 16 (2), 533–545.

Bickenbach, J. (1993). *Physical disability and social policy.* Toronto: University of Toronto Press.

Bickenbach, J. E. (1993). *Physical disability and social policy.* Toronto: University of Toronto Press.

Bissoondath, N. (1994). *Selling illusions: the cult of multiculturalism in Canada.* Toronto: Penguin.

Bishop, A. (1994). *Becoming an ally: breaking the cycle of oppression.* Halifax: Fernwood.

Black, J. Watering down the milk: women coping on Alberta's minimum wage. *The Post,* 3 (2), 18–19.

Blake, R., Bryden, P. & Strain, F. (1997) (Eds.). *The welfare state in Canada: past, present and future.* Concord, ON: Irwin.

Boase, J. P. (1996). *Health care reform or health care rationing? A comparative study.* Orono, ME: Canadian-American Center, University of Maine

Bopp, J., Bopp, M., Brown, L., & Lane, P. (1985). *The sacred tree.* Lethbridge: Four Worlds Development Press.

Bourgeault, R. (1988). Race and class under mercantilism: indigenous people in nineteenth-century Canada. In B. Bolaria, and P. Li (Eds.). *Racial oppression in Canada.* (2nd ed.). Toronto: Garamond Press.

Boychuk, G. W. (1998). *Patchworks of purpose: the development of provincial social assistance regimes in Canada.* Kingston/Montreal: McGill-Queen's University Press.

Brager, G., Specht, H. & Torczyner, J. (1987). *Community organizing.* New York: Columbia University Press.

Braybrooke, D. & Lindblom, C. E. (1963). *The strategy of decision.* New York: Free Press.

Brebner, J. B. (1960). *Canada: a modern history.* Ann Arbor: University of Michigan Press.

Broad, D. (2000). Living a half life? Part-time work, labour standards, and social welfare. *Canadian Social Work Review,* 17(1), 11–32.

Bruce, M. (1961). *The coming of the welfare state*. London: B.T. Batsford.

Bryden, K. (1974). *Old age pensions and policy-making in Canada*. Kingston and Montreal: McGill-Queen's University Press.

Burns, T. J., Batavia, A. I., & DeJong, G. (1994). The health insurance work disincentive for persons with disabilities. *Research in the Sociology of Health Care*, 11, 57–68.

CASSW (1998). *The manual of standards and procedures for the accreditation of Canadian programs of social work education*. Ottawa: Canadian Association of Schools of Social Work.

Caledon Institute of Social Policy (CISP) (1995a). *The comprehensive reform of social programs: brief to the Standing Committee on Human Resources Development*. Ottawa: Renouf Publishing.

Caledon Institute of Social Policy (1995b). Government fights growing gap between rich and poor. *Caledon Commentary*, February.

Caledon Institute of Social Policy (1996). *Roundtable on Canada's aging society and retirement income system*. Ottawa: Caledon Institute of Social Policy.

Caledon Institute of Social Policy (1997). *The down payment budget*. Ottawa: Renouf Publishing Company.

Callahan, M. (1993). Feminist approaches: Women recreate child welfare. In B. Wharf (Ed.) *Rethinking child welfare in Canada*. Toronto: McClelland and Stewart.

Canada (1966). Canada Assistance Plan. Ottawa: Queen's Printer (Repealed in 1995).

Canada (1997). Canada Health and Social Transfer Regulations. Ottawa: Queen's Printer.

Canada (1985, 1995). Federal-Provincial Fiscal Arrangements Act. Ottawa: Queen's Printer.

Canada (1984). The Health Act. Ottawa: Queen's Printer.

Canadian Association of Social Workers (1995). *Statement on the impact of HIV*. Ottawa: Canadian Association of Social Workers.

Canadian Council on Social Development (CCSD) (1984). *Not enough: the meaning and measurement of poverty in Canada*. Ottawa: Canadian Council on Social Development.

Canadian Council on Social Development (1991). *Social policy in the 1990s: the challenge*. Ottawa/Montreal: CCSD.

Canadian Council on Social Development (1998). *The progress of Canada's children*. Ottawa: Canadian Council on Social Development.

Canadian Council on Social Development Undated. Children and youth with special needs: Summary Report of Findings. Ottawa.

Caragata, L. (1997). How should social work respond? Deconstructing practice in mean times. *Canadian Social Work Review*, 14 (2), 139–154.

Careless, J.M.S. (1954). Frontierism, metropolitanism, and Canadian history. *Canadian Historical Review*, 35, 1–21.

Carniol, B. (1987). *Case critical: challenging social work in Canada*. (2nd ed.). Toronto: Between the Lines.

Chappell, R. (1997). *Social welfare in Canadian society*. Scarborough, ON: ITP International Thomson Publishing.

Chappin, R. K. (1995). Social policy development: The strengths perspective. *Social Work*, 40 (4), 506–514.

Chomsky, N. (1991). *Deterring democracy*. London: Verso.

Christensen, C. (1995). Immigrants and minorities in Canada. In J. Turner & F. Turner (Eds.). *Social welfare in Canada*. (3rd ed., 179–212). Scarborough, ON: Allyn and Bacon Canada.

Christian, W., & Campbell, C. (1990). *Political parties and ideologies in Canada*. (3rd ed.). Toronto: McGraw-Hill Ryerson Ltd.

Citizenship and Immigration Canada (2001). Planning Now for Canada's Future. **www.cic.gc.ca/english/pub/**

Clarke, T. (1997). *Silent coup: Confronting the big business takeover of Canada*. Ottawa: Canadian Centre for Policy Initiatives & Toronto: James Lorimer & Co.

Collier, K. (1997). *After the welfare state.* Vancouver: New Star.

Collier, K. (1993). *Social work with rural peoples* (2nd ed.). Vancouver: New Star.

Coolidge, D. (2001). Reaffirming marriage: A presidential priority. *Harvard Journal of Law and Public Policy.* Spring 2001, 24, 2: 65.

Copp, T. (1974). *The anatomy of poverty; the conditions of the working class in Montreal, 1897–1929.* Toronto: McClelland and Stewart.

Cossman, B. (1996). Same-sex couples and the politics of family status. In Brodie, J. (Ed.). *Women and Canadian Public Policy.* Toronto: Harcourt Brace and Company.

Courchene, T.J. (2000). Equalization payments. In *Canadian Encyclopedia 2001.* Toronto: Stewart Publishing.

Courchene, T. J. (1994). *Social Canada in the millennium: reform imperatives and restructuring principles.* Toronto: C.D. Howe Institute, 1994.

Courchene, T. J. & Harris, R. G. (1999). *From fixing to monetary union: options for North American currency integration.* Toronto: C. D. Howe Institute.

Courchene, T. J. & Purvis, D.D. (Eds.) (1993). *Productivity, growth and Canada's international competitiveness: proceedings of a conference held at Queen's University 18–19 September 1992.* Kingston, ON: John Deutsch Institute for the Study of Economic Policy.

Coyne, A. (1995, August 15). A more level playing field for taxpayers. *The Globe and Mail,* A11.

Crane, D. (1980). *A dictionary of Canadian economics.* Edmonton: Hurtig Publishers.

Dahl, R. (1970). *After the Revolution.* New Haven: Yale University Press.

Dare, B. (1997). Harris' first year: attacks and resistance. In D. Ralph, A. Regimbald & N. St-Amand (Eds.). *Open for Business, closed to people* (20–26). Halifax: Fernwood.

Delaney, R. (1995). The philosophical base. In J. Turner, & F. Turner (Eds.), *Canadian social welfare.* (3rd ed., 12–27). Scarborough, ON: Allyn and Bacon Canada.

Delaney, R. & Brownlee, K. (Eds.). (1995). *Northern social work practice.* Thunder Bay: Lakehead University Centre for Northern Studies.

Delaney, R., Brownlee, K. & Graham, J.R. (Eds.). (1997). *Strategies in northern social work practice.* Thunder Bay: Centre for Northern Studies.

Delaney, R., Brownlee, K. & Sellick, M. (2001). Surviving globalization: Empowering rural and remote communities in Canada's provincial norths. *Australian Rural Social Work* 6(3). 4–11.

Delaney, R., Brownlee, K. & Zapf, K.M. (Eds.). (1996). *Issues in northern social work practice.* Thunder Bay: Centre for Northern Studies.

Department of Canadian Heritage. August 9, 2000. A Graphic Overview of Diversity in Canada. **www.pch.gc.ca/multi/assets/ppt/jedsite_e.ppt**

de Schweinitz, K. (1943). *England's road to social security.* Philadelphia: University of Pennsylvania Press.

Desert, G. (1976). Une source historique trop oublie: Les archives hospitaliers. *Gazette des Archives,* 94, 145–164.

Dictionary of government and politics. (1988). Middlesex: Peter Collin Publishing.

Djao, A. (1983). *Inequality and social policy.* Toronto: John Wiley & Sons.

Doern, B. & Aucoin, P. (Eds.) (1971). *The structures of policy-making in Canada.* Toronto: Macmillan.

Dolgoff, R., & Feldstein, D. (1984). *Understanding social welfare.* (2nd ed.). London: Longman.

Dominelli, L. (1988). *Anti-racist social work.* London: Macmillan.

Dominelli, L. (1997). *Sociology for social work.* London: MacMillan.

Dominelli, L., & McLeod, E. (1989). *Feminist social work.* London: Macmillan.

Drover, G. (2000).Redefining social citizenship in a global era. *Canadian Social Work Review,* special issue, social work and globalization, 17, 29–49.

Drover, G., & Kerans, P. (1993). New approaches to welfare theory: foundations. In Drover, G., & Kerans, P. (Eds.) *New approaches to welfare theory*. Brookfield, VT: Edward Elgar.

Drover, G. (1988). Social Work. In *The Canadian encyclopedia* (2034–2035). Edmonton: Hurtig.

DuBois, B., & Miley, K. K. (1996). *Social work: An empowering profession*. (2nd ed.). Boston: Allyn and Bacon.

Durst, D. (Ed.). (1999). *Canada's national child benefit, phoenix or fizzle?* Halifax, Nova Scotia: Fernwood.

Easterbrook, W. T., & Aitken, H. G. J. (1956). *Canadian economic history*. Toronto: Macmillan, 1956.

Eichler, M. (1987). Social policy concerning women. In S. Yelaga (Ed.). *Canadian social policy* (Rev. ed. 139–156). Waterloo, ON: Wilfrid Laurier University Press.

Esping-Anderson, G. (1990). *The three worlds of welfare capitalism*. Cambridge, UK: Polity Press.

Etzioni, A. (1968). *The active society*. New York: The Free Press.

Etzioni, A. (1975). *A comparative analysis of complex organizations*. (2nd ed.). New York: Free Press.

Evans, P. (1997). Divided citizenship? Gender, income security, and the welfare state. In P. Evans, & G. Wekerle (Eds.). *Women and the Canadian welfare state: challenges and change* (91–116). Toronto: University of Toronto Press.

Evans, P. (1995). Women and social welfare: Exploring the connections. In J. C. Turner, & F. Turner (Eds.). *Canadian social welfare*. (3rd ed. 150–64). Scarborough, ON: Allyn and Bacon Canada.

Evans, P., Jacobs, L., Noel, A., & Reynolds, E. (1995). *Workfare: Does it work? Is it fair?* Montreal: Institute for Research on Public Policy.

Evans, P., & Wekerle, G. R. (Eds.). (1997). *Women and the Canadian welfare state: challenges and change*. Toronto: University of Toronto Press.

Federal-Provincial/Territorial Ministers Responsible for the Status of Women. (1997). *Economic gender equality indicators*. Ottawa.

Federico, R. (1983). *The social welfare institution*. (4th ed.). Toronto: D.C. Heath.

Feehan, K., & Hannis, D. (Eds.). (1993). *From strength to strength. Social work education and Aboriginal people*. Edmonton: Grant MacEwan Community College.

Figuera-McDonough, J. (1993). Policy practice: the neglected side of social work interventions. *Social Work*, 38, March, 179–88.

Fingard, J. (1989). *The dark side of life in Victorian Halifax*. Porters Lake, N.S.: Pottersfield Press.

Finlayson, A. (1996). *Naming Rumpelstiltskin: Who will profit and who will lose in the workplace of the 21st century*. Toronto, ON: Key Porter Books.

Flynn, J. P. (1992). *Social agency policy*. (2nd ed.). Chicago: Nelson-Hall.

Foucault, M. (1972). *Power/knowledge: selected interviews and other writings*. NY: Pantheon Books.

Frankl, V. (1969). *The will to meaning*. Scarborough: Plume.

Fraser, N. (1989). *Unruly practices: power, discourse and gender in contemporary social theory*. Minneapolis: University of Minneapolis Press.

Freeman, H. & Sherwood, C. (1970). *Social research and social policy*. Englewood Cliffs, N.J.: Prentice-Hall.

Freiler, C. (2000). Social inclusion as a focus of well-being for children and families. Unpublished paper. Toronto: Laidlaw Foundation.

Freiler, C., & Cerny, J. (1998). *Benefiting Canada's children: perspectives on gender and social responsibility*. Ottawa: Status of Women Canada.

Freire, P. (1994). *Pedagogy of hope*. New York: Continuum.

Freire, P. (1985). *The politics of education: culture, power and liberation*. South Hadley, Mass.: Bergin and Garvey.

Freire, P. (1968). *Pedagogy of the oppressed.* New York: Seabury Press.

Frideres, J. (1998). *Aboriginal peoples in Canada.* (5th ed.). Scarborough, ON: Prentice Hall Allyn and Bacon Canada.

Fromm, E. (1967). The psychological aspects of the guaranteed income. In R. Theobald (Ed.). *The guaranteed income.* Garden City: Anchor, 183–193.

Fromm, E. (1955). *The sane society.* Greenwich, Fawcett.

Fukuyama, F. (1992). *The end of history and the last man.* New York: Avon Books.

Galbraith, J. K. (1983). *The anatomy of power.* Boston: Houghton Mifflin.

Galper, J. (1975). *The politics of social services.* Englewood Cliffs, NJ: Prentice-Hall.

Galster, G. (1996). *Reality and research: social science and U.S. urban policy since 1960.* Washington: Urban Institute Press.

Gambrill, E. (1997). *Social work practice: a critical thinker's guide.* New York: Oxford University Press.

Garrett, L. (2000). *Betrayal of trust: the collapse of global public health.* New York: Hyperion.

Germain, C., & Gitterman, A. (1980). *Social work practice, people and environments: an ecological perspective.* NY: Columbia University Press.

Gil, D. (1998). *Confronting injustice and oppression: concepts and strategies for social workers.* New York: Columbia University Press.

Gil, D. (1992). *Unravelling social policy* (rev. 5th ed.). Rochester: Schenkman Books.

Gil, D. (1970). A systematic approach to social policy analysis. *Social Service Review,* 44 (4), 411–426.

Gil, D. (1976). *The challenge of social inequality.* Cambridge: Schenkman.

Gil, D. (1990). Implications for conservative tendencies for practice and education in social welfare. *Journal of Sociology and Social Welfare,* XVII (2).

Gil, D. (1992). *Unravelling social policy.* (5th ed.). Rochester, Vermont: Schenkman Books.

Gil, D. (1998). *Confronting injustice and oppression: concepts and strategies for social workers.* New York: Columbia University Press.

Gilbert, N. & Specht, H. (1974). *Dimensions of social welfare policy.* Englewood Cliffs, N.J.: Prentice-Hall.

Gilpin, R. (2001). *Global political economy: understanding the international economic order.* Princeton: Princeton University Press.

Gilroy, J. (1990). Social work and the women's movement. In B. Wharf (Ed.). *Social work and social change in Canada.* Toronto: McClelland and Stewart.

Giugni, M. (1999). Introduction: how social movements matter. Past research, present problems, future developments. In Giugni, M., McAdan, D., and Tilly, C. (Eds.). *How Social movements matter* (iii–xxxiii) Minneapolis: University of Minnesota Press.

Gonthier, N. (1978). Dans le Lyon medival: vie et mort d'un pauvre. *Cahiers d'Histoire,* 23 (3), 335–347.

Gordon, L. (1990). The new feminist scholarship on the welfare state. In L. Gordon (Ed.). *Women, the state and welfare.* Madison: University of Wisconsin Press.

Government of Canada. (1999a). Human Resources and Development Canada Web site. Accessed at **www.hrdc-drhc.gc.ca**

Government of Canada (1999b). The Citizenship and Immigration Canada Web site. Accessed at **www.cic.gc.ca**

Graham, J. R. (1992). The Haven, 1878–1930. A Toronto charity's transition from a religious to a professional ethos. *Histoire Sociale/Social History,* 25 (50), 283–306.

Graham, J. R. (1995). Lessons for today: Canadian municipalities and Unemployment Relief during the 1930s Great Depression. *Canadian Review of Social Policy,* 35, 1–18.

Graham, J. R. (1996a). A History of the University of Toronto School of Social Work, 1914–1970, PhD dissertation, University of Toronto.

Graham, J. R. (1996b). A practical idealism: A theoretical values conception for northern social work practice. In R. Delaney, K. Brownlee, & J. R. Graham (Eds.). *Strategies in northern social work practice* (95–103). Thunder Bay: Centre for Northern Studies.

Graham, J. R. (1996c). An analysis of Canadian social welfare historical writing. *Social Service Review*, 70 (1), 140–58.

Graham, J. R. & Al-Krenawi, A. (2000). Canadian approaches to income security. In Francis J. Turner & Joanna C. Turner (Eds.), *Canadian social welfare* (403–20). 4th Edition. Toronto: Prentice Hall/Allyn and Bacon.

Graham, J.R., & Barter, K. (1999). Collaboration: A social work practice method. *Families in Society: The Journal of Contemporary Human Services*, 80(1), 6–13

Graham, J.R., Swift, K., & Delaney, R. (2000). *Canadian social policy: an introduction.* Toronto: Allyn and Bacon.

Gramsci, A. (1971). *Prison notebooks*. New York: International Publishers.

Grant, G. (1965). *Lament for a nation: the defeat of Canadian nationalism.* Toronto: Anansi.

Grant, G. (1969). *Technology and empire: perspectives on North America.* Toronto: Anansi.

Greenspon, E. (1997, November 28). Child poverty lock gets fiscal key. *The Globe and Mail*, A4.

Grob, G. (1992). How policy is made and how evaluators can affect it. *Evaluation-Practice*, 13 (3), 175–183.

Guest, D. (1997). *The emergence of social security in Canada*, (3rd ed.). Vancouver: University of British Columbia Press.

Gwyn, R. (1995). *Nationalism without walls: the unbearable lightness of being Canadian.* Toronto: McClelland and Stewart.

Gwyn, T. (1997). A return to feudalism. Syndicated column, *Chronicle Journal*.

Hage, J. & Hollingsworth, J. R. (1977). The first steps toward the integration of social theory and social policy. *Annals of the American Academy of Political and Social Science*, 434, 1–23.

Handler, J. (1979). *Protecting the social service client: legal and structural controls on official discretion.* NY: Academic Press.

Handler, J. F., & Hasenfeld, Y. (1991). *The moral construction of poverty: welfare reform in America.* Newbury Park, CA: Sage.

Hansen, P. (1999). The welfare state as political community. In Broad, D. & Antony, W. (Eds.). *Citizens or consumers? Social policy in a market society* (314–21). Halifax: Fernwood Publishing.

Hargrove, B. (1999). Unions and social policy; confronting a challenging future. In Broad, D. & Antony, W. (Eds.). *Citizens or consumers? Social policy in a market society* (73–82). Halifax: Fernwood Publishing.

Hartman, A., & Laird, J. (1983). *Family-centred social work practice.* NY: The Free Press.

Hay, D. (1997). Campaign 2000: Child and family poverty in Canada. In J. Pulkingham, & G. Ternowetsky (Eds.). *Child and family policies: struggles, strategies and options.* Halifax: Fernwood Publishing.

Help for poor children. (1997, January 16). *The Globe and Mail*, A16.

Henry, F., Tator, C., Mattis, W., & Rees, T. (1995). *The colour of democracy: racism in Canadian society.* Toronto: Harcourt Brace & Company, Canada.

Hepworth, P. (1980). *Foster care and adoption in Canada.* Ottawa: Canadian Council on Social Development.

Herberg, D., & Herberg, E. (1995). Canada's ethno-racial diversity: policies and programs for Canadian social welfare. In J. Turner, & F. Turner (Eds.). *Social welfare in Canada.* (3rd ed., 179–212). Scarborough, ON: Allyn and Bacon Canada.

Hess, M. (1993). *An overview of Canadian social policy.* Ottawa: Canadian Council on Social Development.

Hogwood, B., & Gunn, L. (1984). *Policy analysis for the real world.* Toronto: Oxford University Press.

Homan, M. (1994). *Promoting community change: making it happen in the real world.* Pacific Grove, Cal.: Brooks/Cole Publishing Company.

Hoover, K. R. (1992). Conservatism. In M. Hawkesworth and M. Kogan (Eds.). *Encyclopedia of government and politics* (Vol. I, 139–154). New York: Routledge.

Horowitz, G. (1970). In W. Kilbourn (Ed.), *Canada: a guide to the peaceable kingdom* (254–260). Toronto: Macmillan of Canada.

Hudson, P., & McKenzie, B. (1981). Child welfare and native people: The extension of colonialism. *The Social Worker,* 49 (2), 63–66, 87–88.

Hutchinson, Y., et al. (1992). *Profile of clients in the Anglophone youth network: examining the situation of the black child.* Montreal: Joint Report of Ville Marie Social Service Centre and McGill University School of Social Work.

Ignatieff, M. (2000). *The rights revolution.* Toronto: Anansi.

Indian and Northern Affairs (2000). First Nations Child and Family Services Program. **www.ainc-inac.gc.ca**

Indian and Northern Affairs (2000). Social Development: Health and Social Indicators. **www.ainc-inac.gc.ca/gs/soci_e.html**

Irving, A. (1987). Federal-provincial issues in social policy. In S. A. Yelaja (Ed.). Canadian social policy (326–349). Waterloo, ON: Wilfrid Laurier University Press.

Irving, A., Parsons, H., & Bellamy, D. (1995). *Neighbours: three social settlements in downtown Toronto.* Toronto: Canadian Scholars Press.

Ismael, J. (Ed.). (1985). *Canadian social welfare policy, federal and provincial dimensions.* Kingston and Montreal: McGill-Queen's University Press.

Ismael, J. (1987). *The Canadian welfare state: evolution and transition.* Edmonton: University of Alberta Press.

Jackson, A. and Robinson. (2000). *Falling behind: the state of working Canada, 2000.* Ottawa: Canadian Centre for Policy Alternatives.

Jackson, A. & Sanger, M. (1998). Dismantling democracy: the multilateral agreement on investment (MAI) and its impact. Ottawa, ON: Canadian Centre for Policy Alternatives and James Lorimer & Co.

Jacobs, L. A. (1995). What are the normative foundations of workfare? In A. Sayeed (Ed.). *Workfare: Does it work? Is it fair?* (13–37).

Jansson, B. (1990). *Social welfare policy: from theory to practice.* Belmont, CA: Wadsworth Publishing Company.

Jenson, J. (1998). *Mapping social cohesion: the state of Canadian research.* Canadian Policy Research Network Study No. F103. Ottawa: Renouf Publishing Co.

Johnson, L. (1986). *Social policy: a generalist approach* (2nd ed.). Boston, MA.: Allyn and Bacon, Inc.

Johnson, P. (1983). *Native children and the child welfare system.* Toronto: James Lorimer and Company.

Jones, A. & Rutman, L. (1981). *In the children's aid: J. J. Kelso and child welfare in Ontario.* Toronto: University of Toronto Press.

Justice for Children and Youth. (1996). *Tout seul: les moins de 18 ans et l'aide sociale.* Toronto: Justice for Children and Youth.

Kadushin, A., & Martin, J. (1988). *Child welfare services.* (4th ed.). NY: Macmillan.

Kalbach, W.E. (1998). Population. *The 1998 Canadian & world encyclopedia.* CD ROM. Toronto: McClelland and Stewart.

Kallen, E. (1989). *Label me human: minority rights of stigmatized Canadians.* Toronto: University of Toronto Press.

Kallen, E. (1995). *Ethnicity and human rights in Canada.* (2nd ed.). Toronto: Oxford University Press.

Kealey, G. S. (1980). *The working class response to industrial capitalism in Toronto, 1867–1892.* Toronto: University of Toronto Press.

Kealey, L. (Ed.). (1979). *A not unreasonable claim: women and reform in Canada, 1880s–1920s.* Toronto: The Women's Press.

Kent, T. (1999). *Social policy 2000: an agenda*. Ottawa: Caledon Institute of Social Policy.

Kerans, P. (1994). In A. Johnson, S. McBride, & P. Smith (Eds.). *Continuities and discontinuities: the political economy of social welfare and labour market policy in Canada* (44–59). Toronto: University of Toronto Press.

Kitchen, B. (1997). The new child benefit: much ado about nothing. *Canadian Review of Social Policy*, 30.

Klasen, S. (1998). Social exclusion and children in OECD countries.

Klein. N. (2000). *No logo: taking aim at the brand bullies*. Toronto: Vintage Canada.

Krieger, J. (Ed.). (1993). *The Oxford companion to politics of the world*. New York: Oxford University Press.

Lafitte, F. (1962). *Social policy in a free society*. Birmingham: Birmingham University Press.

Lalonde, M. (1973). *Working paper on social security in Canada*. Ottawa: Government of Canada.

Lamarshe, L. 1999. New governing arrangements, women and social policy. In Broad, D. & Antony, W. (Eds.). *Citizens or consumers? Social policy in a market society* (5–72). Halifax: Fernwood Publishing.

Landes, R. (1998). *The Canadian polity: a comparative introduction* (5th Ed.). Scarborough: Prentice-Hall.

Lasch, C. (1995). *The revolt of the elites and the betrayal of democracy*. New York: Norton.

Latouche, D. (1998). Quebec. *The 1998 Canadian & world encyclopedia*. CD ROM. Toronto: McClelland and Stewart.

Laxer, J. (1997). *In search of a new left: Canadian politics after the neo-conservative assault*. Toronto: Penguin.

Leiby, J. (1978). *A history of social welfare and social work in the United States*. New York: Columbia University Press.

Leira, A. (1994). Concepts of caring: loving, thinking, doing. *Social Service Review*, 68 (2), 185–201.

Leonard, P. (1975). Towards a paradigm for radical practice. In R. Bailey & M. Brake (Eds.). *Radical social work* (46–61). London: Edward Arnold, Ltd.

Leonard, P. (1984). *Personality and ideology: towards a materialist understanding of the individual*. Atlantic Highlands, NJ: Humanities Press.

Leonard, P. (1997). *Postmodern welfare: reconstructing an emancipatory project*. London: Sage Publications.

Lessard, H. (1997). Creative stories: social rights and Canada's Constitution. In P. Evans, and C. Wekerle (Eds.). *Women and the Canadian welfare state: challenges and change*. Toronto: University of Toronto Press.

Lewin, A. C., & Hasenfeld, Y. (1995). AFDC and marital dissolution: does welfare policy reduce the gains from marriage? *American Sociological Association Papers*.

L'Heureux-Dube, C. (2000). A conversation about equality. *Denver Journal of International Law and Policy*. Winter 2000, 29, 1: 65.

Lightman, E. (1982). Time for a divorce. *The Social Worker. Le travailleur social*, 50 (4), 154, 156.

Lightman, E. (1997). It's not a walk in the park: Workfare in Ontario. In E. Schragge (Ed.). *Workfare: ideology for a new under-class*. Toronto: Garamond Press.

Lipsky, M. (1980). *Street-level bureaucracy: dilemmas of the individual in public services*. NY: Russell Sage Foundation.

Little, B. (2001, August 27). Hot to grasp governments' tax expenditures. *The Globe and Mail*, B2.

Little, B. (1995, June 26). Why there's less in our pockets than in 1980. *The Globe and Mail*, A9.

Little, B. (1996, December 30). Where Canada is the leader of the pack. *The Globe and Mail*, 48.

Little, B. (1997, February 19). Balanced budget on horizon, analysts predict. *The Globe and Mail*, A14.

Little, B. (1997, February 24). How to put the tax picture into focus. *The Globe and Mail*, 48.

Little, B. (1997, September 8). Why your taxman is smiling. *The Globe and Mail*, 48.

Little, M. M. (1999). The limits of Canadian democracy: the citizenship rights of poor women. *Canadian Review of Social Policy*, 43, 59–76.

Lonergan, A., & Richards, C. (Eds.) (1988). *Thomas Berry and the new cosmology*. Mystic, Connecticut: Twenty-Third Publications.

Lower, A. (1958). *Canadians in the making. A social history of Canada*. Toronto: Longmans, Green, and Company.

Lubove, R. (1965). *The professional altruist: the emergence of social work as a career, 1880–1930*. Cambridge: Harvard University Press.

Luttwak, E. (1999). *Turbo-capitalism: winners and losers in the global economy*. New York: Harper Collins.

Luxton, M., & Reiter, E. (1997). Double, double, toil and trouble...women's experience of work and family in Canada, 1980–95. In Evans, P. and Wekerle, G. (Eds.). *Women and the Canadian welfare state: challenges and change* (197–22). Toronto: University of Toronto Press.

Macarov, D. (1995a). *The design of social welfare*. New York: Holt, Rinehart and Winston.

Macarov, D. (1995b). *Social welfare structure and practice*. Thousand Oaks, CA: Sage.

Macmillan dictionary of modern economics. (1992). (4th ed.). London: The Macmillan Press Ltd.

Mannheim, K. (1936). *Ideology and utopia*. New York: Harcourt, Brace & World.

Marchak, M. P. (1988). *Ideological perspectives on Canada*. (3rd ed.). Toronto: McGraw-Hill Ryerson Ltd.

Marfleet, P. (1998). Against the globalist paradigm. International conference on globalization: political, social, and economic perspectives, held at Eastern Mediterranean University (TRNC), November 19–21, 1998.

Marno, P. (1997). Empowerment in the social work literature. Unpublished Master's thesis, School of Social Work, York University.

Marshall, T. H. (1949). Citizenship and social class. Reprinted in D. Held et al., *States and societies*. 1983. London: Open University.

Marshall, T. H. (1965). *Social policy*. London: Hutchinson, 1965.

Marx, K., & Engels, F. (1846, trans. 1947). *The German ideology*, parts 1 and 3. New York: International Publishers.

Maslow, A. H. (1954). *Motivation and personality*. New York: Harper.

Mason, D., Talbott, S. & Leavitt, J. (1993). *Policy and politics for nurses*. (2nd ed.). Toronto: W. B. Saunders Co.

Mawhiney, A. (1995). The First Nations in Canada. In J. Turner, & F. Turner (Eds.). *Canadian social welfare*. (3rd ed., 213–230). Scarborough, ON: Allyn and Bacon Canada.

McArthur, K. (1997 July 9). Women rely more on government transfers. *The Globe and Mail*, A6.

McGilly, F. (1998). *An introduction to Canada's public social services*. Toronto: Oxford University Press.

McGilly, F. (1998). *Canada's public social services: understanding income and health programs*. (2nd ed.). Toronto: Oxford University Press.

McInnis-Dittrich, K. (1994). *Integrating social welfare policy and social work practice*. Pacific Grove, CA: Brooks/Cole Publishing Company.

McKenzie, B. (1997). Connecting policy and practice in First Nations child and family services: A Manitoba case study. In J. Pulkingham & G. Ternowetsky (Eds.). *Child and family policies: struggles, strategies and options*. Halifax: Fernwood Publishing.

McMenemy, J. (1995). *The language of Canadian politics: a guide to important terms and concepts*. Waterloo, ON: Wilfrid Laurier University Press.

McPherson, D., & Rabb, D. (1994). *Indian from the inside: A study in ethno-metaphysics.* Thunder Bay: Centre for Northern Studies.

McQuaig, L. (1993). *The wealthy banker's wife.* Toronto: Penguin Books.

McQuaig, L. (1995). *Shooting the hippo: death by deficit and other Canadian myths.* Toronto, ON: Viking

McQuaig, L. (1998). *The cult of impotence: selling the myth of powerlessness in the global economy.* Toronto: Viking.

McRae, K. (Ed.). (1974). *Consociational democracy.* Toronto: McClelland and Stewart.

Melichercik, J. (1995). Canadian approaches to income security. In F. Turner & J. Turner (Eds.). *Canadian social welfare* (3rd ed.). Toronto: Allyn Bacon, 474–494.

Mendelson, M., & Battle, K. (1999). *Aboriginal people in Canada's labour market.* Ottawa: Caledon Institute of Social Policy.

Miller, D. (Ed.). (1987). *Blackwell encyclopaedia of political science.* Oxford & New York: Basil Blackwell Ltd.

Mills, C. (1959). *The sociological imagination.* NY: Oxford University Press.

Mills, C. W. (1963). *Power, politics and people.* New York: Ballantine Books.

Minor, K. (1995). Special status groups. In J. Turner, & F. Turner (Eds.). *Canadian social welfare.* (3rd ed., 332–359). Scarborough, ON: Allyn and Bacon Canada.

Minoto, H. & Cross, P. (1991). The growth of the federal debt. *Canadian Economic Observer*, June, 3.1–3.17.

Mishra, R. (1981). *Society and social policy: theories and practice of welfare.* (2nd ed.). London: Macmillan.

Mishra, R. (1990). *The welfare state in capitalist society, policies of retrenchment and maintenance in Europe, North America and Australia.* Toronto: University of Toronto Press.

Mishra, R. (1995). The political bases of Canadian social welfare. In J. Turner & F. Turner (Eds.). *Canadian social welfare.* (3rd ed., 59–74). Scarborough, ON: Allyn and Bacon Canada.

Mishra, R. (1999). *Globalization and the Welfare State.* Cheltenham, UK: Edward Elgar.

Mitchell, A. (1993, November 16). Tax hikes eat into food, clothing: survey finds less spent on basics as income levy leaps 42 per cent. *The Globe and Mail*, A1.

Moreau, M. (1989). *Empowerment through a structural approach to social work.* Ottawa: Carleton University School of Social Work.

Morris, M. (2000). Women and poverty. Canadian Research Institute for the Advancement of Women. **www.criaw-icref.ca**

Morrison, I. (1997). Rights and the right: ending social citizenship in tory Ontario. In D. Ralph, A. Regimbald, & N. St-Amand (Eds.). *Open for business, closed to people.* Halifax: Fernwood.

Morton, W.L. (1969). *The kingdom of Canada.* Toronto: McClelland and Stewart.

Moscovitch, A. (1985). *The welfare state since 1975.* Occasional papers series, No. 3. Social Administration Research Unit, University of Regina.

Moscovitch, A., & Albert, J. (Eds.). (1987). *The benevolent state: the growth of welfare in Canada.* Toronto: Garamond Press.

Moscovitch, A., & Drover, G. (Eds.). (1981). *Inequality: essays on the political economy of social welfare.* Toronto: University of Toronto Press.

Mullaly, R. (1993). *Structural social work.* Toronto: McClelland and Stewart.

Mulvale, J.P. (2001). *Reimagining social welfare: beyond the Keynsian welfare state.* Toronto: Garamond.

Muszynski, L. (1987). *Is it fair? What tax reform will do to you.* Ottawa: Canadian Centre for Policy Alternatives.

Muszynski, L. (1992). *Universality and selectivity: the social and political ideas, and the policy issues.* Toronto: Premier's Council on Health, Well-being and Social Justice.

Myles, J. (1994). *Old wine in new bottles: privatizing old age pensions.* Ottawa: Caledon Institute of Social Policy.

NAPO (1994). *Think again: a training resource for service providers*. Ottawa: National Anti-Poverty Organization.

National Council of Welfare. (1993). *Incentives and disincentives to work*. Ottawa: Ministry of Supply and Services Canada.

National Council of Welfare. (1995). *The 1995 budget and block funding*. Ottawa: National Council of Welfare.

National Council of Welfare. (1996a). *A pension primer*. Ottawa: National Council of Welfare.

National Council of Welfare. (1996b). *Improving the Canada Pension Plan*. Ottawa: National Council of Welfare.

National Council of Welfare. (1996c). *A guide to the proposed seniors benefit*. Ottawa: National Council of Welfare.

National Council of Welfare. (1997–98). *Welfare incomes 1996*. Ottawa: National Council of Welfare.

National Council of Welfare. (1998). *Child benefits: kids are still hungry*. Ottawa: National Council of Welfare.

National Council of Welfare. (1999). *A new poverty line: Yes, no, or maybe?*. Ottawa: National Council of Welfare.

National Council of Welfare. (2001). *Child poverty profile 1998*. Ottawa: National Council of Welfare.

Naylor, C. D. (1986). *Private practice, public payment*. Montreal/Kingston: McGill-Queen's University Press.

Nelles, H. V. (1974). *The politics of development: forests, mines, & hydro-electric power in Ontario, 1849–1941*. Toronto: Macmillan.

O'Brien, C. (1998). *Sexual regulation and Ontario social policies in the 1990s*. Doctoral Dissertation. Faculty of Social Work, University of Toronto.

O'Brien, C., & Weir, L. (1995). Lesbians and gay men inside and outside families. In N. Mandell, & A. Duffy (Eds.). *Canadian families: diversity, conflict and change*. Toronto: Harcourt Brace and Company.

Offe, C. (1984). *Contradictions of the welfare state*. Cambridge: MIT Press.

Ontario (1997). Ontario Works Act. Government of Ontario: Queen's Printer for Ontario.

The Oxford English dictionary. (2nd ed.). (1989). Oxford: Clarendon Press.

Pal, K. A. (1988). *State, class, and bureaucracy, Canadian unemployment insurance and public policy*. Kingston and Montreal: McGill-Queen's University Press.

Palmer, B. D. (1979). *A culture in conflict: skilled workers and industrial capitalism in Hamilton, Ontario, 1860–1914*. Montreal/Kingston: McGill-Queen's University Press.

Panitch, L. (Ed.). (1977). *The Canadian state, political economy and political power*. Toronto: University of Toronto Press.

Pascal, G. (1993). Citizenship—A feminist analysis. In G. Drover & P. Kerans (Eds.). *Welfare theory*. Aldershot, UK: Edward Elgar Publishing.

Patterson, E. (1987). Native peoples and social policy. In S. Yelaja (Ed.). *Canadian social policy* (Rev. ed., 175–194). Waterloo, ON: Wilfrid Laurier University Press.

Payne, S. (1992). Fascism. In M. Hawkesworth and M. Kogan (Eds.). *Encyclopedia of government and politics* (Vol. I, 167–178). New York: Routledge.

Pearson, G. (1975). Making social workers: bad promises and good omens. In R. Bailey, & M. Brake (Eds.). *Radical social work*. London: Edward Arnold, Ltd.

Penner, N. (1992). *From protest to power : social democracy in Canada 1900–present*. Toronto: Lorimer.

Pierce, D. (1984). *Policy for the social work practitioner*. New York: Longman.

Pierson, C. (1991). *Beyond the welfare state: the new political economy of social welfare*. University Park: Pennsylvania State University Press.

Pincus, A., & Minahan, A. (1973). *Social work practice: model and method*. Itasca, Illinois: F. E. Peacock Publishers.

Polese, M. (1998). Regional economics. *The 1998 Canadian and world encyclopedia*. CD ROM. Toronto: McClelland and Stewart.

Popple, P., & Leighninger, L. (1998). *The policy-based profession: an introduction to social welfare policy for social workers*. Boston: Allyn and Bacon.

Prentice, A., Bourne, P., Cuthbert Brandt, G., Light, B., Mitchinson, W., & Black, N. (1988). *Canadian women: a history*. Toronto: Harcourt, Brace, Jovanovich.

Rachlis, M., & Kushner, C. (1994). *Strong medicine: how to save Canada's health care system*. Toronto: Harper Collins.

Rebick, J. (2000). *Imagine democracy*. Toronto: Stoddart.

Rein, M. (1974). Social policy analysis and the interpretation of beliefs. *The American Institute for Planners Journal*, September, 297–310.

Rein, M. (1983). *From policy to practice*. Armonk, NY: M. E. Sharpe Inc.

Report for the Interprovincial Conference of Ministers Responsible for Social Services (1980). *The income security system in Canada*. Ottawa: Canadian Inter-governmental Conference Secretariat.

Ricciutelli, L., Larkin, J., & O'Neill, E. (1998). *Confronting the cuts: a sourcebook for women in Ontario*. Toronto: Inanna Publications and Education Inc.

Rice, J.J., & Prince, M.J. (2000). *Changing politics of Canadian social policy*. Toronto: University of Toronto Press.

Riches, G. (1986). *Food banks and the welfare crisis*. Ottawa: Canadian Council on Social Development.

Riches, G., & Ternowetsky, G. (Eds.). (1990). *Unemployment and welfare: social policy and the work of social work*. Toronto: Garamond Press.

Richmond, M. (1930). *The long view*. New York: Russell Sage Foundation.

Rioux, M. (1997). Disability: the place of judgement in a world of fact. *Journal of Intellectual Disability Research*, 41(2), 102–111.

Roeher Institute. (1996). *Disability, community and society*. Toronto: Roeher Institute.

Rokeach, M. (1973). *The nature of human values*. New York: The Free Press.

Rooke, P. T., & Schnell, R. L. (1987). *No bleeding heart: Charlotte Whitton, a feminist on the right*. Montreal/Kingston: McGill-Queen's University Press.

Rose, N. (1996). Psychiatry as a political science: advanced liberalism and the administration of risk. *History of the Human Sciences*. 9(2): 1–23.

Ross, D.P., & Lochhead, C. (1998). Poverty. In *1998 Canadian encylopedia* CD ROM. Toronto: McClelland and Stewart.

Ross, D. P., Scott, K.J., & Smith, P.J. (2000). *The Canadian fact book on poverty*. Ottawa: The Canadian Council on Social Development.

Ross, D. P., Shillington, E. R., & Lochead, C. (1994). *The Canadian fact book on poverty—1994*. Ottawa: The Canadian Council on Social Development.

Sachs, W. (1999). Globalization and sustainability. Public lecture, the University of Calgary, March 19, 1999.

Sachs, W., Loske, R., Linz, M., et al. (1998). *Greening the North: a post-industrial blueprint for ecology and equity*. New York: Zed.

Saul, J. R. (1995). *The unconscious civilization*. Concord, ON: House of Anansi Press.

Schansberg, D. E. (1996). *Poor policy: how government harms the poor*. Boulder, Colo: Westview Press.

Schorr, A. (1985). Professional practice as policy. *Social Service Review*, 59, June, 185–86.

Schragge, E. (Ed.). (1997). *Workfare: ideology for a new under-class*. Toronto: Garamond Press.

Schragge, E., & Deniger, M. (1997). Workfare in Quebec. In Schragge, E. (Ed.). *Workfare: ideology for a new under-class*. Toronto: Garamond Press.

Schumacher, E.F. (1973). *Small is beautiful: economics as if people mattered*. New York: Harper and Row.

Schwartz, W. (1974). Private troubles and public issues: one social work job or two? In P. E. Weinberger (Ed.). *Perspectives on social welfare*. (2nd ed.). NY: Macmillan.

Scott, K. (1998). *Women and the CHST: a profile of women receiving social assistance in 1994.* Ottawa: Status of Women, Canada.

Sen, A. (1992). *Inequality reexamined.* New York: Harvard University Press.

Senate Committee on Poverty (1971). *Poverty in Canada.* Ottawa: Canadian Government Publishing Centre.

Sennett, R. (1998). *The corrosion of character: the personal consequences of work in the new capitalism.* New York: Norton.

Shah, P. J., & Smith, P. K. (1995). Do welfare benefits cause the welfare caseload? *Public Choice* 85 (1–2), 91–105.

Shewell, H., & Spagnut, A. (1995). The First Nations of Canada: social welfare and the quest for self-government. In J. Dixon, & R. Scheurell (Eds.). *Social welfare with indigenous peoples.* London: Routledge.

Silver, H. (1994). Social exclusion and social solidarity: three paradigms. *International Labour Review.* 1333(5–6): 531–78.

Simon, H. (1957). *Administrative behavior: a study of decision-making processes in administrative organization* (3rd Ed.). New York: Free Press.

Sirico, R. A. (1997, July 27). Work is moral and so is workfare. *New York Times*, E15.

Smith, P. K. (1993). Welfare as a cause of poverty: a time series analysis. *Public Choice*, 75 (2), 157–170.

Soros, G. *The crisis of global capitalism: open society endangered.* New York: Public Affairs.

Splane, R. B. (1965). *Social welfare in Ontario 1791–1893: a study of public welfare administration.* Toronto: University of Toronto Press.

Stainton, T. (1994). *Autonomy and social policy.* Aldershot: Avebury.

Statistics Canada and Citizenship and Immigration Canada. (1996). *Profiles: total immigrant population.* Immigration Research Series.

Stelter, G. A. & Artibese, A. F. J. (Eds.). (1977). *The Canadian city: essays in urban history.* Toronto: McClelland and Stewart.

Stroman, D. (1989). *Mental retardation in social context.* Lanham, MD: University Press of America, Inc.

Strong-Boag, V. (1976). *The parliament of women: the national council of women of Canada, 1893–1929.* Ottawa: National Museum of Man.

Struthers, J. (1994). *Limits to affluence: welfare in Ontario, 1920–1970.* Toronto: University of Toronto Press.

Struthers, J. (1983). *No fault of their own: unemployment and the Canadian welfare state 1914–1941.* Toronto: University of Toronto Press.

Swift, K. (1995). *Manufacturing bad mothers: a critical perspective on child neglect.* Toronto: University of Toronto Press.

Swift, K. (1997). Canada: Trends and issues in child welfare. In N. Gilbert (Ed.). *Combating child abuse* (38–71). New York: Oxford University Press.

Swift, K. (2001). The case for opposition: challenging contemporary child welfare policy directions. *Canadian Review of Social Policy.*

Swift, K., & Birmingham, M. (1999). Caring in a globalizing economy: single mothers on assistance. In D. Durst (Ed.). *Canada's new National Child Benefit: phoenix or fizzle?* Halifax: Fernwood Publishing.

Taylor-Henley, S., & Hudson, P. (1992). *Aboriginal self-government and social services: First Nations-provincial relationships.* Canadian Public Policy, 18 (1), 13–26.

Teeple, G. (1995). *Globalization and the decline of social reform.* Toronto: Garamond Press.

Teilhard de Chardin, P. (1955). *The phenomenon of man.* New York: Harper & Brothers.

Thomlison, R. J., & Bradshaw, C. (1999). Canadian political processes and social work practice. In F. J. Turner (Ed.). *Social work practice: a Canadian perspective* (164–177). Toronto: Free Press.

Thompson, N. (1993). *Anti-discriminatory practice.* London: Macmillan.

Thorsell, W. (April 11, 1998). Why April is truly the cruelest month for Canadians. *The Globe and Mail*, D6.

Tilly, C. (1999). From interactions to outcomes in social movements. In Giugni, M., McAdan, D. & Tilly, C. (Eds.). *How social movements matter*. (253–270.). Minneapolis: University of Minnesota Press. **www.civitas.org.uk**

Titmuss, R.M. (1958). *Essays on the welfare state*. London: George Allen and Unwin.

Titmuss, R. (1970). *The gift relationship: from human blood to social policy*. London: George Allen & Unwin.

Titmuss, R. (1974). *Social policy: an introduction*. London: George Allen & Unwin Ltd.

Titmuss, R.M. (1987). *Selected writings of Richard M. Titmuss: the philosophy of welfare*. London: Allen and Unwin.

Torjman, S. (1996a). *Workfare: a poor law*. Ottawa: Caledon Institute of Social Policy.

Torjman, S. (1996b). *History/hysteria*. Ottawa: Caledon Institute of Social Policy.

Torjman, S. (1997). *Welfare warfare*. Ottawa: Caledon Institute of Social Policy.

Torjman, S. (1998a). *Community-based poverty reduction*. Ottawa: Caledon Institute of Social Policy.

Torjman, S. (1998b). *Welfare reform through tailor-made training*. Ottawa: Caledon Institute of Social Policy.

Torjman, S. (1999). *Dumb and dumber governments*. Ottawa: Caledon Institute of Social Policy.

Torjman, S., & Battle, K. (1995a). *Can we have national standards?* Ottawa: Caledon Institute of Social Policy.

Torjman, S., & Battle, K. (1995b). *The dangers of block funding*. Ottawa: Caledon Institute of Social Policy.

Torjman, S. & Battle, K. (1999). *Good work: getting it and keeping it*. Ottawa: Caledon Institute of Social Policy.

Torrie, R. (2000, May 19). A clear and present danger. *Globe and Mail*, A13.

Trofimenkoff, S.M. (1983). *The dream of nation*. Toronto: McClelland and Stewart.

Trudeau, P. E. (1990). The values of a just society. In T. Axworthy & P. E. Trudeau (Eds.). *Towards a just society*. (357–385). Markham: Viking.

Turk, J. & Wilson, G. (1996). *Unfair shares: corporations and taxation in Canada*. Don Mills: Ontario Coalition for Social Justice & Ontario Federation of Labour.

Turner, F. (1995). Social welfare in Canada. In J. Turner, & F. Turner (Eds.). *Canadian social welfare*. (3rd ed., 1–11). Scarborough, ON: Allyn and Bacon Canada.

Turner, J. C., & Turner, F. J. (1999). *Canadian social welfare* (4th ed.). Scarborough, ON: Allyn and Bacon Canada.

United Nations. (1996). *Istanbul declaration on human settlements*.

Ursel, J. (1992). *Private lives, public policy; one hundred years of state intervention in the family*. Toronto: Women's Press.

Valentine, F. (2001). Enabling citizenship: full inclusion of children with disabilities and their parents. Discussion paper No. F/13. Ottawa: Canadian Policy Research Network.

Valpy, M. (1994, September 23). What do Canadians consider to be poverty? *The Globe and Mail*, A2.

Van Wormer, K. (1997). *Social welfare: a world view*. New York: Nelson Hall.

Webb, D. (1981). Radical and traditional social work. *British Journal of Social Work* 11, 143–58.

Weber, Max. (1930, trans. 1958). *The Protestant ethic and the spirit of capitalism*. New York: Charles Scribner's Sons.

Webster's New World Dictionary. (3rd College ed.). (1988). New York: Simon & Schuster.

Wein, F. (1991). *The role of social policy in economic restructuring*. Halifax, NS: The Institute for Research on Public Policy.

Wharf, B. (1978). Citizen participation and social policy. In S. Yelaja (Ed.). *Canadian social policy* (227–242). Waterloo, ON: Wilfrid Laurier University Press.

Wharf, B. (1986). Social welfare and the political system. In J. Turner & F. Turner (Eds.). *Canadian social welfare* (2nd ed., 103–120). Don Mills: Collier Macmillan.

Wharf, B. (Ed.).(1990). *Social work and social change in Canada*. Toronto: McClelland and Stewart.

Wharf, B. (1992). *Community and social policy in Canada*. Toronto: McClelland and Stewart.

Wharf, B & Cossom, J. (1987). Citizen participation and social welfare policy. In S. Yelaja (Ed.). *Canadian social policy*. (Rev. ed., 266–287). Waterloo, ON: Wilfrid Laurier University Press.

Wharf, B. & Cossom, J. (1987). Citizen participation and social welfare policy. In S. Yelaja (Ed.) *Canadian social policy* (2nd. Ed.)(p. 267).Waterloo, On: Wilfrid Laurier University Press.

Wharf, B. & McKenzie, B. (1998). *Connecting policy to practice in the human services*. Toronto: Oxford University Press.

Wilensky, H. L., & Lebeaux, C.N. (1958). *Industrial society and social welfare*. New York: Russell Sage Foundation.

Williams, F. (1989). *Social policy: a critical introduction*. Cambridge: Polity Press.

Wintemute, R. (1995). *Sexual orientation and human rights*. Oxford: Clarendon Press.

Woodsworth, D. (1986). Canadian realities. In J. Turner & F. Turner (Eds.). *Canadian social welfare*. (2nd ed.). Don Mills: Collier Macmillan.

Yelaja, S. (1987). Canadian social policy: perspectives. In S. Yelaja (Ed.). *Canadian social policy* (Rev. ed.). Waterloo, ON: Wilfrid Laurier University Press.

Yelaja, S. (Ed.) (1987). *Canadian Social Policy* (Rev. ed.). Waterloo, ON: Wilfrid Laurier University Press.

Young, C. (1994). Taxing times for lesbians and gay men: equality at what cost? *Dalhousie Law Journal*, 17 (2), 534–559.

Zapf, K. (1991). Educating social work practitioners for the north: A challenge for conventional models and structures, *The Northern Review*, (7), Summer, 35–52.

Zapf, M.K. (1999). Geographic factors. In F. Turner (Ed.). *Social work practice: a Canadian perspective* (344–358). Scarborough, ON: Allyn and Bacon Canada.

Index

Credits

Statistics Canada Information is used with the permission of the Minister of Industry, as Minister responsible for Statistics Canada. Information on the availability of the wide range of data from Statistics Canada can be obtained from Statistics Canada's Regional Offices, its World Wide Web site at **www.statcan.ca**, and its toll-free access number, 1-800-263-1136.

Chapter 2:
Figure 2.1 Total Social Spending in Canada 1945–1992/93; **Figure 2.2** Total Social Spending in Canada Per Capita, 1945/46–1992/93; and **Figure 2.3** Total Social Spending in Canada as Percentage of GDP, 1945/46–1992/93: Caledon Institute of Social Policy. (1995). The comprehensive reform of social programs: Brief to the Standing Committee on Human Resources Development. Ottawa, ON: Renouf Publishing.

Figure 2.4 Total Government (federal, provincial and municipal) Income security expenditures, 1980–81 to 1998–99; **Figure 2.5** Total Government (federal, provincial and municipal) Income security expenditures per capita, 1980–81 to 1998–99; and **Figure 2.6** Total Government (federal, provincial and municipal) Income security expenditures as % of GDP and total spending, 1980–81 to 1998–99: The Centre for the Study of Living Standards and the Institute for Research on Public Policy. *The Review of Economic Performance and Social Progress. The Longest Decade: Canada in the 1990s.*

Chapter 3:
Figure 3.1 Total federal transfers, 2001–02: $47 billion to Provinces and Territories Website: **www.fin.gc.ca/FEDPROV/FTPTe.html**

Reproduced with the permission of the Minister of Public Works and Government Services Canada, 2000.

Table 3.1 Social Assistance Nation-wide, 1999.

Chapter 4:
Figure 4.2 Maslow's Hierarchy of Needs. Haber, A., & Runyon, R. (1986). *Fundamentals of Psychology.* (4th ed.). New York: McGraw-Hill Company.

Figure 4.3 Poverty in Canada Compared with Other OECD Countries. OECD Employment Outlook June 2001. Copyright OECD, 2001.

Figure 4.4 Child Poverty in Canada Compared with Other Countries, mid-1990s. UNICEF Innocenti Research Centre, Florence, Italy. Innocenti Report Card No. 1, June 2000. "A league table of child poverty in rich nations." ISSN:1605-7317

Figure 4.5 Class Struggle. Adapted from the Statistics Canada publication "Labour Force Survey, Labour Force Historical Review" Catalogue No. 71F0004XCB, 1999.

Graph Reprinted with permission from *The Globe and Mail.*

Figure 4.6 Education makes a Difference. Adapted from the Statistics Canada publication *The Daily*, Catalogue No. 11-001, Thursday March 15, 2001, page 5.

Figure 4.7 Income Distribution in Canada: The Gini Coefficient. Adapted from Statistics Canada publication, "Income after tax, distribution by size in Canada", Catalogue No. 13-210 and "Income in Canada," Catalogue No. 75-202.

Graph Reprinted with permission from *The Globe and Mail*.

Figure 4.8 Income Tax Payment in Canada. Statistics Canada CANSIM database at http://loansima.statcan.ca/cgi-win/CNSMCGI.EXE, Matrix Nos. 3800034, 3800033 and 3800004.

Graph Reprinted with permission from *The Globe and Mail*.

Chapter 5:
Figure 5.1 Canada in the Global Economy. Adapted from the Statistics Canada publication *The Daily*, Catalogue 11-001, Wednesday, March 29, 2000, page 2.

Figure 5.2 How Canadians are Wired. Adapted from the Statistics Canada publication "Analytical paper series – Service Industries Division", Catalogue 63F0002XPB, November 1999, No. 27, page 4.

Graph Reprinted with permission from *The Globe and Mail*.

Chapter 6:
Figure 6.1 Annual Number of Immigrants Arriving in Canada, Immigration—Historical Perspective (1860-2000) Citizenship and Immigration Canada. *Facts and Figures 2000: Immigration Overview*. Cat. No. MP43-333/2001E August 2001; and **Figure 6.2** Number of Immigrants, as a Percentage of the Population of Canada, 1901–1991: Immigration Research Series—*Profiles*—Total Immigration Population. Catalogue No. 62-2/13/1996. ISBN 0-662-62491-2 1996. Reproduced with the permission of the Minister of Public Works and Government Services Canada, 2002.